D1608736

AMERICAN COMIC STRIP COLLECTIONS, 1884–1939

AMERICAN COMIC STRIP COLLECTIONS, 1884–1939

THE EVOLUTIONARY ERA

Denis Gifford

G.K.HALL &CO.

70 LINCOLN STREET, BOSTON, MASS.

PN
6726
.G54
1990

Published 1990 in the United States of America and Canada by G.K. Hall & Co., 70 Lincoln Street, Boston, Massachusetts 02111, U.S.A.

First published 1990 by **Mansell Publishing Limited**
A Cassell imprint
Villiers House, 41/47 Strand, London WC2N 5JE, England under the title
The American Comic Book Catalogue: The Evolutionary Era, 1884–1939

© Denis Gifford, 1990

All rights reserved. No part of this publication may be reproduced or transmitted in any form or by any means, electronic or mechanical, including photocopy, recording or any information storage or retrieval system, without permission in writing from the publishers or their appointed agents.

ISBN 0-8161-7270-6

Library of Congress Cataloging-in-Publication Data forthcoming.

Printed and bound in Great Britain.

DABNEY LANCASTER LIBRARY
LONGWOOD COLLEGE
FARMVILLE, VIRGINIA 23901

Dedication

For Fred Schwab
The first comic book artist I learned to look for – and tried to draw like – when I
was nine years old, and whom I was thrilled to meet almost half a century later!

DABNEY LANCASTER LIBRARY
1000149389

Contents

Acknowledgements

Special thanks for special help from Randall W. Scott, curator of comics at the Michigan State University Libraries in East Lansing; and to Mark Johnson and his brother Cole, collectors and historians of the American newspaper strip, of Levittown, Pennsylvania.

Introduction

This catalogue is the first attempt to trace chronologically the origins and evolution of that familiar, world-wide division of illustrated literature known as the American comic book. It begins with the first stumbling step of reprinting previously published comic strips in book format and concludes with the firm establishment of the original comic book as an ongoing format in its own right. The period covered runs fifty-five years, from 1884 to 1939.

The earliest traced comic book is *Stuff and Nonsense*, a compilation in hardback format of comic strips and cartoons drawn by Arthur Burdett Frost for the magazine *Harper's Monthly*, assembled and published in 1884 by Charles Scribner's Sons at their offices in 743 Broadway, New York. The last comic book in this catalogue is number one of *The Blue Beetle*, a super hero title published by Victor Fox Publications of Springfield, Massachusetts, dated Winter 1939. Between these 472 titles may be found the whole history of a popular art form which has encircled the world.

The American comic book as we now know it evolved quite differently from the British comic paper and its similar European counterparts. In the beginning there were the humorous magazines for adults, *Life*, *Judge* and *Puck*, which included comic strips among their illustrations. Some of these were intended for the children of their grown-up readers, and there was a demand for collections of strips to be reprinted in more permanent form.

A little later the circulation war between New York press barons led to the expansion of their Sunday newspapers into sections, one of which was designed as a humorous or comic supplement. Beginning as a mixture of illustrations, jokes, essays, short stories, etc., these sections, with the addition of colour from new, cheap colour presses, turned into totally pictorial supplements. With titles like *The Funny Side*, these supplements soon became known colloquially as 'the funnies', and each strip cartoon was called 'a comic'. Once the serialized adventure strip had been introduced, funnies seemed an inappropriate term and the term comics began to take over. The earliest comic books, being reprints of newspaper strips, generally used the word funnies — *The Funnies* (1929), *Famous Funnies* (1933) — while the word comics was more frequently applied to the growing area of original strip material — *The Comics Magazine* (1936). The continuing difference between the two terms is illustrated by *The Complete Book of Comics and Funnies*, published as late as 1944.

Perhaps here is the point to emphasize that the American newspaper strips or funnies are not covered by this book, except where they are reprinted in comic book format. The first of this type was *The Yellow Kid* (1897), Richard Felton Outcault's panel-cum-strip for *The American Humorist*, the Sunday colour supplement to William Randolph Hearst's *New York Sunday Journal*, which lasted for but one issue. There was also one known issue of *The Children's Christmas Book*, a coloured comic supplement included with the 12 December 1897 issue of the *Journal's* rival, the *New York Sunday World*. This 16-page prototype comic book is the earliest known example of its kind, and is therefore included in this catalogue.

All American newspapers were broadsheets at this time, which made a straight reprinting of the strip cartoons impractical. Some strips were only half-pages, however, and a collection of these on a music hall theme by Carl Schultze, who signed his work 'Bunny', was published by Isaac H. Blanchard in 1900. Although the size and shape was an awkward landscape, cardboard covers gave it some durability, and it set the format for the comic book for more than thirty years. A volume of Schultze's series *Foxy Grandpa* followed in December 1900, and this juvenile geriatric quickly became a long-running favourite of early comic books. Indeed, he reappeared as a star of original comic books as drawn by a new cartoonist, Charles Biro, so may be regarded as the longest-lived cartoon hero of our period.

The first actual series of comic books started on 23 November 1902 with a special announcement in the *New York Journal* funnies supplement. A set of five uniform books was published by William R. Hearst's *New York American and Journal* featuring Alphonse and Gaston, Happy Hooligan, The Katzenjammer Kids, The Tigers, and On and Off Mount Ararat. They cost 50 cents each, and were reprinted the following year as 'new editions with many additional pictures'. This major onslaught on the market may be seen as the official birthdate of the American comic book.

Many more landscape books in cardboard covers followed, the most popular being the series starring Richard Outcault's naughty boy, Buster Brown. Frederick A. Stokes and Co. published these, which were the first to receive British editions published in London and Edinburgh by W. & R. Chambers Ltd. To conform to the landscape shape, Outcault's full-page strips were sliced in half, so that each covered two pages.

Most of the early comic books featured the collected strips of a single character. It was not until 1908 that several different strips were tried by Stokes, who issued *The Three Funmakers*, a book combining adventures of Frederick Burr Opper's Happy Hooligan, Maude the Mule by the same artist, and Rudolph Dirks' Katzenjammer Kids. This variety format would become standard in the 10 cent comic book, thirty years later.

The first daily newspaper strip to appear in book format was Bud Fisher's popular Mutt and Jeff. Originally an idea of the Ball Publishing company of Boston, Massachusetts, this was perhaps the most awkward of all early comic books, being in the narrow landscape format of $15\frac{1}{2}$ by $5\frac{1}{2}$ inches, one strip to a page (1910). Two years later the problem had still not been solved: M.A. Donohue published Thomas A. Dorgan's strip, *Silk Hat Harry's Divorce Suit* as a book of virtually the same shape, adding a quarter of an inch to the depth. It was not until 1919 that Cupples and Leon of New York, a company with long experience in juvenile publishing, solved the problem by cutting daily strips in half and arranging them on a square ten by ten inch page. Their first comic book, *Bringing Up Father* by George McManus, was so successful that Cupples and Leon became the prime publishers of strip cartoon reprints well into the 1930s. It was not until M.C. Gaines created the comic book as we know it in 1933, that the familiar cardboard-covered comics of Cupples and Leon and their imitators began to lose favour.

The first successful comic book created for newsstand publication was *The Funnies*, which went on sale weekly from 16 January 1929. Published by George T. Delacorte, Jr. (Dell Publications) it was in tabloid format and followed the layout of the Sunday supplements combined with the part-text fiction style of the British comic papers, which had been established since 1875. It was not a great success because it was too close to the format of the free supplements: Americans failed to see why they should pay for something that resembled their regular Sunday funnies. The price was reduced from 10 cents to five, and the frequency of publication changed to monthly, but *The Funnies* failed and was discontinued at No. 36. However, Dell Publishing would return once the smaller comic book format became established, as indeed would their title of *The Funnies*.

Another format for reprinting newspaper strips was the *Big Little Books* series, founded by the Whitman Publishing Company in late 1932. *The Adventures of Dick Tracy, Detective* was the first to go on sale, a thick little book of 320 pages. Many more followed, all with the same design: text on the left hand page, one large strip panel minus any speech ballons on the right. What syndicated strips were left untouched by Whitman were signed by Saalfield Publishing, who began issuing their rip-off version, the *Little Big Books*, in 1934. Other publishers followed the formula, and for a while it seemd as though this style of comic book would win the day.

It was Max Charles Gaines, a salesman with the Eastern Color Printing Company of New York, who fathered the perfect format for the American comic book. With his sales manager, Harry I. Wildenberg, he put together a one-shot publication called *Funnies On Parade*, a 32-page reprint of some of the strips Eastern used in the Sunday colour supplements they printed for various newspapers. Set in a coloured cover, four pages of better quality paper, the comic books were taken by Proctor and Gamble as a promotional giveaway. The year was 1933, and before it closed Gaines had produced further comic books, *Famous Funnies: A Carnival of Comics* in September, and *Century of Comics*, a bumper 100-page edition. These were still giveaway comic books. The first comic book to be sold on newsstands arrived in 1934: *Famous Funnies Series 1*. It was so successful that *Famous Funnies* was put into production as a regular monthly publication, starting afresh with No. 1 in July 1934. It would run until July 1955, a total of 218 editions.

A fresh attempt at an original comic book started in February 1935 with No. 1 of *New Fun*, designed and published by Malcolm Wheeler-Nicholson's National Allied Publications. This reverted to the tabloid format of *The Funnies* and like that 1929 weekly, failed to click. However, with a gradually reduced page size and change of title to *More Fun*, this comic book notched up a total run of 127 editions, closing in November 1947. It became, through changes of ownership, the founding father of what today is the National Comics/D.C. Comics publishing empire. A companion comic book, *New Comics*, was the first all-original publication in standard comic book format. It was started by Wheeler-Nicholson in December 1935 and ran, with adjustments of title to *New Adventure Comics* (No. 12, 1937) and *Adventure Comics* (No. 32, 1938), for 503 issues (September 1983).

It is the publication of No. 1 of *Action Comics* in June 1938 that sets the seal on comic books as a popular art form in their own right. Gone for good were the secondary rights in old newspaper strips; here at last was the perfect comic book starring the perfect original comic book character: Superman. With this unique hero, created in their youth by the talented teenagers Jerome (Jerry) Siegel and Joseph (Joe) Shuster as writer and artist respectively, comic books found their own feet at last, Superman caught on with the young readers immediately, and soon the word was out among the other publishers. By the end of the decade, no comic book seemed complete without its caped clone. The American comic book was here to stay.

How To Use the Catalogue

The main entries are arranged chronologically by year, and alphabetically within each year. Each main entry is given an item number, which is the reference number used in both Title Index and Name Index. The chronological arrangement enables this book to be read as an historic survey of the development of the comic book from its varied beginnings to the ultimate format in which it has continued from the late 1930s to the present day. The two Indexes enable the specific enquirer to track down a title or artist/author to their point in history.

Ideal entries consist of the following information:

1. Item number.
2. Title.
3. Subtitle.
4. Date of publication: year, month, day. Length of run: date and number of last issue.
5. Original publication price.
6. Page count (including covers).
7. Page size in inches: width by height; with variations.
8. Publishing house (publisher's name in brackets); address.
9. Editorial: names of editor and staff, with address if different from publisher.
10. Artist, where book is the work of a single artist.
11. Syndicate.

Following this block of information, details of the contents of each comic book are given thus:

12. *Contents*: each fresh item in the book is shown by title, with page number, and artist (where there is more than one contributor).
13. *Advertisements*: names of advertisers taking space within the book.
14. *Editorial* or *Introduction*: the first editorial or introduction to a book or series is quoted in full.

15. Descriptive comment: each entry includes a detailed physical description of the book as to printing techniques, colouring, layout of strips, etc., and comments on the book's significance or place in history. Also included are details of any British editions, with publishers' names.

16. In the case of series entries such as *Big Little Books*, *Feature Books*, etc., only those titles reprinting comic strips are listed, and only those falling within our period. Where series of comic books continue beyond December 1939, note is made in the 'run' entry (see '4' above) only.

17. Where a comic book undergoes a change of title, a separate entry is made for the new title, and cross-references made for the previous and/or subsequent title.

Abbreviations

(BW)	black and white
¢.	cents
No.	number
pp.	pages
(R)	reprint
V.	volume

The Catalogue

1 Stuff and Nonsense

1884. $1.50. 100 pp. $7^3/_4 \times 10^1/_4$. Publisher: Charles Scribner's Sons, 743 Broadway, New York. Artist: Arthur Burdett Frost.

Contents
1 Title page
5 Contents
15–27 (R) The Fatal Mistake: A Tale of a Cat
35–41 (R) Ye Aesthete. Ye Boy and Ye Bullfrog
51–57 (R) The Balloonists
73–82 (R) The Power of the Human Eye

Compilation of strips and cartoons drawn by A.B. Frost, who drew an original cover, title page, and illustrated content pages for the book. The strips are reprinted from the magazine *Harper's Monthly*, and are rearranged so that each page of the book contains a single picture. The strips are designated 'Stuff' and the cartoon pages, which are mostly illustrated limericks, are designated 'Nonsense'. Only the strips are listed above. These strips belong to the primitive period before regular characters were developed. A.B. Frost is best remembered as the original illustrator of Joel Chandler Harris's *Uncle Remus* stories. *Stuff and Nonsense* was published in Britain by John C. Nimmo, and reprinted in 1889 and 1896. A new edition, rearranged to fit 64 pages, was published by George Routledge & Sons in 1910.

2 Comic Sheets

No. 1–No. 60: 1888. $11^3/_4 \times 15^3/_4$. Publisher: Humoristic Publishing Co., 38 Hall Building, Walnut and Ninth Street, Kansas City, Missouri.

No. 1 *Impossible Adventures*
No. 2 *Francis the Foundling*
No. 3 *The Discreet Child*
No. 4 *The Selfish Little Boy*
No. 5 *Theodorus the Slovenly*
No. 6 *The Little Boys in Our Days*
No. 7 *The Black Man*
No. 8 *If I Was a Little Boy*
No. 9 *The Adventures of a Voyage*
No. 10 *Cecilia the Babbler*

No. 11 *The Price of a Lie*
No. 12 *Mary the Disobedient Girl*
No. 13 *Louisette and the Lamb*
No. 14 *Courage Recompensed*
No. 15 *True Story of John Serinet*
No. 16 *Charles the Disobedient Boy*
No. 17 *The Little Girls in Our Days*
No. 18 *The Enchanted Whistle*
No. 19 *Calino's Simplicity*
No. 20 *The Magic Lantern*
No. 21 *The Misadventures of Mr. Heedless*
No. 22 *The King of the Moon*
No. 23 *William Tell*
No. 24 *Genevieve of Brabant*
No. 25 *The Sailor-boy's Dream*
No. 26 *The Costly Disobedience*
No. 27 *The Disobedient Little Girls*
No. 28 *The Disobedient Little Boys*
No. 29 *The Urchins*
No. 30 *The Inquisitive Little Girl*
No. 31 *Little Tom Thumb*
No. 32 *Little Red Riding Hood*
No. 33 *The Flying Trunk*
No. 34 *Jack Simpleton*
No. 35 *The Land of Cocagne*
No. 36 *Don Quichotte*
No. 37 *Blonda and Fairy Caprice*
No. 38 *Un-business-like Jack*
No. 39 *Captain Goodman*
No. 40 *The Lion and the Two Sailors*
No. 41 *The Little Mama, or The Doll's Education*
No. 42 *A Real Fairy*
No. 43 *John Laughing and John Crying*
No. 44 *The Uncomfortable Neighbours*
No. 45 *The Bells*
No. 46 *The Untruthful Boy*
No. 47 *Julian the Coward*
No. 48 *Master Unfortunate*
No. 49 *Advice to Everybody*
No. 50 *The Proud Matilda*
No. 51 *The Museum of Little Children*
No. 52 *The Museum of Little Children* (continued)
No. 53 *The Story of a Little Mouse*
No. 54 *Martha the Good Negress*
No. 55 *The Interesting Adventures of Mr. Sponger*
No. 56 *Father Flog*
No. 57 *The Imprudent Children*

No. 58 *The Pearl Necklace*
No. 59 *Cinderella*
No. 60 *Wisdom of the Nations*

The first comics for children to be published in the United States were this series of sixty numbered sheets, printed in four colours. They were translations into English of selected comic sheets originally published in France in the series *Imagerie d'Epinal*, and were printed in Epinal by the French publishers, Pellerin, for export to the U.S.A. Each sheet bears the indicia: 'Printed expressly for the Humoristic Publishing Co., Kansas City, Mo. Imagerie d'Epinal — Pellerin, imp.-edit.' The sheets are undated, but according to a local directory held at the Kansas City Public Library, the Humoristic Publishing Co. was located at the north-west corner of Walnut and Ninth Street, at No. 38 in the Hall Building, during the year 1888. How much each sheet cost is not known, nor if they were sold singly or in sets. The colours are bright, but the paper is extremely thin.

3 The Bull Calf and Other Tales

1892. 120 pp. 8¹/₂×6³/₄. Publisher: Charles Scribner's Sons, 743 Broadway, New York. Artist: Arthur Burdett Frost.

Contents
1 Title Page
3 Contents
5 (R) The Humane Man and the Bull Calf
19 (R) A Warning to Mutton That Thinks Itself Lamb
29 (R) Antonio and Jeremiah; An Inharmonious Tale
37 (R) Dizzy Joe
55 (R) Violet's Experience
63 (R) The Entire Discomfiture of Uneasy Walker
73 (R) 'Twas a Poem about Gentle Spring
87 (R) The Kidnapping of Private Jean Français
101 (R) A Low Down Trick; or Louisa's Capitulation
109 (R) A Tail of Two Tails

Compilation of strips drawn by A.B. Frost, who drew an original cover, title page and contents page for the book. The strips are reprinted from the magazine *Life*, and are rearranged so that each page of the book contains one single picture. These strips belong to the primitive period before regular characters were developed. A British edition was published by John C. Nimmo of London in 1892, with a new edition in 1896 in which the contents were rearranged to fit 60 pages. A 'new revised' edition was published in 1924, price $1.50. This contained seven additional strips reprinted from *Life* magazine, dating from 21 May 1921 to 13 July 1922. This edition was reprinted in 1969 in a reduced size by Dover Publications of New York.

4 The Yellow Kid

No. 1: 1897. 5¢. Publisher: Howard Ainslee & Co., New York. Artist: Richard Felton Outcault.

The first attempt at a regular publication built around a comic strip character, although only 'No. 1, Vol. 1' is known to exist. Richard Felton Outcault, the original artist, drew the special full-colour cover, and the advertisement on the back cover for the *New York Sunday Journal*. This was William Randolph Hearst's newspaper, in *The American Humorist* section of which the Yellow Kid regularly appeared. Hal L. Cohen's *Official Guide to Comic Books* (House of Collectibles, 1974) reproduces the covers of this book and describes it as 'the first true comic book'. However, Bill Blackbeard in *The World Encyclopedia of Comics* describes it as 'a joke magazine with the strip name (but contains no strips)'.

5 The Yellow Kid in McFadden's Flats

1897. 50¢. Publisher: G.W. Dillingham Co., 12 East 22nd Street, New York. Artist: Richard Felton Outcault.

Contents
Compilation of cartoons reprinted from the Sunday comic supplement of William Randolph Hearst's *New York Journal*, drawn by Richard Felton Outcault. The drawings are linked with a narrative written by E.W. Townsend, well known as the author of the 'Chimmie Fadden' stories. As Townsend was more famous than Outcault at the time, it is his name under which the book is listed in contemporary American trade catalogues. The book was published by G.W. Dillingham as No. 24 in their series, *The American Authors Library*.
The Yellow Kid is generally considered the first American comic strip hero: see Bill Blackbeard's entry in *The World Encyclopedia of Comics* (Chelsea House, 1976). Originally a supporting character in R.F. Outcault's series of large panels, Hogan's Alley, in the *New York World*, the Kid made his debut on 5 May 1895. The character was not immediately christened the Yellow Kid, his first appearance in that bright colour being on 5 January 1896. After 17 May 1896 the artist left the *New York World* for Hearst's *New York Journal*, and it was in this paper's Sunday supplement, *The American Humorist*, that Outcault first turned his weekly panel into a comic strip proper. The Yellow Kid now became the central character. Meanwhile, Outcault's old paper, *The World*, continued Hogan's Alley (and the Yellow Kid), now drawn by George B. Luks. The rival Yellow Kids led to a legal battle and, it is said, to the coining of the phrase 'yellow journalism'. Bill Blackbeard comments that 'this reprint book ... consisting of Hearst strip reprints with an accompanying text, constituted the first true comicbook'.

6 The Children's Christmas Book

12 December 1897. Free (supplement). 16 pp. 8³/₄ × 10¹/₄. Publisher: The New York Sunday World.

Contents
1 Santa Claus	George B. Luks
2 The Boy Who Discovered Santa Claus (text)	G.H. Grant
3 Danny Murphy's Santa Claus Goat (text)	B.
4 Christmas with Mother Goose	J.B.L.
5 Christmas in Gay Gazoozaland	J.B.L.

6 Sammy and Santa Claus (text)
7 Simple Christmas Gifts (text)
8 Robbie's Exciting Dream Will Crawford
10 Old and New Christmas Games (text) G.H. Grant
11 The Doll's Christmas Story (text) B.
12 A Puzzle Map of Greater New York
13 A Pictorial Christmas Puzzle J.B.L.
14 Tommy's Christmas Thoughts Lester
15 Some Christmas Novelties G.H. Grant
16 The Regal Beverage

B.

If *Famous Funnies* and its prototype giveaways are the fathers of the modern American Comic Book, then this must be the grandfather. It is a 16-page book, an unnumbered one-shot complete in itself, issued as a Christmas supplement to the *New York Sunday World*. Printed in virtually full colour (red, blue and yellow) on eight pages, black-and-white on alternate spreads, it contains a mixture of full-page cartoons and strips with text stories and features, and thus in format resembles the traditional British comic paper of the period. All material is original, created for the book, and the artists include George B. Luks who, at the time, was drawing the Yellow Kid for the *Sunday World*'s comic supplement.

7 Funny Folks

1899. $5.00. 90 pp. 16¹/₂×12. Publisher: E.P. Dutton & Co., 31 West 23rd Street, New York. Artist: Franklin Morris Howarth.

Contents
Compilation of comic strips reprinted from *Puck* magazine, 'reproduced by kind permission of Keppler & Schwarzmann, publishers of that periodical'. Hardback volume with cover specially drawn by the artist, Franklin Morris Howarth. Contains 40 strips printed on one side of the paper only, 14 of them in full colour, 26 in black-and-white. A British edition was published by J.M. Dent & Co., with the additional credit, 'Published in Great Britain by the courteous permission of Mr. James Henderson, the proprietor of the English copyright.' The title of the book is that of Henderson's weekly comic, *Funny Folks*, which began on 12 December 1874 and was still running at the time of this book's publication.
The beginnings of the first popular comic book format may be seen in this book, although its cloth-bound hardback binding and high-quality art paper set it above the low-cost requirements of the true newsstand comic book, and place it in the realms of the modern 'coffee table' book.

8 Vaudevilles and Other Things

1900. 20 pp. 10¹/₂×13. Publisher: Isaac H. Blanchard Co., 268 Canal Street, New York. Artist: Carl Schultze ('Bunny'). Syndicate: New York Herald Co.

Contents
Compilation of newspaper strips originally published in the *New York Herald* Sunday supplement. Reprinted in full colour with cardboard covers. This strip, originally entitled 'The Herald's Vaudeville Show', was the first regular series to appear in the comic section. The first episode, depicting 'Signor

Umptitumtino and the Magic Wheatcakes', was published in the *Herald* on 31 December 1899. The artist, 'Bunny' (Carl E. Schultze), drew a special cover for the book.

With its oblong format, necessitated by its reprinting of half-page broadsheet strips without reduction, and cardboard covers, necessitated by the unwieldy size of the book, this reprint edition set the format for the standard comic book in the early years of the twentieth century.

9 Folks in Funnyville

October 1900. $1.50. Publisher: R.H. Russell, Franklin Square, New York. Artist: Frederick Burr Opper.

Contents

Compilation of cartoons and strips originally published in the Sunday supplement, *American Humorist*, to William Randolph Hearst's *New York Journal*. Cardboard covers, specially drawn by the artist, F.B. Opper.

10 Foxy Grandpa

December 1900. 75¢. 20 pp. 15×9. Publisher: Foxy Grandpa Co. Artist: Carl Schultze ('Bunny'). Syndicate: New York Herald Co.

Contents

Compilation of strips originally published in the *New York Herald* Sunday supplement, reprinted in full colour. Cardboard covers, specially drawn by the artist, 'Bunny'. This strip first appeared on 7 January 1900, and this book is the first of a long series of reprints that was to run for sixteen years.

11 The Further Adventures of Foxy Grandpa

December 1901. 75¢. Publisher: Frederick A. Stokes Co., 5 East 16th Street, New York. Artist: Carl Schultze ('Bunny').

Contents

Compilation of half-page strips originally published in the Sunday supplement of the *New York Herald*. Reprinted in full colour, on one side of the page only. With cardboard covers, specially drawn by the artist, 'Bunny' (Carl Schultze).

12 The Latest Larks of Foxy Grandpa

1902. 32 pp. 15½×9½. Publisher: Lewis R. Hammersly Co., 1510 Chestnut Street, Philadelphia. Artist: Carl Schultze ('Bunny'). Syndicate: New York Herald Co.

Contents

Compilation of newspaper strips reprinted in four colours from the Sunday supplement of the *New York Herald*. Had cardboard covers, with special artwork by the artist, 'Bunny'. Reprinted in 1905 and published by M.A. Donohue & Co.

13 Pore Li'l Mose

1902. 30 pp. 15×10½. Publisher: Grand Union Tea Co., Brooklyn, New York. Artist: Richard F. Outcault. Syndicate: New York Herald Co.

Contents
Compilation of newspaper strips reprinted in four colours from the Sunday supplement of the *New York Herald*. Cardboard covers, with special artwork by the artist, Richard Felton Outcault. 'Pore Li'l Mose' made his comic strip debut on 2 December 1900.
This comic book was published as an advertising premium for Grand Union Tea, and was the first use of a comic strip or comic book for this purpose.

14 Alphonse and Gaston and Their Friend Leon

23 November 1902. 50¢. 15¼×10. Publisher: New York American and Journal (W.R. Hearst). Artist: Frederick Burr Opper.

Contents
Compilation of strips originally published in the William Randolph Hearst Sunday supplements, and reprinted in full colour. Special cover drawn by the artist; cardboard covers. First advertised in the *New York Journal* supplement on Sunday, 23 November 1902:

> *Announcement! The popular characters of the comic supplement have been published in book form. Your newsdealer can get them for you. They are the best comic-books that have ever been published. For sale everwhere at 50 cents each.*

This book is one of a set of five uniform comic books published on the same day by this publisher. Thus the official birth of the American comic book as a publishing enterprise may be marked as 23 November 1902. A new edition of this book was published in 1906 by Cupples & Leon, price 75¢.

15 Happy Hooligan

23 November 1902. 50¢. 50 pp. 15¼×10. Publisher: New York American and Journal (W.R. Hearst). Artist: Frederick Burr Opper.

Contents
Compilation of strips originally published in the William Randolph Hearst Sunday supplements, and reprinted in full colour. Special cover drawn by the artist; cardboard covers. Further information, see *Alphonse and Gaston and Their Friend Leon* above. A new edition of this book was published in 1906 by Cupples & Leon, price 75¢.

16 The Katzenjammer Kids

23 November 1902. 50¢. 50 pp. 15¼×10. Publisher: New York American and Journal (W.R. Hearst). Artist: Rudolph Dirks.

Contents

Compilation of strips originally published in the William Randolph Hearst Sunday supplements, reprinted in full colour. For further information, see *Alphonse and Gaston and Their Friend Leon* above. Special cover drawn by the artist; cardboard covers.

17 On and Off Mount Ararat

23 November 1902. 50¢. 50 pp. 15¹/₄×10. Publisher: New York American and Journal (W.R. Hearst). Artist: James Swinnerton.

Contents

Compilation of strips originally published in the William Randolph Hearst Sunday supplements, reprinted in full colour. Special cover drawn by the artist; cardboard covers. For futher information, see *Alphonse and Gaston and Their Friend Leon* above.

18 The Tigers

23 November 1902. 50¢. 50 pp. 15¹/₄×10. Publisher: New York American and Journal (W.R. Hearst). Artist: James Swinnerton.

Contents

Compilation of strips originally published in the William Randolph Hearst Sunday supplements, reprinted in full colour. Special cover drawn by the artist; cardboard covers. For further information, see *Alphonse and Gaston and Their Friend Leon* above.

19 The Merry Adventures of Foxy Grandpa

December 1902. $1.00. 15¹/₄×10¹/₄. Publisher: Foxy Grandpa Co. Artist: Carl Schultze ('Bunny').

Contents

Compilation of half-page strips reprinted from the Sunday supplements. Printed in full colour on one side of the page only, with cardboard covers specially drawn by the artist, 'Bunny' (Carl Schultze).

20 The Latest Adventures of Foxy Grandpa

1903. 24 pp. 15×9. Publisher: Lewis R. Hammersly Co., 1510 Chestnut Street, Philadelphia. Artist: Carl Schultze ('Bunny'). Syndicate: New York Herald Co.

Contents

Compilation of strips reprinted from the Sunday supplement of the *New York Herald*. Printed in full colour, with cardboard covers specially drawn by the artist, 'Bunny'. This book was reprinted in 1905 and published by M.A. Donohue & Co.

21 Alphonse and Gaston and Their Friend Leon

November 1903. 82 pp. $15^{1}/_{4} \times 10$. Publisher: New York American and Journal (W.R. Hearst). Artist: Frederick Burr Opper.

Contents
Compilation of 38 strips originally published in the William Randolph Hearst Sunday supplements, reprinted in full colour, with cardboard covers. This is a new edition of the book first published on 23 November 1902, advertised as 'New edition with many additional pictures'. Strips are printed on one side of the page only.

22 The Katzenjammer Kids

November 1903. 82 pp. $15^{1}/_{4} \times 10$. Publisher: New York American and Journal (W.R. Hearst). Artist: Rudolph Dirks.

Contents
Compilation of 38 strips originally published in the William Randolph Hearst Sunday supplements, reprinted in full colour, with cardboard covers. This is a new edition of the book first published on 23 November 1902, advertised as 'New edition with many additional pictures'. Strips are printed on one side of the page only.

23 Buster Brown and His Resolutions

December 1903. 60¢. 68 pp. $16 \times 11^{1}/_{4}$. Publisher: Frederick A. Stokes Co., 5 East 16th Street, New York. Artist: Richard F. Outcault. Syndicate: New York Herald Co.

Introduction
'The author wishes to say in presenting Buster Brown that Buster is not a bad or naughty boy as the thousands of parents of Buster know. He is an industrious person, full of energy and ingenuity. If all the energy of the vast army of Busters around us could be directed into some useful channel and brought to bear upon some practical work it would accomplish wonders. Buster is a kind little chap and his faithful dog finds in him a gentle but busy companion. He is not an invention; these pictures of his pranks are simply records of the usual everyday happenings in any healthy household.'

Contents
1 Cover
3 Title page; Introduction
5 (R) Buster Brown Just Puts On the Finishing Touches
7 (R) Buster Brown Has His Portrait Painted
9 (R) Buster Brown Controls His Temper
11 (R) Buster Brown's Dog Meets His Old Side Partner
13 (R) Buster Brown Takes a Little of His Own Medicine
15 (R) Buster Brown Hunts His Mama's Purse

R. F. Outcault

9

17 (R) Buster Brown and a Cut-glass Salad Bowl
19 (R) Buster Brown Gets Even with the Postman
21 (R) Buster Brown Saves the Life of a Cat
23 (R) Buster Brown, He's a Wonder with the Ladies
25 (R) Buster Brown Just Sits in the Glue
27 (R) Buster Brown Makes More Trouble for Himself
31 (R) Buster Brown's Happy New Year
35 (R) Buster Brown Starts for his Grandma's
39 (R) Just Buster Brown That's All
43 (R) Buster Brown's Unlucky Day
47 (R) Buster Brown: His New Goat
51 (R) Buster Brown He Acquires a Pet Monkey
55 (R) Buster Brown Plays Another Little Innocent Trick
59 (R) Buster Brown and a Pair of Roller Skates
63 (R) Buster Brown's Double

The first comic book collection of Buster Brown strips, reprinted from Sunday comic supplements syndicated by the New York Herald Company. An awkward-sized book, dictated by the large broadsheet plates of the original strips, which were cut into halves. The outsize format also necessitated the use of cardboard covers. The strips in the books are copyrighted 1902 and 1903, and the first twelve are half-page strips, the remainder being full-page strips divided into halves. Thus there are actually 21 complete strips in the book. The printing is full four-colour throughout, save for the title page, which is black-and-white, and specially drawn for the book. The cover is also original for the book. The reverse sides of all pages are blank paper. British edition published by W. & R. Chambers Ltd., London and Edinburgh.

24 Foxy Grandpa's Mother Goose

December 1903. Publisher: Frederick A. Stokes Co., 5 East 16th Street, New York. Artist: Carl Schultze ('Bunny').

Contents
Oblong book in cardboard covers, specially drawn by the artist, 'Bunny' (Carl Schultze). It is not known whether this is an original book featuring the character Foxy Grandpa from the Sunday comic strip, or a reprint of such strips.

25 The New Adventures of Foxy Grandpa

December 1903. 60¢. 66 pp. 15¼ × 10¼. Publisher: Frederick A. Stokes Co., 5 East 16th Street, New York. Artist: Carl Schultze ('Bunny').

Contents
Compilation of 30 half-page strips reprinted from the William Randolph Hearst Sunday supplements. Strips are printed in four colours on one side of the page only, with a title page and full-colour cover specially drawn by the artist, 'Bunny' (Carl Schultze). Cardboard covers. The strips are copyrighted 1902 and 1903. British edition published by W. & R. Chambers, London and Edinburgh.

26 Buster Brown, His Dog Tige, and Their Troubles

October 1904. 70¢. 66 pp. 16×11¹/₄. Publisher: Frederick A. Stokes Co., 5 East 16th Street, New York. Artist: Richard F. Outcault. Syndicate: New York Herald.

Contents
Compilation of strips reprinted from Sunday newspaper supplements and copyrighted 1903 and 1904 by the *New York Herald*. The original full-page strips have been divided into halves, and printed in four colours on one side of the page only. Thus there are 15 complete strips in the book, plus a specially drawn cover and title page by the artist, R. F. Outcault. Cardboard covers. British edition published by W. & R. Chambers, London and Edinburgh. This book was reprinted in 1974 by Dover Publications, with a new introduction by August Derleth, and a new cover designed by Theodore Menten. It was entitled *Buster Brown*, and incorrectly credited as a republication of the earlier book, *Buster Brown and His Resolutions* (1904). The original book was republished by Stokes in 1917 in a cheap 25¢ edition.

27 Foxy Grandpa Up-to-Date

October 1904. 60¢. 66 pp. 15¹/₄×10¹/₄. Publisher: Frederick A. Stokes Co., 5 East 16th Street, New York. Artist: Carl Schultze ('Bunny'). Syndicate: American Journal–Examiner; William R. Hearst.

Contents
Compilation of half-page strips reprinted from Sunday supplements. Contains 30 strips in full colour, printed on one side of the page only, plus black-and-white title page and full-colour cover specially drawn by the artist, 'Bunny' (Carl Schultze). The strips are copyrighted 1903 by W.R. Hearst and 1904 by the *American Journal–Examiner*. Seventeen of the strips are entitled 'Foxy Grandpa and Smart Uncle Alex'. Cardboard covers. British edition published by W. & R. Chambers Ltd., London and Edinburgh.

28 Buster Brown Abroad

November 1904. $1.00. 86 pp. 8×10¹/₄. Publisher: Frederick A. Stokes Co., 5 East 16th Street, New York. Artist: Richard F. Outcault.

Contents
The first novelization of a comic strip character. The artist, Richard F. Outcault, here adapted his Sunday supplement strips into a narrative concerning Buster Brown and his family and pets on an ocean cruise to foreign parts. Profusely illustrated, but not to be considered a comic book.

29 Buster Brown's Blue Ribbon Book of Jokes and Jingles

No. 1–No. 2: 1905. Free (promotional). Publisher: Brown Shoe Co., St. Louis, Missouri. Artist: Richard F. Outcault.

The first original comic book to be produced as an advertising premium, this short-run series was built around Richard Outcault's popular comic strip, Buster Brown, which first appeared on 4 May 1902 in the *New York Herald.* Buster Brown was an obvious choice of symbol for the Brown Shoe Company of St. Louis, and they launched a special line called Buster Brown Blue Ribbon Shoes for boys and girls. The book, with its full-colour covers, was specially drawn by the artist, and introduced Buster and his gang: Tige the dog, Mary Jane, and even Outcault's earlier comic hero, the Yellow Kid, all of whom lined up on the back cover to sing perhaps the world's first commercial jingle: 'And all our days we'll sing the praise of Buster Brown Blue Ribbon Shoes!' Buster continued to be identified with Brown's Shoes long after the demise of both his strip and his creator. A new series of their *Buster Brown Comics* ran from 1945 to 1960.

30 Dreams of the Rarebit Fiend

1905. 68 pp. $7^1/_2 \times 10^1/_4$. Publisher: Frederick A. Stokes Co., 5 East 16th Street, New York. Artist: 'Silas' (Winsor McCay).

Introduction
'The happy creations which appear inside are the reproductions of a comic series now running in the *New York Evening Telegram.* They have caused many people to laugh and some, perchance, to weep, for it frequently happens that one man's food is another's poison. Nevertheless, the popularity of this series has so grown and the manifestations of approval have become so numerous, along with a suggestion that the creations be given some permanent form, that the *New York Evening Telegram* has generously permitted the author and publisher to make the book possible. The very vitality of the series lies in the public's appreciation, and, grounded on this fact, the present volume is submitted for further approval.'

Contents
Compilation of 61 daily newspaper strips reprinted from the *New York Evening Telegram.* Printed in black-and-white, with a new cover and title page drawn by the artist, 'Silas' (Winsor McCay), who also wrote an introduction. Included are the additional articles 'Rarebit Symbolism' by Randolph C. Lewis, 'On the History of the Welsh Rabbit' by T.B. Hanly, and 'Concerning the Symptoms' by John W. Harrington. All were hand-lettered by McCay. A new edition was published in 1973 by Dover Publications Inc., New York, which dropped one of the original strips as 'unpalatable', and added a new Publisher's Note on the artist and his film versions.

31 Foxy Grandpa and Flip-Flaps

1905. 60¢. 68 pp. $15^1/_4 \times 10^1/_4$. Publisher: Frederick A. Stokes Co., 5 East 16th Street, New York. Artist: Carl Schultze ('Bunny'). Syndicate: American Journal–Examiner.

Contents
Compilation of 30 half-page strips reprinted from the William Randolph Hearst Sunday supplements, printed in four colours on one side of the page only. Cardboard covers.

32 Jimmy

1905. 50¢. 40 pp. 15×10. Publisher: New York American & Journal (W.R. Hearst). Artist: James Swinnerton.

Contents
Compilation of newspaper strips from the William Randolph Hearst Sunday supplements, reprinted in full colour. Special cover drawn by the artist, James Swinnerton; cardboard covers. 'Jimmy' started as a strip on 14 February 1904, and was later retitled 'Little Jimmy'.

33 The Upside-Downs of Little Lady Lovekins and Old Man Muffaroo

1905. 32 pp. Publisher: G.W. Dillingham Co., 12 East 22nd Street, New York. Artist: Gustave Verbeck. Syndicate: New York Herald Co.

Contents
Compilation of 24 half-page-size comic strips reprinted in four colours from the Sunday supplement of the *New York Herald*, and copyrighted 1904. The strip was unique in that after the six panels had been read, it could be turned upside down and read as a further, different six panels. The British edition was published by W. & R. Chambers, London and Edinburgh, and a reprint in much reduced format was published by Rajah Press in 1963.

34 Foxy Grandpa's Surprises

August 1905. 70¢. 64 pp. $15^1/_4 \times 10^1/_4$. Publisher: Frederick A. Stokes Co., 5 East 16th Street, New York. Artist: Carl Schultze ('Bunny'). Syndicate: American Journal–Examiner.

Contents
Compilation of 29 half-page strips reprinted from the William Randolph Hearst Sunday supplements. Strips are copyrighted 1904 and 1905 by the *American Journal–Examiner*, and are printed in three colours on one side of the page only. British edition published by W. & R. Chambers, London and Edinburgh. Cardboard covers.

35 Buster Brown's Pranks

December 1905. 70¢. 66 pp. $16 \times 11^1/_4$. Publisher: Frederick A. Stokes Co., 5 East 16th Street, New York. Artist: Richard F. Outcault. Syndicate: New York Herald.

Contents
Compilation of newspaper strips reprinted from the *New York Herald* Sunday supplement, and copyrighted 1903 and 1904. The original full-page strips are divided into halves and printed in four colours on one side of the page only. Original title page and full-colour cover drawn by the artist, R.F. Outcault. British edition published by W. & R. Chambers, London and Edinburgh. Cardboard covers.

36 Little Sammy Sneeze

December 1905. 70¢. 62 pp. $16^1/_2 \times 11$. Publisher: Frederick A. Stokes Co., 5 East 16th Street, New York. Artist: Winsor McCay. Syndicate: New York Herald.

Contents
Compilation of half-page strips reprinted from the Sunday comic supplements. Contains 28 strips copyrighted 1905 by the *New York Herald*, printed in full colour on one side of the page only, plus an original title page and full-colour cover drawn by the artist, Winsor McCay. British edition published by W. & R. Chambers Ltd., London and Edinburgh. Cardboard covers. 'Permission to print this series in book form, kindly granted by the *New York Herald*, was received with thanks by the author and publisher.'

37 Tige: His Story

December 1905. $1.25. Publisher: Frederick A. Stokes Co., 5 East 16th Street, New York. Artist: Richard F. Outcault.

Contents
Fictitious 'biography' of Buster Brown's pet dog, written as a text story and illustrated by the artist, Richard Felton Outcault. British edition published in 1906 by W. & R. Chambers, London and Edinburgh. Not considered a true comic book.

38 Buster Brown, His Dog Tige, and Their Jolly Times

1906. 60¢. 66 pp. 16½×11. Publisher: Cupples & Leon, 443 Fourth Avenue, New York. Artist: Richard F. Outcault. Syndicate: New York Herald Co.

Contents
Compilation of 30 newspaper strips reprinted from the Sunday supplement of the *New York Herald*, and copyrighted 1905. Printed in four colours, on one side of the page only, with a full-colour cover and title page drawn by C. Nuttall. Cardboard covers. This was the first comic book of Buster Brown to be published by Cupples & Leon, who had taken over the reprinting rights from the Frederick A. Stokes Co. when the original artist, Richard Felton Outcault, left the *New York Herald* to draw Buster for William Randolph Hearst's *American Journal–Examiner*. Outcault's original Buster continued as a reprint comic book with the Stokes company. British edition published by Dean & Son, London. The book was reprinted in 1916 by Cupples & Leon in a cheap 35¢ edition.

39 Buster Brown's Antics

1906. 60¢. 66 pp. 16×11. Publisher: Frederick A. Stokes Co., 5 East 16th Street, New York. Artist: Richard F. Outcault. Syndicate: American Journal–Examiner; Denver Post.

Contents
Compilation of strips reprinted from the Sunday comic supplements. This book contains 15 broadsheet pages divided into halves, printed in four colours on one side of the paper only. Strips are copyrighted 1905 and 1906 by the *American Journal–Examiner*, with one strip copyright 1906 the *Denver Post* and R.F. Outcault. Unusually in this series, the printer is given credit: the Charles Francis

Press. British edition published by W. & R. Chambers Ltd., Edinburgh and London. Cardboard covers.

40 Foxy Grandpa's Frolics

1906. 60¢. 66 pp. 15¼×10¼. Publisher: Frederick A. Stokes Co., 5 East 16th Street, New York. Artist: Carl Schultze ('Bunny'). Syndicate: American Journal–Examiner.

Contents
Compilation of 30 half-page strips reprinted from the William Randolph Hearst Sunday supplements. Strips are printed in four colours on one side of the page only, and are copyrighted 1904, 1905, 1906 by the *American Journal–Examiner*. Cardboard covers. British edition published by W. & R. Chambers Ltd., London and Edinburgh. A cheap 25¢ edition was published by Stokes in 1917.

41 Jimmy and His Scrapes

1906. 66 pp. 15¼×10¼. Publisher: Frederick A. Stokes Co., 5 East 16th Street, New York. Artist: James Swinnerton. Syndicate: American Journal–Examiner.

Contents
Compilation of half-page strips reprinted from the William Randolph Hearst Sunday supplements. Contains 30 strips printed in four colours on one side of the page only, plus black-and-white title page and full-colour cover specially drawn by the artist, James Swinnerton. The strips are copyrighted 1905 and 1906 by the *American Journal–Examiner*. Cardboard covers. British edition published by W. & R. Chambers Ltd., London and Edinburgh.

42 Maud

1906. 70 pp. 15½×10¼. Publisher: Frederick A. Stokes Co., 5 East 16th Street, New York. Artist: Frederick Burr Opper. Syndicate: American Journal–Examiner.

Contents
Compilation of half-page strips reprinted from the William Randolph Hearst Sunday supplements. Contains 30 strips printed in three colours, on one side of the page only, plus black-and-white title page and full-colour cover specially drawn by the artist, F. Opper. The strips, originally titled 'And Her Name Was Maud', are copyrighted 1904, 1905, 1906 by the *American Journal–Examiner*. Cardboard covers. British edition published by Dow & Lester, Forester's Hall Place, Clerkenwell Road, London, E.C.

43 Sam and His Laugh

1906. 60 pp. 15¼×10¼. Publisher: Frederick A. Stokes Co., 5 East 16th Street, New York. Artist: James Swinnerton. Syndicate: American Journal–Examiner.

Contents
Compilation of half-page strips reprinted from the William Randolph Hearst Sunday supplements. Contains 27 strips printed in four colours on one side of the page only, plus black-and-white title page and full-colour cover specially drawn by the artist, James Swinnerton. Copyrighted 1904 and 1905 by the *American Journal–Examiner*. Cardboard covers. British edition published by W. & R. Chambers Ltd., London and Edinburgh.

44 The Travels of Happy Hooligan

1906. 66 pp. 15¼×10¼. Publisher: Frederick A. Stokes Co., 5 East 16th Street, New York. Artist: Frederick Burr Opper. Syndicate: American Journal–Examiner.

Contents
Compilation of half-page strips reprinted from the William Randolph Hearst Sunday supplements. Contains 30 strips printed in four colours on one side of the page only, plus black-and-white title page and full-colour cover specially drawn by the artist, F. Opper. The strips are copyrighted 1905 and 1906 by the *American Journal–Examiner*, and feature the two tramps, Happy Hooligan and Gloomy Gus, on a world trip. Cardboard covers. British edition published by W. & R. Chambers Ltd., London and Edinburgh. *Note:* this title was incorrectly advertised in other Stokes publications as *Happy Hooligan's Travels*.

45 The Trials of Lulu and Leander

1906. 62 pp. 15¼×10¼. Publisher: Frederick A. Stokes Co., 5 East 16th Street, New York. Artist: Franklin Morris Howarth. Syndicate: American Journal–Examiner.

Contents
Compilation of half-page strips reprinted from the William Randolph Hearst Sunday supplements. Contains 28 strips printed in three colours on one side of the paper only, plus a new black-and-white title page and full-colour cover drawn by the artist, F.M. Howarth. The strips, originally titled 'The Love of Lulu and Leander', are copyrighted 1905 by the *American Journal–Examiner*. Cardboard covers. British edition published by W. & R. Chambers Ltd., London and Edinburgh.

46 The Tricks of the Katzenjammer Kids

1906. 66 pp. 15¼×10¼. Publisher: Frederick A. Stokes Co., 5 East 16th Street, New York. Artist: Rudolph Dirks. Syndicate: American Journal–Examiner.
47
Contents
Compilation of strips reprinted from the William Randolph Hearst Sunday supplements. Contains 30 strips printed in four colours on one side of the page only, plus a new black-and-white title page and full-colour cover drawn by the artist, Rudolph Dirks. The strips are copyrighted 1905 by the *American Journal–Examiner*. Cardboard covers. British edition published by W. & R. Chambers Ltd., London and Edinburgh. No. 1 of *The Katzenjammer Kids* series (by this publisher).

47 Willie Westinghouse Edison Smith the Boy Inventor

1906. 70 pp. 16×10¹/₄. Publisher: Frederick A. Stokes Co., 5 East 16th Street, New York. Artist: Frank Crane.

Introduction
This book is most cordially dedicated by the author to all the little 'Jack-knife Carpenters' of the world.

Contents
  1 Cover
  3 Title page; Introduction
  5 (R) Willie Westinghouse's Auto Life-saving Device
  7 (R) Willie Westinghouse Teaches Cousin Tommy How to Swim
  9 (R) Willie Westinghouse Stops the Chimney from Smoking but —
 11 (R) Willie Westinghouse on the Farm: His Patent Churn
 13 (R) Willie Westinghouse Tries to Cure a Runaway Colt
 15 (R) The Automatic Door Was All Right but Papa Was Careless
 17 (R) Willie Westinghouse Gives his Papa a Whirl on the Ice
 19 (R) Willie Westinghouse Improves Papa's Patent Fire Extinguisher
 21 (R) Willie Westinghouse Has a New Airship Scheme
 23 (R) Willie Gives Papa and the Minister a Swift Ride Down Hill
 25 (R) Willie Westinghouse Tries to Roll the Lawn by Electric Power
 27 (R) Willie on the Farm: The Airbrake That Worked Too Well
 29 (R) Willie Westinghouse Goes Out for the Dust and Gets It
 31 (R) Papa Didn't Know the Bank Messenger's Satchel Was Loaded
 33 (R) Willie's Safety Appliance Puts the Automobile Out of Commission
 35 (R) Willie Westinghouse's Patent Paint Brush Causes Trouble
 37 (R) Willie Westinghouse Opens the Baseball Season
 39 (R) Willie Westinghouse Tries to Teach the Twins to Skate
 41 (R) Willie Westinghouse Invents a Lightning Stencil Brush
 43 (R) Willie Westinghouse Builds a Swell Easter Bonnet for Cook
 45 (R) Willie Westinghouse Gives Jim's Twins a Rid on His Snow Carrousel
 47 (R) Willie Westinghouse Invents a Newfangled Sweeper
 49 (R) Willie's Fire Escape Is a Good Scheme
 51 (R) Willie's Automatic Scarecrow and How It Worked
 53 (R) Willie Westinghouse Gives the Minister a Shaking Up
 55 (R) Willie Westinghouse Builds a Shoot-the-chute
 57 (R) Willie Westinghouse Shakes Up the Police Department
 59 (R) Willie Westinghouse Gets into More Trouble in the Kitchen
 61 (R) Willie Converts Santa Claus into a Cider Fountain
 63 (R) Willie Westinghouse Greets the New Year with a New Invention

Compilation of half-page strips reprinted from Sunday newspaper supplements. Contains 30 strips printed in four colours, on one side of the page only, plus black-and-white title page and full-colour cover specially drawn by the artist, Frank Crane, Cardboard Covers. British edition published by Alston Rivers Ltd., Arundel Street, London, W.C.

48 The Merry Pranks of Foxy Grandpa

May 1906. 75¢. 60 pp. 15½×9½. Publisher: M.A. Donohue & Co., 407 Dearborn Street, Chicago. Artist: Carl Schultz ('Bunny'). Syndicate: New York Herald.

Contents
Compilation of 28 half-page strips reprinted in four colours from the *New York Herald* Sunday supplements. Cardboard covers, specially drawn by the artist, 'Bunny'.

49 Little Nemo in Slumberland

September 1906. 75¢. 30 pp. 16½×11. Publisher: Duffield & Co., 36 West 37th Street, New York. Artist: Winsor McCay. Syndicate: New York Herald.

Contents
Compilation of the weekly newspaper strip published in the Sunday supplement of the *New York Herald* (first appearance: 15 October 1905). Reprinted in four colours, with each broadsheet page divided into halves. The strip concerns the vivid dreams of a small boy, and his nightly adventures with the strange people who live in Dreamland. Compare with the same artist's version of adult dreams in *Dreams of the Rarebit Fiend*.

50 My Resolutions by Buster Brown

November 1906. 75¢. 68 pp. Publisher: Frederick A. Stokes Co., 5 East 16th Street, New York. Artist: Richard F. Outcault. Syndicate: American Journal–Examiner.

Contents
Compilation of 60 'resolutions', extracted from Buster Brown comic strips originally published in the William Randolph Hearst Sunday supplements. Buster Brown always ended each adventure with a 'resolution'. Printed in black-and-white as a small volume with cardboard covers, including a photograph of the artist, Richard F. Outcault, signed 'sincerely yours'. British edition published by W. & R. Chambers Ltd., London and Edinburgh. A paper-covered reprint of this book, entitled *Buster Brown's Maxims for Men*, was published by Chambers, in 1907, price 1s.

51 Little Johnny and the Teddy Bears

1907. 50¢. 32 pp. 10½×14½. Publisher: Reilly & Britton Co., (No. F1292), 1006 Michigan Avenue, Chicago. Artist: John Randolph Bray.

Contents
Compilation of the weekly strip reprinted in four colours from *Judge* magazine. The original advertisement read:

> *Sets forth the uproarious adventures of six stuffed Teddy Bears who come to life by means of a wonderful elixir and with Johnny get into and out of all kinds of mischief. The funniest*

pictures imaginable by J.R. Bray, reproduced in brilliant colors, and ridiculous rhymes by R.D. Tane, editor of Judge. Bound in stiff card board and printed in many colors.

The strip ran on the back page of *Judge* from 1903 to 1910, and was the first strip to feature the Teddy Bear toys made popular through President Theodore ('Teddy') Roosevelt. The artist, John Randolph Bray, left strip cartooning to become the leading producer of animated cartoon films in the silent era.

52 Military Willie

1907. 16 pp. 9½×7. Publisher: J.I. Austen Co., Chicago. Artist: F.R. Morgan.

Contents
Compilation of strips, printed with half the pages in black-and-white, half in colour. The strips, which have nine pictures to each page, have not been traced to any newspaper, so may be original for the book.

53 The Newlyweds and Their Baby

1907. 68 pp. 10×13. Publisher: Saalfield Publishing Co., Akron, Ohio. Artist: George McManus. Syndicate: Press Publishing Co.

Contents
Compilation of 57 daily newspaper strips syndicated by Joseph Pulitzer's *New York World*. Hardcover, with four introductory illustrations specially drawn for the book by the artist, George McManus. Printed black-and-white with alternate pages in single colours.
Ten years later the same publisher, Saalfield, reprinted several of these strips in a new, shorter edition entitled *The Newlyweds and Their Baby's Comic Pictures*.

54 The Outbursts of Everett True

1907. 35¢. 100 pp. 4½×9. Publisher: Saalfield Publishing Co., Akron, Ohio. Artist: A.D. Condo.

Introduction
'JUST A MINUTE —
We're all of us mollycoddles — more or less. We have a valuable hour which somebody wearies away in recitals of his troubles with his furnace. We look pleasant when a neighbor hurls at us the "bright sayings" of his Little Willie. We graciously permit a man to give the hot air treatment to some question of politics — and dinner growing colder every minute. We tolerate the nuisance and the boor, even smiling, at times, instead of resenting intrusions and impertinences. And all for the sake of peace. Everett True lacks our weakness in treatment of the human pest. He is a living protest against the incarnate irritants that are with us always. He is not a reformer, but rather an executioner, inflicting punishment where he comes in contact with fit subjects of penal treatment. Mr. True's victims call him a "grouch". In reality he is a humanitarian.'

Contents

Compilation reprinting the daily newspaper strip drawn by A.D. Condo and written by J.W. Raper. It includes 77 strips arranged over 94 pages printed in black-and-white. A facsimile edition was published in 1983 by the Vestal Press Ltd. of New York.

55 Peck's Bad Boy and Cousin Cynthia

1907. 11³/₄×15³/₄. Publisher: Thompson, Chicago. Artist: Walt McDougall.

Contents

Compilation of Sunday newspaper supplement strips reprinted in four colours, with cardboard covers specially drawn by the artist, Walt McDougall. The strip depicted the further adventures of the characters created in a series of popular short stories by George W. Peck.

56 Buddy Tucker (Buster Brown Nuggets)

December 1907. 25¢. 32 pp. 6¹/₄×7¹/₄. Publisher: Cupples & Leon Co., 443 Fourth Avenue, New York. Syndicate: New York Herald. Artist: Richard F. Outcault.

No. 1 *Buddy Tucker Meets Alice in Wonderland*
No. 2 *Buddy Tucker Visits the House That Jack Built*

Contents

Listed by the publisher as No. 9 and No. 10 of the *Buster Brown Nuggets* series (see *Buster Brown Nuggets*). Reprints of strips from the *New York Herald* Sunday supplement, copyright date 1905. The strips, originally a half-page series of six pictures, are arranged one picture to each page, printed in full colour. Cardboard covers with special cover illustration are printed in full colour, with a frontispiece in black-and-white.

57 Buster Brown and Mary Jane's Painting Book

December 1907. 75¢. 16×11¹/₄. Publisher: Frederick A. Stokes Co., 5 East 16th Street, New York. Artist: Richard F. Outcault.

Contents

Series of large pictures adapted from the Sunday newspaper strip published by William Randolph Hearst. Cardboard covers, printed in full colour, specially drawn by the artist, R.F. Outcault. British edition published by the University Press, Cambridge.

58 Buster Brown's Autobiography

December 1907. $1.25. Publisher: Frederick A. Stokes Co., 5 East 16th Street, New York. Artist: Richard F. Outcault.

Contents
Fictional autobiography of the comic strip character, written as a text story and illustrated by the artist, Richard Felton Outcault. British edition published in November 1909 by W. & R. Chambers, London and Edinburgh. Not considered a true comic book.

59 Buster Brown's Latest Frolics

December 1907. 60¢. 66 pp. 16×11. Publisher: Cupples & Leon Co., 443 Fourth Avenue, New York. Artist: Richard F. Outcault. Syndicate: New York Herald.

Contents
Compilation of newspaper strips reprinted from the *New York Herald* Sunday supplement. Contains 15 full-page strips divided into halves and printed in four colours on one side of the page only. Strips are copyrighted 1905 and 1906. By the time this book was published, the original artist, R.F. Outcault, had moved to the William Randolph Hearst newspapers, hence the covers and title page for this book are drawn by another artist, C. Nuttall. Cardboard covers. British edition published by Dean & Son, London. Cupples & Leon republished the book in 1916 in a cheap 35¢ edition.

60 Buster Brown Nuggets

December 1907. 25¢. 32 pp. 6¼×7¼. Publisher: Cupples & Leon Co., 443 Fourth Avenue, New York. Syndicate: New York Herald. Artist: Richard F. Outcault.

No. 1 *Buster Brown Goes Fishing*
No. 2 *Buster Brown Goes Swimming*
No. 3 *Buster Brown Plays Indian*
No. 4 *Buster Brown Goes Shooting*
No. 5 *Buster Brown Plays Cowboy*
No. 6 *Buster Brown on Uncle Jack's Farm*
No. 7 *Buster Brown, Tige and the Bull*
No. 8 *Buster Brown and Uncle Buster*

Contents
Series of 'Six Funny Books for Children' (also listed as 10 books). Reprints of strips from the *New York Herald* Sunday supplement, copyright date 1905. The strips are arranged with one picture to each page, printed in full colour. Cardboard covers with special cover illustration printed in full colour. British edition published by Dean & Son, London. The last two *Buster Brown Nuggets* (No. 9 and No. 10) were, in fact, *Buddy Tucker* books: see *Buddy Tucker (Buster Brown Nuggets)*. This series was reprinted in 1908 by Saalfield & Co., in an untearable format as *Buster Brown Muslin Books*.

61 The Cruise of the Katzenjammer Kids

December 1907. 60¢. 62 pp. 15×10. Publisher: Frederick A. Stokes Co., 5 East 16th Street, New York. Artist: Rudolph Dirks. Syndicate: New York Journal.

Contents

Compilation of strips reprinted from the Sunday supplement of the *New York Journal*. Contains 14 full-page strips divided into half pages and printed in four colours on one side of the page only. The strips comprise a serial continuity of the Katzenjammer family's voyage aboard the *Prosit*. No. 2 of *The Katzenjammer Kids* series.

62 Foxy Grandpa's Triumphs

December 1907. 60¢. 62 pp. 15¼×10¼. Publisher: Frederick A. Stokes Co., 5 East 16th Street, New York. Artist: Carl Schultze ('Bunny'). Syndicate: American Journal–Examiner.

Contents

Compilation of half-page strips reprinted from the William Randolph Hearst Sunday supplements. Contains 28 strips printed in four colours on one side of the paper only. Cardboard covers with an original drawing by the artist, 'Bunny', plus title page in black-and-white. British edition published by W. & R. Chambers, London and Edinburgh. A cheap 25¢ edition was published by Stokes in 1917.

63 Happy Hooligan Home Again

December 1907. 60¢. 66 pp. 15¼×10¼. Publisher: Frederick A. Stokes Co., 5 East 16th Street, New York. Artist: Frederick Burr Opper. Syndicate: American Journal–Examiner.

Contents

Compilation of strips reprinted from the William Randolph Hearst Sunday supplements. Contains 30 strips printed in four colours on one side of the page only, plus black-and-white title pages and four-colour cover specially drawn by the artist, F. Opper. Cardboard covers.

64 Maud the Matchless

December 1907. 60¢ 70 pp. 15¼×10¼. Publisher: Frederick A. Stokes Co., 5 East 16th Street, New York. Artist: Frederick Burr Opper. Syndicate: American Journal–Examiner.

Contents

Compilation of half-page strips reprinted from the William Randolph Hearst Sunday supplements. Contains 30 strips printed in colour on one side of the page only, plus a black-and-white title page and full-colour cover specially drawn by the artist, F. Opper. The strip's original title is 'And Her Name Was Maud'. Cardboard covers. No. 2 in the *Maud* series.

65 Outcault's Buster Brown and Co., Including Mary Jane

December 1907. 60¢ 66 pp. 16×11. Publisher: Frederick A. Stokes Co., 5 East 16th Street, New York. Artist: Richard F. Outcault. Syndicate: American Journal–Examiner.

Contents

Compilation of newspaper strips reprinted from the William Randolph Hearst Sunday supplements. Contains 15 full-page strips divided into halves and printed in four colours on one side of the page only. Strips are copyrighted 1906–1907 by the *American Journal–Examiner*, and include the sequence featuring Buster Brown's goat. Also included are the headings of the comic supplements with cartoons by Gus Mager. The artist's name is in the book's title to distinguish it from the other Buster Brown series, published by Cupples & Leon. Cardboard covers. British edition published by W. & R. Chambers of London and Edinburgh.

66 The Teddy Bear Books

1907(?). 20 pp. 5½ × 6¾. Publisher: Merrimack Publishing Corporation, 85 Fifth Avenue, New York. Artist: John Randolph Bray.

No. 1 *The Teddy Bears Come to Life*
No. 2 *The Teddy Bears in a Smashup*
No. 3 *The Teddy Bears on a Lark*
No. 4 *The Teddy Bears in Hot Water*

Contents

Small books each containing reprints of two strips from the weekly series, 'Little Johnny and the Teddy Bears', first published in *Judge* magazine, 1907. Reprinted one picture to each page, in three colours (black, red, green), with new cover, back cover, and frontispiece drawings by the artist, John R. Bray.

This series by the Merrimack Publishing Corporation appears to be a reprinting of an earlier series of books as yet untraced. These books are printed in Hong Kong by a lithographic or gravure process. The series carries no date, but the cover art is dated 1907. See entry for **Little Johnny and the Teddy Bears**.

67 Adventures of Peck's Bad Boy in Pictures

1908. 11¾ × 15¾. Publisher: Stanton & Van Liet Co. Artist: Walt McDougall.

Contents

Compilation of Sunday newspaper supplement strips reprinted in four colours, with cardboard covers specially drawn by the artist, Walt McDougall. The strip depicted the further adventures of the characters created by George W. Peck in his popular series of short stories and books. Third collection of the strip, but the first by this publisher.

68 Buster Brown's Amusing Capers

1908. 60¢. 58 pp. 16¼ × 11¼. Publisher: Cupples & Leon Co., 443 Fourth Avenue, New York. Syndicate: New York Herald Co.

Contents
Compilation of Buster Brown strips, reprinted from Sunday comic supplements syndicated by the New York Herald Company, and copyrighted 1906–1907. The book contains 13 broadsheet pages divided into halves, printed in full colour on one side of the page only. The only new material is the cover drawing, which is reprinted black-and-white as a title page. Cardboard covers. British edition published by Dean & Son Ltd., 160a Fleet Street, London, E.C. These strips are not drawn by the creator, Richard F. Outcault, but by an anonymous substitute artist. A cheap editon of this book was published in 1916, price 35¢.

69 Foxy Grandpa Sparklets

1908. 24 pp. $6^1/2 \times 7^3/4$. Publisher: M.A. Donohue & Co., 407 Dearborn Street, Chicago. Artist: Carl Schultze ('Bunny').

No. 1 *Foxy Grandpa Rides the Goat*
No. 2 *Foxy Grandpa Playing Ball*
No. 3 *Foxy Grandpa Fun on the Farm*
No. 4 *Foxy Grandpa Fancy Shooting*
No. 5 *Foxy Grandpa Shows the Boys Up*
No. 6 *Foxy Grandpa Plays Santa Claus*

Contents
Series of six small booklets reprinting newspaper strips from the Sunday supplements. The strips are rearranged as one picture to each page, with four strips in each book.

70 The Mischievous Monks of Crocodile Isle

1908. 12 pp. $8^1/2 \times 11^1/2$. Publisher: J.I. Austen Co., Chicago. Artist: F.R. Morgan.

Contents
Compilation of strips reprinted 4 pages in colours, 8 pages in black-and-white. The strips are arranged longwise so that the book must be turned to be read.

71 Peck's Bad Boy and His Chums

1908. $11^3/4 \times 15^3/4$. Publisher: Thompson, Chicago. Artist: Walt McDougall.

Contents
Compilation of Sunday newspaper supplement strips reprinted in four colours, with cardboard covers specially drawn by the artist, Walt McDougall. The strip depicted the further adventures of the characters created by George W. Peck in a popular series of short stories. Second in this publisher's series.

72 The Three Funmakers

1908. 60¢. 68 pp. $15^1/4 \times 10^1/4$. Publisher: Frederick A. Stokes Co., 5 East 16th Street, New York. Syndicate: American Journal–Examiner.

Contents
Compilation of three different series of strips reprinted from the Sunday supplements of William Randolph Hearst newspapers: 'Happy Hooligan' by Fred Opper, 'And Her Name Was Maud' by Fred Opper, and 'The Katzenjammer Kids' by Rudolph Dirks. Printed in four colours on one side of the page only. Cardboard covers. This might be regarded as the prototype of the modern comic book, as it is the first compilation of several different strips.

73 Foxy Grandpa and His Boys

August 1908. 60¢. 64 pp. 15¼×10¼. Publisher: Frederick A. Stokes Co., 5 East 16th Street, New York. Artist: Carl Schultze ('Bunny'). Syndicate: American Journal–Examiner.

Contents
Compilation of 25 half-page strips and two full-page strips reprinted from the William Randolph Hearst Sunday supplements. Strips are copyright 1904, 1907 and 1908 by the *American Journal–Examiner*, and include some adventures entitled 'Foxy Grandpa Abroad' featuring his visit to the Alps in 1904. Strips are printed in four colours on one side of the page only. British edition published by W. & R. Chambers, London and Edinburgh. A cheap 25¢ edition was published in 1917 by Stokes.

74 Handy Happy Hooligan

August 1908. 60¢. 70 pp. 15¼×10¼. Publisher: Frederick A. Stokes Co., 5 East 16th Street, New York. Artist: Frederick Burr Opper. Syndicate: American Journal–Examiner.

Contents
Compilation of strips reprinted from the William Randolph Hearst Sunday supplements. Contains 30 strips printed in four colours on one side of the page only, plus black-and-white title page and full-colour cover drawn by the artist, F. Opper. Cardboard covers.

75 The Komical Katzenjammers

August 1908. 60¢. 62 pp. 15×10. Publisher: Frederick A. Stokes Co., 5 East 16th Street, New York. New York. Artist: Rudolph Dirks. Syndicate: New York Journal.

Contents
1 Cover
4 (R) Such Is Life at the North Pole
6 (R) Der Captain's Relief Party Is a Fizzle
8 (R) My, Such a Relief!
10 (R) So Nearovitch! It Was Toughsky!
12 (R) Allee Samee Comes Chinese Explorer!
14 (R) Oh Such a Mean Trick!
16 (R) An Off Day on Board the *Prosit*

18 (R) Fritz Gets a Camera! Hans Gets Jealous!
20 (R) It Vas der Captain's Cousin!
22 (R) The Katzies Have the Measles!
24 (R) Yes Thank You! The Katzenjammer Kids Are Well Again
26 (R) In Addition to Which the Kids Wish You All a Happy New Year
28 (R) Introducing Sandy the New Butcher Boy
30 (R) No, the Katzenjammer Kids Couldn't Stand the Strain

Compilation of Sunday supplement comic strips, copyrighted 1906–1907 by the *New York Journal*. Contains 14 full-page strips divided into half-pages, printed in full colour on one side of the page only. Eight of the strips deal with the Katzenjammer family's voyage to the North Pole aboard the *Prosit*. A facsimile edition was published in 1974 by Dover Publication Inc., with a new introduction by August Derleth. No. 3 of *The Katzenjammer Kids* series.

76 Maud the Mirthful Mule

August 1908. 60¢. 70 pp. 15¼×10¼. Publisher: Frederick A. Stokes Co., 5 East 16th Street, New York. Artist: Frederick Burr Opper. Syndicate: American Journal–Examiner.

Contents
Compilation of strips reprinted from the William Randolph Hearst Sunday supplements. Contains 30 strips printed in colours on one side of the page only, plus an original title page in black-and-white and a full-colour cover drawn by the artist, F. Opper. The title of the strip is actually 'And Her Name Was Maud'. Cardboard covers. No. 3 in the *Maud* series.

77 Outcault's Buster, Mary Jane, and Tige

August 1908. 60¢ 66 pp. 16×11. Publisher: Frederick A. Stokes Co., 5 East 16th Street, New York. Artist: Richard F. Outcault. Syndicate: American Journal–Examiner.

Contents
Compilation of newspaper strips reprinted from the William Randolph Hearst Sunday supplements. Contains 15 full-page strips divided into halves and printed in four colours on one side of the page only. The title identifies this as being drawn by the original artist, R.F. Outcault, as opposed to the rival series of books being issued by Cupples & Leon. Outcault also drew a special full-colour cover, and black-and-white title page. Cardboard covers. British edition published by W. & R. Chambers Ltd., London and Edinburgh.

78 Angelic Angelina

1909. 30 pp. 17×11½. Publisher: Cupples & Leon Co., 443 Fourth Avenue, New York. Artist: Munson Paddock.

Contents
Compilation of newspaper strips reprinted from Sunday supplements. Printed in two colours on one side of the page only. Cardboard covers, with special cover drawn by the artist, Munson Paddock.

79 Buffalo Bill's Picture Stories

1909. Publisher: Street & Smith Publications, 7th Avenue, New York..

Contents
Strips in a card cover. No further details known, but may be the first comic book with original artwork, rather than reprints.

80 Little Nemo in Slumberland

1909. 14×10. Publisher: Cupples & Leon Co., 443 Fourth Avenue, New York. Artist: Winsor McCay. Syndicate: New York Herald.

Contents
Compilation of the weekly newspaper strip published in the Sunday supplement of the *New York Herald*. Reprinted in four colours, with each broadsheet page divided into halves to make a large oblong book, printed on one side of the page only. Cardboard covers, specially drawn by the artist, Winsor McCay.

81 The Monkey-Shines of Marseleen

1909. 17×11½. 28 pp. Publisher: Cupples & Leon Co., 443 Fourth Avenue, New York. Artist: Norman Jenner.

Contents
Compilation of the weekly newspaper strip published in Sunday comic supplements. Reprinted in two colours, on one side of the page only. Cardboard covers, specially drawn by the artist, Norman E. Jenner.

82 Buster Brown the Busy Body

December 1909. 60¢. 58 pp. 16×11. Publisher: Cupples & Leon, 443 Fourth Avenue, New York. Syndicate: New York Herald.

Contents
Compilation of 13 newspaper strips reprinted from the *New York Herald* Sunday supplement. Each strip is divided into halves and printed in four colours on one side of the page only. The strips are copyright 1908 and are not drawn by R.F. Outcault, the original artist. They include a series of Buster's travels with his uncle. Cardboard covers. British edition published by Dean & Son, London. Cupples & Leon issued a cheap 35¢ edition of this book in 1917.

83 Foxy Grandpa and Little Brother

December 1909. 60¢. 58 pp. 15×10. Publisher: Frederick A. Stokes Co., 5 East 16th Street, New York. Artist: Carl Schultze ('Bunny').

Contents
Compilation of newspaper strips reprinted in four colours from Sunday supplements. Cardboard covers.

84 Outcault's Real Buster and the Only Mary Jane

December 1909. 60¢. 66 pp. 16×11. Publisher: Frederick A. Stokes Co., 5 East 16th Street, New York. Artist: Richard F. Outcault. Syndicate: American Journal–Examiner.

Contents
Compilation of 15 newspaper strips reprinted from William Randolph Hearst's Sunday supplements. Each strip is divided into halves and printed in four colours on one side of the page only. The artist has drawn a new title page and coloured cover, and the title of the book is intended to counteract the rival series of *Buster Brown* books published by Cupples & Leon. Cardboard covers. British edition published by W. & R. Chambers Ltd., London and Edinburgh.

85 Kaptin Kiddo and Puppo

1910. 60¢. 62 pp. 16½×11. Publisher: Frederick A. Stokes Co., 5 East 16th Street, New York. Artist: Grace G. Wiederseim. Syndicate: North American Co.

Contents
Compilation of Sunday newspaper strips reprinted in four colours. Strips are arranged as half to a page, printed on one side of the paper only. Contains 14 full-page strips (28 half-pages) copyright 1910 by the North American Company. Original title 'The Turrible Tales of Kaptin Kiddo'. The strip is a collaboration on the part of two women, writer Margaret G. Hays and artist Grace G. Wiederseim, who designed the original coloured cover, printed on cardboard, and the title page sketch. A British edition was published by W. & R. Chambers Ltd., of Edinburgh and London. First book in a series of two.

86 Outcault's Buster Brown Up To Date

July 1910. 60¢. 66 pp. 16×11. Publisher: Frederick A. Stokes Co., 5 East 16th Street, New York. Artist: Richard F. Outcault. Syndicate: American Journal–Examiner.

Contents
Compilation of 15 full-page strips from the William Randolph Hearst Sunday comic supplements. Each strip is divided into half pages, and printed in four colours on one side of the page only. The artist has also drawn a new cover in colours, and a new title page. Strips are copyrighted 1909 by the *American Journal–Examiner*. The presence of the artist's name in the title was intended to identify the strips as 'genuine' Buster Brown adventures, as distinct from the rival series of books concurrently being published by Cupples & Leon. British edition published by W. & R. Chambers, London and Edinburgh.

87 The Mutt and Jeff Cartoons

October 1910. 50¢. 68 pp. 15^1/$_2$×5^1/$_2$. Publisher: Ball Publishing Co., Boston, Massachusetts. Artist: Bud Fisher. Syndicate: H.C. Fisher, Star Publishing Co.

Introduction
'No book is a regular book without a preface; hence this bundle of junk. A dedication is supposed to give class to a book, and Mutt is always on the job with the classy stuff. Sometimes one starts a preface by exposing the author's real name, but I shall cut that out for were I to impart my real label, I might get six months for obtaining money under false pretenses. Books are published for two reasons: First, to get the author's name into print. Second, to get money into the author's pocket. (Of course, the publisher gets some too, but the author is not supposed to know that.) This book is different. There is only one excuse for putting it before the public — to get the money. (Thank you for buying this one.) The Mutt and Jeff cartoons have been running daily in the Hearst papers for three years, making a total of close onto one thousand pictures. It can readily be seen that it would be almost impossible to place this entire collection in one book. If such were done, this publication would look like the city directory of Greater New York, and a truck would be necessary to move this book from the store to the purchaser's home which would greatly handicap its sale. Not desiring to put the crusher on the marketing of this flock of debris, we have been forced to make a selection of a number of the most representative pictures, selected from the various periods of Mutt's career. We give some of Mutt's earlier adventures and end with his most recent, thereby covering the most important events in the life of this eccentric gentleman and his side kick, Little Jeff. And now if the people who read this crime have as much fun as I did in drawing the contents, I shall be satisfied. Bud Fisher.'

Compilation of daily newspaper strips, copyright 1908 and 1910 by Harry Conway Fisher and the Star Publishing Company. Printed in black-and-white throughout, with cardboard covers, black on brown. Cover and title page specially drawn by the artist. Contains 60 strips printed one to a page. A new edition of this book was published in 1987 by Arcadia Publications of Greenfield, Wisconsin, including a new historic introduction. Unlike the original, however, this book is hinged at the top, not at the side.

88 Buster Brown on His Travels

December 1910. 60¢. 58 pp. 16×11. Publisher: Cupples & Leon Co., 443 Fourth Avenue, New York. Syndicate: New York Herald.

Contents
Compilation of newspaper strips reprinted from the Sunday supplement of the *New York Herald*. Contains 13 full-page strips divided into halves and printed in four colours on one side of the page only. Note that these strips are not drawn by the original artist, R.F. Outcault. The story line covers a world cruise taken by Buster in company of Bill the Bosun. British edition published by Dean & Son, London. A cheap 35¢ edition was published by Cupples & Leon in 1917.

89 Foxy Grandpa's Latest Tricks

1911. 60¢. 62 pp. 15×10. Publisher: Frederick A. Stokes Co., 5 East 16th Street, New York. Artist: Carl Schultze ('Bunny').

Contents

Reprints of the newspaper strip published in the Sunday supplements, printed in four colours with cardboard covers. Strips are copyrighted 1910 and 1911.

90 Nervy Nat's Adventures

1911. 85¢. Publisher: Leslie-Judge Co., (Frank Leslie), New York. Artist: James Montgomery Flagg.

Contents

Compilation of full-page comic strips reprinted from the weekly humorous magazine, *Judge*. 'Nervy Nat' by James Montgomery Flagg was a top-hatted tramp who made his debut in 1903. Many strips were printed in four colours, but this reprint is in black-and-white.

91 Bunny's Blue Book

July 1911. 60¢. 15×10. Publisher: Frederick Stokes Co., 5 East 16th Street, New York. Artist: Carl Schultze ('Bunny').

Contents

Reprints of newspaper strips published in the Sunday supplements, printed in four colours with specially drawn cardboard covers. First book in the 'Bunny' series.

92 Buster Brown's Fun and Nonsense

July 1911. 60¢. 66 pp. 16×11. Publisher: Frederick A. Stokes Co., 5 East 16th Street, New York. Artist: Richard F. Outcault. Syndicate: American Journal–Examiner.

Contents

Compilation of 15 full-page strips from the William Randolph Hearst Sunday supplements, copyrighted 1910–1911. Each strip is divided into half pages, and printed in four colours on one side of the page only. The artist has drawn a special coloured cover, printed on boards. British edition published by W. & R. Chambers, London and Edinburgh.

93 Ducky Daddles

July 1911. 50¢. 15×10. Publisher: Frederick A. Stokes Co., 5 East 16th Street, New York. Artist: Grace Wiederseim.

Contents

Reprints of the newspaper strip published in the Sunday supplements. Printed in four colours, with cardboard covers in colour specially designed by the artist, Grace Wiederseim. The strips are written by the artist's sister, Margaret G. Hayes.

94 Buster Brown's Happy Days

September 1911. 60¢. 58 pp. 16×11. Publisher: Cupples & Leon Co., 443 Fourth Avenue, New York. Syndicate: New York Herald.

Contents
Compilation of 13 full-page strips reprinted from the *New York Herald* Sunday supplement. Each strip is divided into halves and printed in four colours on one side of the paper only. The strips are copyrighted 1908, but are not drawn by the original artist, R.F. Outcault. Cardboard covers. British edition published by Dean & Son, London.

95 Bunny's Red Book

1912. 60¢. 15×10. Publisher: Frederick A. Stokes Co., 5 East 16th Street, New York. Artist: Carl Schultze ('Bunny').

Contents
Reprints of newspaper strips published in the Sunday supplements, printed in four colours with specially drawn cardboard covers. Second in the 'Bunny' series

96 Buster Brown in Foreign Lands

1912. 35¢. 58 pp. 16×10. Publisher: Cupples & Leon Co., 443 Fourth Avenue, New York. Syndicate: New York Herald.

Contents
Compilation of newspaper strips reprinted from the Sunday supplement of the *New York Herald*. Contains 26 strips in four colours, printed on one side of the page only, copyrighted 1908 and 1909. The strips, which are not drawn by the original artist, R.F. Outcault, concern Buster Brown's serialized trip around the world. British edition published by Dean & Son, London.

97 Buster Brown the Fun Maker

1912. 60¢. 66 pp. 16×10. Publisher: Frederick A. Stokes Co., 5 East 16th Street, New York. Artist: Richard F. Outcault. Syndicate: American Journal–Examiner.

Contents
Compilation of Buster Brown strips, reprinted from Sunday comic supplements syndicated by the *American Journal–Examiner*, and copyrighted 1908, 1909, 1910. The book contains 15 broadsheet pages divided into halves, printed in four colours on one side of the page only. The only new material is the full-colour cover and black-and-white title page, drawn by the artist, R.F. Outcault. Cardboard covers. British edition published by W. & R. Chambers Ltd., Edinburgh and London. *Note:* in the final strip, 'Buster Brown Has Company', Outcault's earlier creation, 'The Yellow Kid', makes a guest appearance.

98 The Monk Joke Book

1912. 16 pp. Publisher: New York American (W.R. Hearst). Artist: Gus Mager.

Contents
Compilation of newspaper strips reprinted from William Randolph Hearst Sunday supplements, and published as a free premium with the *New York American.*

99 Silk Hat Harry's Divorce Suit

1912. 15¹/₂×5³/₄. Publisher: M.A. Donohue & Co., 407 Dearborn Street, Chicago. Artist: Thomas Aloysius Dorgan. Syndicate: American Journal–Examiner.

Contents
Compilation of daily newspaper strips printed black-and-white throughout, bound in a cardboard cover. Cover specially drawn by the artist, 'Tad' (Thomas Aloysius Dorgan).

100 Bunny's Green Book

1913. 60¢. 15×10. Publisher: Frederick A. Stokes Co., 5 East 16th Street, New York. Artist: Carl Schultze ('Bunny').

Contents
Compilation of newspaper strips reprinted from Sunday supplements. Printed in four colours, with specially drawn cardboard covers by the artist, 'Bunny'. Third and last in this 'Bunny' series.

101 Buster Brown and His Pets

1913. 60¢. 58 pp. 16×10. Publisher: Cupples & Leon Co., 443 Fourth Avenue, New York. Syndicate: New York Herald.

Contents
Compilation of newspaper strips reprinted from the *New York Herald* Sunday supplements. There are 13 full-page strips divided into halves and printed in four colours on one side of the page only. The strips are copyrighted 1909 and are not drawn by the original artist, R.F. Outcault. They feature a series about Buster's travels with Bill the Bosun and his uncle. Cardboard covers. British editon published by Dean & Son Ltd., London. A cheap 35¢ edition was published by Cupples & Leon in 1916.

102 Buster Brown at Home

1913. 60¢. 58 pp. 16×10. Publisher: Frederick A. Stokes Co., 5 East 16th Street, New York. Artist: Richard F. Outcault. Syndicate: American Journal–Examiner.

Contents

Compilation of 13 full-page strips reprinted from the Sunday comic supplements. Each strip is divided in halves and printed on two pages. Pages are printed in three colours on one side of the paper only. The strips are copyrighted 1906, 1908, 1909 and 1910 by the *American Journal–Examiner*. Cardboard covers with original artwork by the artist. British edition published by W. & R. Chambers Ltd., Edinburgh and London.

103 Carlo

1913. 120pp. 9½×8. Publisher: Doubleday Page & Co., Garden City, New York. Artist: Arthur Burdett Frost.

Contents

Compilation of a regular strip cartoon featuring Carlo the dog, reprinted in black-and-white. The strip is enlarged so that it reads one single panel to the page. The book contains 105 panels. Hardback edition, with special cover drawing and title page by the artist, Arthur Burdett Frost.

104 The Mutt and Jeff Cartoons: Book 2

1913. 50¢. 68 pp. 15½×5½. Publisher: Ball Publishing Co., Boston, Massachusetts. Artist: Bud Fisher. Syndicate: H.C. Fisher.

Contents

Compilation of daily newspaper strips, printed black-and-white and bound in a cardboard cover. Contains 60 strips printed one to a page. Special cover and title page drawn by the artist.

105 Kaptin Kiddo's 'Speriences

July 1913. 60¢. 62 pp. 16½×11. Publisher: Frederick A. Stokes Co., 5 East 16th Street, New York. Artist: Grace G. Drayton. Syndicate: North American Co.

Contents

Compilation of Sunday newspaper strips reprinted in four colours. Strips are arranged as half to a page, printed on one side of the paper only. Contains 14 full-page strips (28 half-pages) copyright 1911 and 1912 by the North American Company, original title 'The Turrible Tales of Kaptin Kiddo'. This strip is the collaboration of two women, writer Margaret G. Hayes and artist Grace G. Drayton, who designed the original coloured cover and title page. She married during the run of the strip, as those dated before January 1912 are signed Grace G. Wiederseim. A British edition was published by W. & R. Chambers Ltd. of Edinburgh and London.

106 Mr. Twee-Deedle

August 1913. 60¢. 16×10. Publisher: Cupples & Leon Co., 443 Fourth Avenue, New York. Artist: John B. Gruelle. Syndicate: New York Herald.

Contents

Compilation of strips reprinted from the Sunday newspaper supplements syndicated by the *New York Herald*. Printed in four colours with cardboard covers specially drawn by the artist, Johnny Gruelle. 'Mr. Twee-Deedle' was the result of Gruelle's winning the *Herald's* $2,000 contest to discover a new comic artist.

107 Buster and Tige Here Again

1914. 60¢. 62pp. 16×10. Publisher: Frederick A. Stokes Co., 5 East 16th Street, New York. Artist: Richard F. Outcault. Syndicate: Newspaper Feature Service.

Contents

Compilation of 14 full-page strips from the William Randolph Hearst Sunday supplements. Each strip is divided in halves and printed in four colours, on one side of the paper only. The artist has drawn a special cover and title page. Strips are copyrighted 1913 and 1914 by the Newspaper Feature Service. Cardboard covers.

108 Buster Brown's Funny Tricks

1914. 60¢. 58 pp. 16×10. Publisher: Cupples & Leon Co., 443 Fourth Avenue, New York. Syndicate: New York Herald.

Contents

Compilation of newspaper strips reprinted from the *New York Herald* Sunday supplement. Thirteen full-page strips have been divided into halves, and printed in four colours on one side of the paper only. The strips are copyrighted 1908, and are not drawn by the original artist, Richard Outcault. Cardboard covers. British edition published by Dean & Son, London.

109 Foxy Grandpa

1914. 24 pp. 15½×9½. Publisher: Bunny Publishing Co. Artist: Carl Schultze ('Bunny').

Contents

Compilation of newspaper strips printed in four colours, in cardboard cover. This book was published by the artist, 'Bunny'.

110 The Mutt and Jeff Cartoons: Book 3

1914. 60¢. 68 pp. 15½×5½. Publisher: Ball Publishing Co., Boston, Massachusetts. Artist: Bud Fisher. Syndicate: H.C. Fisher.

Contents

Compilation of daily newspaper strips reprinted in black-and-white, and arranged one to a page. Cardboard covers with new cover picture and title page drawn by the artist.

34

111 The Adventures of Willie Green

1915. 50¢. 30 pp. Publisher: Frank M. Acton Co., 27 South Seventh Street, Philadelphia. Artist: Harris Brown.

Contents
Compilation of newspaper strips in cardboard covers. Issued as 'Book No. 1' but no further books published.

112 Buster Brown and His Chum Tige

1915. 60¢. 62 pp. 16×10. Publisher: Frederick A. Stokes Co., 5 East 16th Street, New York. Artist: Richard F. Outcault. Syndicate: Newspaper Feature Service.

Contents
Compilation of 14 full-page strips from the William Randolph Hearst Sunday supplements. Each strip is divided into halves and printed on one side of the paper only, in four colours. The artist has drawn a new title page and coloured cover. Strips are copyrighted 1914 and 1915 by the Newspaper Feature Service. British edition published by W. & R. Chambers, London and Edinburgh.

113 Dimples

1915. 12 pp. 5¼×6¼. Publisher: Hearst's International Library Co., New York. Artist: Grace G. Drayton.

No. 1 *She Has a Naughty Play Husband*
No. 2 *She Goes for a Walk*
No. 3 *She Had to Sneeze*
No. 4 *Puppy and Pussy*
No. 5 *Wait Till Fido Comes Home*

Contents
Series of five small books, each reprinting one single strip from the William Randolph Hearst Sunday supplements. The strips are arranged one picture to each page, printed in four colours throughout. Special covers drawn by the artist, Grace G. Drayton.

114 Foxy Grandpa Always Jolly

1915. 60¢. 16×10. Publisher: Frederick A. Stokes Co., 5 East 16th Street, New York. Artist: Carl Schultze ('Bunny').

Contents
Compilation of Sunday supplement strips reprinted in four colours on one side of the page only. Cardboard covers, specially drawn by the artist, 'Bunny'.

115 The Mutt and Jeff Cartoons: Book 4

1915. 60¢. 68 pp. 15½×5½. Publisher: Ball Publishing Co., Boston, Massachusetts. Artist: Bud Fisher. Syndicate: H.C. Fisher.

Contents

Compilation of daily newspaper strips, printed black-and-white and bound in a cardboard cover. Contains 60 strips printed one to a page. Special cover and title page drawn by the artist.

116 Roger Bean, R.G.

No. 1: 1915–No. 4: 1917. 34pp. 16×4¾. Publisher: Indiana News Co. Artist: Chic Jackson.

Contents

Compilation of daily newspaper strips reprinted from the *Indiana News*. Printed black-and-white with cardboard covers. *Note:* for No. 3, see *Along the Firing Line with Roger Bean* (1916).

117 Along the Firing Line with Roger Bean

1916. 66 pp. 17×6. Publisher: Indiana News Co. Artist: Chic Jackson.

Contents

Compilation of daily newspaper strips reprinted from the *Indiana News*, 1915. Printed black-and-white with cardboard covers specially drawn by the artist, Charles ('Chic') Jackson. *Note:* this book is bound at the top instead of at the side. No. 3 of the *Roger Bean, R.G.* series.

118 Buster Brown at Play

1916. 60¢. 58 pp. 16×10. Publisher: Cupples & Leon Co., 443 Fourth Street, New York. Syndicate: New York Herald.

Contents

Compilation of newspaper strips reprinted from the *New York Herald* Sunday supplement. Thirteen full-page strips, divided into halves, are printed in four colours on one side of the page only. Strips are copyrighted 1908 and 1909. Cardboard covers. Note that these strips are not by the original 'Buster Brown' artist, Richard F. Outcault, nor are the cover and title page artwork. British edition published by Dean & Son, London.

119 Buster Brown the Little Rogue

1916. 60¢. 58 pp. 16×10. Publisher: Frederick A. Stokes Co., 5 East 16th Street, New York. Artist: Richard F. Outcault. Syndicate: Newspaper Feature Service.

Contents
Compilation of newspaper strips reprinted from the William Randolph Hearst Sunday supplements.
Contains 13 full-page strips divided into halves and printed in four colours on one side of the page
only. Strips are copyright 1914 and 1915 by the Newspaper Feature Service Inc. Cardboard covers.
Coloured cover and title page drawn by the artist, R.F. Outcault.

120 Mutt and Jeff in the Trenches

1916. 60¢. 68 pp. $15^1/_2 \times 5^1/_2$. Publisher: Ball Publishing Co., Boston, Massachusetts. Artist: Bud Fisher.
Syndicate: H.C. Fisher.

Contents
Compilation of daily newspaper strips, printed black-and-white throughout, arranged one strip to a
page. Cardboard covers, specially drawn by the artist, Bud Fisher. This book is No. 5 in the *Mutt and
Jeff* series, and features the wartime adventures of the characters, which were drawn in France while
the artist was serving with the U.S. Army.

121 Foxy Grandpa's Merry Book

August 1916. 25¢. 64 pp. 15×10. Publisher: Frederick A. Stokes Co., 5 East 16th Street, New York.
Artist: Carl Schultze ('Bunny').

Contents
Compilation of newspaper strips reprinted in four colours from the Sunday supplements. Cardboard
covers.

122 Bringing Up Father

1917. 100 pp. $16^1/_2 \times 5^1/_2$. Publisher: Star Company. Artist: George McManus. Syndicate: Star
Company.

Introduction
'To Mr and Mrs Public and all the little Publics:
Dear Folks: In response to the clamoring for a collection of "Bringing Up Father" cartoons that has
been going on for nearly three years, I herewith dedicate this book to you all. It was an awful job to
draw so many pictures and the least you can do in return to help along a poor but honest artist is to
buy a lot of copies. With this income tax business, the high cost of living AND the punky little royalty
that I'm getting out of this, I figure that I've got to sell 600,000,000 copies to make any money. That
makes six copies for every man, woman and child in the United States. I'm thinking of getting out a
Spanish edition to supply Porto Rico and the Philippines and one in Eskimo for Alaska. So loosen up,
good people. Nix on buying just one copy. Every patriot will keep one copy lying on his parlor table,
one in the kitchen for the cop, one for shaving paper and one for the baby to play with — to say
nothing of those that he ought to give away to other patriots. I can also highly recommend the paper in

the book for laying under carpets. Seriously, however, I hope you will all like Father in this form, and that you will sympathize with Maggie in her efforts to train him so that he will adorn the swell, social sphere which Maggie understands as well as a Moro cannibal understands hydrostatics — whatever they may be. Sincerely yours, Geo. McManus.'

Contents
Reprints of 94 daily strips in the series 'Bringing Up Father', which started in 1913 in the William Randolph Hearst newspapers. Strips are variously numbered: M19, A3, D23, J27, F28, etc., and others are not numbered, indicating random and non-chronological order. Oblong book in cardboard covers, cover in red and black on yellow. Cover and title page specially drawn by the artist, George McManus.
After this first edition of the strip, an annual series of reprint books in more manageable size was commenced by another publisher, Cupples & Leon, beginning 1919.

123 Buster Brown and the Cat

1917. 25¢. 58 pp. 16×10. Publisher: Frederick A. Stokes Co., 5 East 16th Street, New York. Artist: Richard F. Outcault. Syndicate: Newspaper Feature Service.

Contents
Compilation of newspaper strips reprinted from the William Randolph Hearst Sunday supplements. Contains 13 full-page strips divided into halves and printed in four colours on one side of the page only. Coloured cover and title page drawn by the artist, R.F. Outcault. Cardboard covers.

124 Buster Brown Disturbs the Family

1917. 25¢. 16×10. Publisher: Frederick A. Stokes Co., 5 East 16th Street, New York. Artist: Richard F. Outcault.

Contents
Compilation of the Sunday newspaper strip, reprinted in four colours with a cardboard cover specially drawn by the artist, R.F. Outcault.

125 Charlie Chaplin in the Army

1917. 20 pp. 16×9³/₄. Publisher: M.A. Donohue & Co., 407 Dearborn Steet, Chicago. Artists: Elzie Segar: Carothers. Syndicate: J. Keeley.

Contents
Compilation of daily newspaper comic strips, copyright 1915–1917 by J. Keeley, by arrangement with the Essany Company. Printed in black-and-white with full-colour covers. Contains 30 strips drawn by Elzie Segar and Carothers. The book is numberd 'No. 318'.

126 Charlie Chaplin in the Movies

1917. 20 pp. 16×9³/₄. Publisher: M.A. Donohue & Co., 407 Dearborn Street, Chicago. Artists: Elzie Segar; Carothers. Syndicate: J. Keeley.

Contents
Compilation of daily newspaper comic strips, copyright 1915–1917 by J. Keeley, by arrangement with the Essanay Company. Printed in black-and-white with full-colour covers. Contains 30 strips drawn by two artists, Segar and Carothers. The book is numbered 'No. 316'.

127 Charlie Chaplin Up in the Air

1917. 20 pp. 16×9³/₄. Publisher: M.A. Donohue & Co., 407 Dearborn Street, Chicago. Artists: Elzie Segar; Carothers. Syndicate: J. Keeley.

Contents
Compilation of daily newspaper comic strips, copyright 1915–1917 by J. Keeley, by arrangement with the Essanay Company. Printed in black-and-white with full-colour covers. Contains 30 strips drawn by Elzie Chrisler Segar and Carothers. The book is numbered 'No. 317'.

128 Charlie Chaplin's Comic Capers

1917. 20 pp. 16×9³/₄. Publisher: M.A. Donohue & Co., 407 Dearborn Street, Chicago. Artists: Elzie Segar; Carothers. Syndicate: J. Keeley.

Contents
1 Cover
2 (R) Charlie Chaplin's Comic Capers
3 Title page
4 Instructions for the Little Artist
5–19 (R) Charlie Chaplin's Comic Capers
20 Back cover

Compilation of daily newspaper comic strips, copyright 1915–1917 by J. Keeley by arrangement with the Essanay Company. Printed in black-and-white throughout, with full-colour covers. Contains 30 strips, 20 of which are signed Segar. The book is numbered 'Series 1' and 'No. 315'.

129 Charlie Chaplin's Funny Stunts

1917. 12¹/₂×16¹/₂. Publisher: M.A. Donohue & Co., 407 Dearborn Street, Chicago. Artist: Elzie Segar. Syndicate: J. Keeley.

Contents
Compilation of broadsheet-sized Sunday supplement pages, reprinted in full colour with full-colour cover. Copyright 1915–1917 by J. Keeley, by arrangement with the Essanay Company, who were the current producers of Charlie Chaplin's films.

130 Comic Painting and Crayoning Book

1917. 36 pp. 10×13¹/₂. Publisher: Saalfield Publishing Co., Akron, Ohio.

Contents
1 Cover
3 Title Page
4 Tidy Teddy   F.M. Follet
16 Clarence the Cop   C.W. Kahles
28 Mr and Mrs Butt-in   C.W. Kahles
34 The Look-Alike Brothers   Ladendorf

Compilation of newspaper strips reprinted in black-and-white with full-colour covers. Panels are enlarged two to a page to make them suitable for children to colour in with paints or crayons.
In 1917 the Saalfield Publishing Company of Akron, New York and Chicago entered comicbook publishing with a series of books compiled from old daily and Sunday newspaper strips. Many of the strips used, such as those in this colouring book, came from an earlier era. For example, the only dated strip in this book is Ladendorf's Look-alike Brothers: 1903.

131 Foxy Grandpa's Adventures

1917. 25¢. 62 pp. 15×10. Publisher: Frederick A. Stokes Co., 5 East 16th Street, New York. Artist: Carl Schultze ('Bunny').

Contents
Compilation of half-page strips reprinted from Sunday supplements. The strips are printed in four colours on one side of the page only. Coloured cover on cardboard specially drawn by the artist, 'Bunny' (Carl Schultze).
Note: in 1917 the Stokes company reissued a number of their earlier comic books in cheap 25¢ editions. This book would appear to be one of the cheap reissues, but an earlier book of this title has not been traced.

132 Funny Larks of Hans und Fritz

1917. 52 pp. 13¾×10. Publisher: Saalfield Publishing Co., Akron, Ohio. Artist: Rudolph Dirks. Syndicate: Press Publishing Co., New York.

Contents
Compilation of Sunday supplement strips reprinted from the *New York World*. The strips are divided so that one full Sunday page is spread over three pages of the book, four panels to the page. Printed on one side of the page only, the book contains seven Sunday strips. Specially-drawn covers (not by the original artist), title page, a page depicting the characters, and six pages of strips are printed in full colour, the remainder being in two colours only: 8 pages in black and red, 8 in black and blue. Strips are copyrighted 1916, Press Publishing Co.
The first republication in comic book form of 'Hans und Fritz', the 'doppelganger' strip created by Rudolph Dirks after he left his original strip, 'The Katzenjammer Kids'. *Note:* this book is incorrectly listed in the 1985 edition of *The Comic Book Price Guide* as Hans and Fritz (1929).

133 The Further Adventures of Mr. Tweedeedle

1917. 35¢. 16×10. Publisher: Cupples & Leon Co., 443 Fourth Avenue, New York. Artist: John B. Gruelle. Syndicate: New York Herald.

Contents
Compilation of strips reprinted from the Sunday newspaper supplements syndicated by the *New York Herald*. Printed in four colours with cardboard covers specially drawn by the artist, Johnny Gruelle.

134 Hawkshaw the Detective

1917. 24 pp. 10½×13½. Publisher: Saalfield Publishing Co., Akron, Ohio. Artist: Gus Mager. Syndicate: Press Publishing Co.

Contents
Compilation of newspaper strips reprinted from the Sunday supplements of the *New York World*. Reprinted in black-and-white, with a two-colour cover specially drawn by the artist, Gus Mager. Reissued in 1927 as *The Adventures of Hawkshaw*. Strips are copyrighted 1916.

135 Lady Bountiful

1917. 24 pp. 13½×10¼. Publisher: Saalfield Publishing Co., Akron, Ohio. Artist: Gene Carr. Syndicate: Press Publishing Co.

Contents
Compilation of newspaper strips reprinted from the Sunday supplements of the William Randolph Hearst papers. Arranged as two panels to each page, and printed black-and-white throughout. Cardboard covers in two colours, specially drawn by the artist, Eugene (Gene) Carr.

136 The Newlyweds and Their Baby's Comic Pictures

1917. 20 pp. 14½×20¼. Publisher: Saalfield Publishing Co., Akron, Ohio. Artist: George McManus. Syndicate: Press Publishing Co.

Contents
Compilation of newspaper comic strips copyrighted 1907. Some pages printed in colours, the rest black-and-white as pages for colouring in paints or crayons. Special cover and title page, but not drawn by the artist, George McManus.

137 Nippy's Pop

1917. 36 pp. 13½×10½. Publishers: Saalfield Publishing Co., Akron, Ohio. Artist: Charles M. Payne. Syndicate: Press Publishing Co. (*New York World*).

Contents
Compilation of 31 newspaper strips reprinted in green ink. Coloured cover on card, specially drawn by the artist, Charles M. Payne.

138 The Real Buster Brown

1917. 25¢. 16×10. Publisher: Frederick A. Stokes Co., 5 East 16th Street, New York. Artist: Richard F. Outcault.

Contents
Compilation of the Sunday newspaper strip, reprinted in four colours with a cover specially drawn by the artist, R.F. Outcault.

139 S'Matter Pop?

1917. 44 pp. 14×10. Publisher: Saalfield Publishing Co., Akron, Ohio. Artist: Charles M. Payne. Syndicate: Press Publishing Co. (*New York World*).

Contents
Compilation of newspaper strips reprinted from Sunday supplements. Strips are printed in four colours on one side of the page only. Cardboard cover in full colour, specially drawn by the artist, Charles M. Payne.

140 The Book of the Gumps Cartoons

1918. 50¢. 64 pp. 13½×5¼. Publisher: Landfield-Kupfer Co., 727 South Dearborn Street, Chicago. Artist: Sidney Smith. Syndicate: Chicago Tribune.

Contents
Compilation of daily newspaper strips syndicated by the *Chicago Tribune*. Reprinted in black-and-white, one strip to the page. Cardboard covers, specially designed by the artist, Sidney Smith. 'The Gumps' started on 12 February 1917.

141 The Gumps: Book 2

1918. 36 pp. 13½×5¼. Publisher: Landfield-Kupfer Co., 727 South Dearborn Street, Chicago. Artist: Sidney Smith. Syndicate: Chicago Tribune.

Contents
Compilation of daily newspaper strips syndicated by the *Chicago Tribune*. Reprinted in black-and-white, one strip to the page. Unlike the first Gumps book (above), this was issued in paper covers.

142 Bringing Up Father

1919. 25¢. 52 pp. 10×10. Publisher: Cupples & Leon Co., 443 Fourth Avenue, New York. Artist: George McManus. Syndicate: International Feature Service Inc.

Introduction
'Bon voyage, Little Book! May you have a long and prosperous journey. May the natives of all the civilized and uncivilized countries of the globe from the dark-skinned Senegambians to the dark-brained Bolsheviks greet you with joy and pungle down their coin. The more that like you the happier I shall be. I have tried to make Father human. He has his faults and his foibles; he is a low-brow, he never went to college and he insists upon spelling geography with a capital J. But his heart is kindly. He enjoys life and loves his fellow man. It is true that he loves Dinty Moore better than he does Van Rennselaer Trelawney de Goof, but who doesn't? Maggie, at times, makes him unhappy. Occasionally — that is, about four times a day — she hits him with a rolling-pin or a soup tureen. But, at the bottom of his heart, he loves her. Go to it, little book! And if you behave nicely and I get reports that everybody likes you, maybe I'll let you travel again. George McManus.'

Contents
Compilation of daily newspaper strips copyright International Feature Service Inc. The book contains 46 strips arranged one to the page, with an original cover, title page, and back cover by the artist. Printed black-and-white throughout, with two-colour (red and black) covers on cardboard.

143 Bringing Up Father: Second Series

1919. 25¢. 52 pp. 10×10. Publisher: Cupples & Leon Co., 443 Fourth Avenue, New York. Artist: George McManus. Syndicate: International Feature Service.

Contents
Compilation of daily newspaper strips copyright International Feature Service Inc. Forty-six strips arranged one to a page, printed black-and-white, with a two-colour cover and title page specially drawn by the artist.
A British edition of this book was published by A.V.N. Jones and Co., London. The caption 'Second Series' was deleted and the price of 1/6 (one shilling and sixpence) inserted. The title page cartoon was also deleted and the legend '194 Pictures' inserted.

144 Bringing Up Father: Third Series

1919. 25¢. 52 pp. 10×10. Publisher: Cupples & Leon Co., 443 Fourth Avenue, New York. Artist: George McManus. Syndicate: International Feature Service Inc.

Contents
Compilation of daily newspaper strips reprinted from dates between January and July 1919, copyright International Feature Service Inc. The book contains 46 strips arranged one to the page, with an original cover, title page and back cover by the artist. Cardboard covers.

145 Mutt and Jeff Cartoons: Book 6

1919. 25¢. 52 pp. 10×9¾. Publisher: Cupples & Leon Co., 443 Fourth Avenue, New York. Artist: Bud Fisher. Syndicate: H.C. Fisher.

Contents
Compilation of 46 daily newspaper strips, arranged one to a page. The artist, Bud Fisher, has drawn an original cover, back cover, and title page. Cardboard covers printed in two colours. The strips, the copyright of H.C. Fisher, are selected from the years 1915–1918.
This was the only Mutt and Jeff book to receive a British edition, which was priced at 2/6 (two shillings and sixpence) and published in 1920 by Dean & Son of London, a specialist in children's books. At the time Mutt and Jeff were well known in Britain from the animated cartoon series released by Fox.

146 School Days

1919. 102 pp. 7³/₄×9¹/₄. Publisher: Harper & Brothers, 49 East 33rd Street, New York. Artist: Clare Victor Dwiggins.

Contents
Compilation of the newspaper cartoon series, a daily panel rather than a strip, which began in syndication in 1917. The book, a hardback, has a cover and title page drawn by the artist, Clare 'Dwig' Dwiggins.

147 Adventures of Mutt and Jeff

1920. 60¢. 48 pp. 16×11. Publisher: Cupples & Leon Co., 443 Fourth Avenue, New York. Artist: Bud Fisher. Syndicate: H.C. Fisher.

Contents
Compilation of 20 Sunday supplement strips reprinted in four colours. with a cardboard cover specially drawn by the artist, Bud Fisher. The first publication in book form of the coloured Sunday strips of 'Mutt and Jeff'.

148 It Happens in the Best Families

1920. 30¢. 52 pp. Publisher: Powers Photo Engraving Co. Artist: Clare Briggs.

Contents
Compilation of newspaper strips reprinted from the Sunday supplements and copyrighted 1914–1920. Printed black-and-white and published as a 'Special Railroad Edition'.
151

149 Keeping Up With the Joneses: First Series

1920. 25¢. 52 pp. 10×9³/₄. Publisher: Cupples & Leon Co., 443 Fourth Avenue, New York. Artist: A.R. Momand.

Introduction
'Dear Folks: Here they are, Clarice and Aloysius, Julie, Ethelbert and Belladonna, in book form for the first time. I hope you will all buy a copy, as the price of ham and eggs, yachts and automobiles are way up; and "artists have to live". In these days of "Looney Living", it's pretty hard to keep up with the Joneses, so if you are having any trouble in "keeping up", a copy of this little book may give you a few helpful hints. I cheerfully recommend it as a complete social guide to those desiring to mingle with the 400 or 4,000,000, as the case may be. After reading it you will have no trouble in distinguishing a demi-tasse from a *café parfait*, or the correct angle at which to hold your finger bowl when drinking therefrom. The leaves in this book are especially suitable for wall paper, now that wall paper is so high. Buy a couple of thousand copies at any news stand, cut out the pages, paper the walls of your drawing room with them, and you will have a design of rare and unusual beauty, combined with an art gallery that none of the old masters could equal. There are many other uses to which this volume can be put, but paper and ink are so expensive and the publisher told me to be very careful and not write too much. No college, home or barber shop is complete without a copy. Sincerely, Pop Momand.'

Contents
Compilation of 46 daily newspaper strips, printed black-and-white and arranged one strip to a page. Cardboard covers in colours, and special title page drawn by the artist, A.R. 'Pop' Momand.

150 Mutt and Jeff: Book 7

1920. 25¢. 52 pp. 10×9³/₄. Publisher: Cupples & Leon Co., 443 Fourth Avenue, New York. Artist: Bud Fisher. Syndicate: H.C. Fisher.

Contents
Compilation of 46 daily newspaper strips, arranged one to a page and printed black-and-white. Two-colour cover on cardboard specially drawn by the artist, Bud Fisher.

151 Uncle Wiggily Series

1920. 36 pp. 5¹/₂×7. Publisher: Charles Graham & Co., 39 Division Street, Newark. Artist: Lang Campbell. Syndicate: McClure Newspaper Syndicate.

No. 1 *Uncle Wiggily's Auto Sled*
No. 2 *Uncle Wiggily's Snow Man*
No. 3 *Uncle Wiggily's Holidays*
No. 4 *Uncle Wiggily's Apple Roast*
No. 5 *Uncle Wiggily's Picnic*
No. 6 *Uncle Wiggily Goes Fishing*

Introduction
'LOOK HERE! UNCLE WIGGILY HAS A MESSAGE FOR YOU
Dear Boys and Girls: I know you will like this little book, and I want to tell you something else that my author-father, Mr. Garis, has done for you. He has made a wonderful game, played on a big, beautiful,

colored board. It's all about me and he calls it "The Uncle Wiggily Game". It is sold by all stores and toy-dealers. Ask for "The Uncle Wiggily Game". Yours for happy hours, Uncle Wiggily.'

Contents
Series of six small-sized books reprinting Sunday supplement strips of 'Uncle Wiggily' (a rabbit), drawn by Lang Campbell and written by Howard R. Garis. Book 1 contains three Sunday pages, dated 8, 15 and 22 February 1920, copyright the McClure Newspaper Syndicate. The strips are arranged with one picture on each page, and the book is printed in four colours throughout. Cardboard covers.

152 Bringing Up Father: Fourth Series

1921. 25¢. 52 pp. 10×10. Publisher: Cupples & Leon Co., 443 Fourth Avenue, New York. Artist: George McManus. Syndicate: International Feature Service.

Contents
Compilation of daily newspaper strips copyright International Feature Service Inc. Strips arranged one to the page and printed black-and-white, with cardboard covers in two colours specially drawn by the artist, George McManus.

153 Bringing Up Father: Fifth Series

1921. 25¢. 52 pp. 10×10. Publisher: Cupples & Leon Co. 443 Fourth Avenue, New York. Artist: George McManus. Syndicate: International Feature Service.

Contents
Compilation of daily newspaper strips copyright International Feature Service Inc. Strips arranged one to the page and printed black-and-white, with cardboard covers in two colours specially drawn by the artist, George McManus.

154 Bughouse Fables

1921. 10¢. 48 pp. 4×4½. Publisher: Embee Distributing Co., 141 East 25th Street, New York. Artist: Billy De Beck. Syndicate: King Features.

Contents
Compilation of newspaper strips syndicated by King Features; printed in black-and-white.

155 The Katzenjammer Kids

1921. 24 pp. 16×10. Publisher: Embee Distributing Co., 141 East 25th Street, New York. Artist: Rudolph Dirks. Syndicate: King Features.

Contents
Reprints of Sunday supplement strips: 20 pages in four colours.

156 Keeping Up with the Joneses: Book 2

1921. 25¢. 52 pp. 10×9³/₄. Publisher: Cupples & Leon Co., 443 Fourth Avenue, New York. Artist: A.R. Momand.

Contents
Compilation of newspaper strips. Forty-six daily strips arranged one to a page and printed black-and-white. Coloured covers on cardboard specially drawn by the artist, Pop Momand. Last in this series.

157 Mutt and Jeff

1921. 24 pp. 15×9. Publisher: Embee Distributing Co., 141 East 25th Street, New York. Artist: Bud Fisher. Syndicate: H.C. Fisher.

Contents
Reprints of Sunday supplement strips in four colours.

158 Percy and Ferdie: First Series

1921. 52 pp. 10×9¹/₂. Publisher: Cupples & Leon Co., 443 Fourth Avenue, New York. Artist: H.A. McGill. Syndicate: Sun Printing & Publishing Association.

Introduction
'Dear People: As the Hallroom Boys are better acquainted with the situation, we'll let Percy be the spokesman. When it comes to hard luck, says Percy, this here Job chap in the Old Testament has nothing on us. We've had it wished onto us for over 16 long years and no part time, either. We're looking for sympathy, so here we are in book form, with all our troubles. Sure we press our own trousers, juggle the frying pan and sell ribbon at Wanacoopers, but did John D. or Andy Carnegie start with a silver spoon in their mouths? Nossir. Five and ten cent store cutlery, same as what we use. Never mind. Financial giants some day we'll be too. Putting up a front costs money, so in the meantime, we need clean collars, our rent must be paid, our creditors are indecently insistent and we get no free passes for our week-end trips. Consequently, we need your financial assistance — whacks of it. Yours very truly, Percy and Ferdie per H.A. MacGill.'

Contents
Reprints of 46 daily newspaper strips, arranged one strip to the page. Printed /black-and-white, with cardboard covers in colours specially drawn by the artist, H.A. MacGill.
Although announced as 'First Series', there were no further editions of *Percy and Ferdie*. The strip was originally entitled 'The Hall-Room Boys' and began in the W.R. Hearst newspapers in 1907.

159 Reg'lar Fellers

1921. 25¢. 52 pp. 10×10. Publisher: Cupples & Leon Co., 443 Fourth Avenue, New York. Artist: Gene Byrnes.

Contents
Compilation of daily newspaper strips printed black-and-white, one to a page. Cardboard covers in two colours, with special artwork and title page drawn by the artist. The strip first appeared in 1918.

160 Toonerville Trolley and Other Cartoons

1921. 25¢. 52 pp. 10×10. Publisher: Cupples & Leon Co., 443 Fourth Avenue, New York. Artist: Fontaine Fox. Syndicate: McNaught Syndicate.

Introduction
'FOREWORD BY THE TERRIBLE TEMPERED MR. BANG
When it was learned that this Fox person had rooked somebody into getting out a book of his stuff, there was called at once an Indignation Meeting at which were present: the Skipper of the Trolley, the Powerful Katrinka, Aunt Eppie Hogg, the Absent-Minded Professor, Jimmy McGuire, Pres. Little Scorpions Club, Edith (Tomboy) Taylor, and several others including me. It was agreed to have the Absent-Minded Professor draw up a dignified but threatening Letter of Protest and mail it to the Publishers. The Professor wrote the letter all right, then very carefully the four-eyed simp blotted it, tossed it aside, and mailed the blotter! Of course we received no reply from the Publishers and when I called on them it was too late to stop the book. However, these Publishers, being square guys, agreed to let me write an introduction for the book in which we could clear ourselves of any responsibility for the d—— thing either direct or indirect. Which we hereby do. Signed, Ira Brimstone Bang.'

Contents
Compilation of 46 daily newspaper cartoons and strips from the series 'Toonerville Folks', copyrighted 1920–1921 by the McNaught Syndicate. Arranged one to a page and printed black-and-white. Cardboard covers in colours, specially drawn by the artist, Fontaine Fox.
Although labelled 'First Series', this was the only book of 'Toonerville Folks' to be published by Cupples & Leon. There were two earlier reprint collections of Fontaine Fox's newspaper cartoons, *F. Fox's Funny Folk* (George H. Doran Co., 1917) and *Cartoons* (Harper Brothers, 1918), but these had no comic connection.

161 The Trouble of Bringing Up Father

1921. 24pp. 15×9. Publisher: Embee Distributing Co., 141 East 25th Street, New York. Artist: George McManus.

Contents
Compilation of Sunday newspaper strips reprinted in full colour. Cardboard covers, specially drawn by the artist, George McManus.

162 Ain't It a Grand and Glorious Feeling

1922. 15¢. 28 pp. 9×9½. Publisher: Whitman Publishing Co., Racine, Wisconsin. Artist: Clare Briggs. Syndicate: New York Tribune.

Contents
Compilation of 11 Sunday newspaper strips, printed in full colour, with a cardboard cover in colour, specially drawn by the artist, Clare Briggs. Strips are copyrighted 1921 by the *New York Tribune*. the strips are arranged so that one full-page strip covers two pages of the book.
This is the second *Mr. and Mrs.* book, the title page carrying the subtitle, 'More of the Married Life of Mr. and Mrs.'. This book was also published in a cheaper black-and-white edition.

163 Bringing Up Father: Sixth Series

1922. 25¢. 52 pp. 10×10. Publisher: Cupples & Leon Co., 443 Fourth Avenue, New York. Artist: George McManus. Syndicate: International Feature Service.

Contents
Compilation of daily newspaper strips printed in black-and-white with cardboard covers in two colours, specially drawn by the artist, George McManus. Strips arranged one to the page.

164 The Doings of the Doo Dads

1922. 50¢. 34 pp. 7¾×7¾. Publisher: Universal Features and Speciality Co. Artist: Arch Dale. Syndicate: Detroit News.

Contents
Compilation of the 'Doo Dads' daily newspaper strip, copyrighted 1921 by the *Detroit News*. Printed in black-and-white with two-colour cover designed by the artist, Arch Dale.

165 Jimmie Dugan and the Reg'lar Fellers

1922. 25¢. 52 pp. 10×10. Publisher: Cupples & Leon Co., 443 Fourth Avenue, New York. Artist: Gene Byrnes.

Contents
Compilation of daily newspaper strips printed black-and-white, one to a page. Cardboard covers in two colours, specially drawn by the artist, Eugene (Gene) Byrnes.

166 Mr. and Mrs.

1922. 15¢. 28 pp. 9×9½. Publisher: Whitman Publishing Co., Racine, Wisconsin. Artist: Clare Briggs. Syndicate: New York Tribune.

Contents

Compilation of 11 Sunday newspaper strips reprinted from the *New York Tribune*, printed in full colour and with a cardboard cover in colour specially drawn by the artist, Clare Briggs. The strips are arranged so that one full-page strip covers two pages of the book.

The 'Mr. and Mrs.' strip started on 14 April 1919. This is the first of two book collections published by Whitman, the second being entitled *Ain't It a Grand and Glorious Feeling*.

167 Mutt and Jeff: Book 8

1922. 25¢. 52 pp. 10×9¾. Publisher: Cupples & Leon Co., 443 Fourth Avenue, New York. Artist: Bud Fisher. Syndicate: H.C. Fisher.

Contents

Compilation of 46 daily newspaper strips copyrighted by H.C. ('Bud') Fisher. Strips are arranged one to a page and printed black-and-white. Coloured cover on cardboard and title page specially drawn by the artist.

168 Pink Laffin

1922. 9×12. Publisher: Whitman Publishing Co., Racine, Wisconsin. Artist: Ray Gleason.

Contents

No. 1 *Pink Laffin: The Lighter Side of Life*
No. 2 *Pink Laffin: He Tells 'Em*
No. 3 *Pink Laffin and His Family*
No. 4 *Pink Laffin's Knockouts*

Series of four small booklets reprinting the daily newspaper strip by Ray Gleason.

169 Comic Monthly

No. 1: January 1922–No. 12: December 1922. 10¢. 28pp. 8½×9. Publisher: Embee Distributing Co., 1493 Broadway, New York. Editor: Rudolph Block Jr.

Contents

No. 1 (R) *Polly and Her Pals*	Cliff Sterrett
No. 2 (R) *Mike and Ike: They Look Alike*	Rube Goldberg
No. 3 (R) *S'Matter Pop*	C.M. Payne
No. 4 (R) *Barney Google*	Billy De Beck
No. 5 (R) *Tillie the Toiler*	Russ Westover
No. 6 (R) *Indoor Sports*	T.A. Dorgan
No. 7 (R) *Little Jimmy*	James Swinnerton
No. 8 (R) *Toots and Casper*	Jimmy Murphy

No. 9 (R) *Foolish Questions*   Rube Goldberg
No. 10 (R) *Foolish Questions*   Rube Goldberg
No. 11 (R) *Barney Google and Spark Plug*   Billy De Beck
No. 12 (R) *Polly and Her Pals*   Cliff Sterrett

The first regular monthly comic book. Each issue is devoted to a single character, and reprints a selection of daily newspaper strips copyrighted 1921 by various syndicates. Strips are arranged one to a page and printed black-and-white, with specially drawn covers in colours. According to *Crawford's Encyclopedia of Comic Books*, the Embee Company went bankrupt in September 1922 and only the first seven issues of *Comic Monthly* were distributed. The name Embee stood for the initials M.B. of cartoonist George McManus and editor Rudolph Block Jr., who founded the publishing company with Alfred Block, Dr. William Rodgers and Frank J. Rice.

170 Barney Google and His Faithful Nag Spark Plug

1923. 25¢. 52 pp. 9^1/$_4$×10. Publisher: Cupples & Leon Co., 443 Fourth Avenue, New York. Artist: Billy De Beck. Syndicate: King Features.

Introduction
'In permitting my friend Barney Google to step from the pages of newspapers into this impressive-looking book, I want to apologize for him. He isn't much to look at. He's a born low-brow. He'd rather be with a stable-boy than with an emperor. And he's thoroughly irresponsible. But he isn't bad at heart. He is devoted to his wife. When the Sweet Woman gets on his nerves, he simply packs up and beats it. But he loves her just the same. And he always sees to it that, no matter how far away he is, she is well provided for. The further away he is, the more she gets. And his feelings for Spark Plug — well, they change from time to time. When Spark Plug wins a race, Barney loves him like a brother. But when Sparky loses, Barney always figures out how much he could get for him at a glue factory. I hope you will like Barney and his horse. You will find that Barney, with all his faults and weaknesses, is human, like the rest of us. And you've simply got to like Spark Plug. If their adventures please you and if you tell me you would like to know more of them, I'll get out other books. Anyway, please accept my thanks for having taken this one.'

Contents
Compilation of daily newspaper strips syndicated by King Features. Contains 44 strips arranged one to a page, printed in black-and-white. Coloured cover on cardboard, plus title page specially drawn by the artist, Billy De Beck. The 'Barney Google' strip started in January 1919.

171 Bringing Up Father: Seventh Series

1923. 25¢. 52 pp. 10×10. Publisher: Cupples & Leon Co., 443 Fourth Avenue, New York. Artist: George McManus. Syndicate: International Feature Service.

Contents
Compilation of daily newspaper strips arranged one to a page and printed black-and-white. Cardboard covers in two colours specially drawn by the artist, George McManus.

172 Canyon County Kiddies

1923. $2.00. 74 pp. Publisher: Doubleday Page & Co., Garden City, New York. Artist: James Swinnerton.

Contents
Compilation of 'Canyon Kiddies' cartoons originally published as a children's feature in *Good Housekeeping*, a monthly magazine.

173 Peter Rabbit

1923. 12 pp. 9¼×6¼. Publisher: John H. Eggers Co. (The House of Little Books). Artist: Harrison Cady. Syndicate: New York Tribune.

Contents
Set of four small books contained in a special cardboard box, 'The House of Little Books'. Books are numbered B1 to B4, and contain reprints of Sunday newspaper strips copyrighted 1922 by the *New York Tribune*. Strips are arranged half to each page, and are printed 8 pages black-and-white, 4 pages in full colour. The character of Peter Rabbit is the American creation of Thornton W. Burgess, not the British one of Beatrix Potter.

174 Adventures of Slim and Spud

1924. 104 pp. 9¾×3¾. Publisher: Prairie Farmer Publishing Co., 223 West Jackson Boulevard, Chicago.

Contents
Compilation of newspaper strips originally published in *The Prairie Farmer*, and reprinted in oblong format, black-and-white thoughout.

175 Andy Gump: His Life Story

1924. $1.00. 192 pp. 5½×8½. Publisher: Reilly & Lee Co., 536 Lake Shore Drive, Chicago. Artist: Sidney Smith. Syndicate: Chicago Tribune.

Contents
'Biography' of the comic strip hero of the daily newspaper strip, 'The Gumps', illustrated with pictures from the strip. Hardback, with cover specially drawn by the artist, Sidney Smith. Not strictly a comic book.

176 Banana Oil

1924. 52 pp. Publisher: M.S. Publishing Co. Artist: Milt Gross.

Contents

Compilation of gag strips originally published in the *New York World*. Printed black-and-white with a cover specially drawn by the artist, Milt Gross.

177 Barney Google and Spark Plug: Book 2

1924. 25¢. 52 pp. 10×9³/₄. Publisher: Cupples & Leon Co., 443 Fourth Avenue, New York. Artist: Billy De Beck.

Contents

Compilation of daily newspaper strips, arranged one to a page and printed black-and-white. Coloured cover on cardboard, and title page specially drawn by the artist, Billy De Beck.

178 Bringing Up Father: Eighth Series

1924. 25¢. 52 pp. 10×10. Publisher: Cupples & Leon Co., 443 Fourth Avenue, New York. Artist: George McManus. Syndicate: International Feature Service.

Contents

Compilation of 46 daily newspaper strips arranged one to the page, printed black-and-white. Cardboard covers in two colours specially drawn by the artist, George McManus.

179 The Diary of Snubs Our Dog

Vol. 1: 1924–Series 5: 1934. £1.50; 60¢. 96 pp.(1); 120 pp. 7×9. Publishers: Belden Press, 2316 Lincoln Avenue, Chicago, Illinois (1); George Sully & Co., 114 East 25th Street, New York (2–4); Associated Authors Service, 222 West Adams Street, Chicago (5). Artist: Paul R. Carmack.

Contents

Reprints of the newspaper comic strip designed for children, first published in *The Christian Science Monitor*. The first collection of 96 pages was published in Chicago by the Belden Press, in 1924. The next three collections numbered Volumes 2, 3 and 4, were published in New York by George Sully & Co., in 1926, 1928 and 1931. These were clothbound hardback books of 120 pages, each reprinting 106 strips. The artist, Paul R. Carmack, drew special dust-wrappers and end-papers. The final collection was published in Chicago by the Associated Authors Service, in 1934.

180 The Gumps

1924. 25¢. 52 pp. 10×9³/₄. Publisher: Cupples & Leon Co., 443 Fourth Avenue, New York. Artist: Sidney Smith. Syndicate: Chicago Tribune.

Contents

Compilation of 46 daily newspaper strips reprinted in black-and-white and arranged one to the page. Two-colour covers on cardboard, and title page specially drawn by the artist, Sidney Smith.

181 Mutt and Jeff: Book 9

1924. 25¢. 52 pp. 10×9³/₄. Publisher: Cupples & Leon Co., 443 Fourth Avenue, New York. Artist: Bud Fisher. Syndicate: H.C. Fisher.

Introduction
'Habit is a terrible thing! When Book No. 1 of this bunch of rubbish first appeared before the patient public, I wrote a preface and thereby hooked myself into writing a preface for each new book of these misdemeanors. As I have said, habit is a terrible thing, and my publisher has gotten the preface habit. Therefore I am writing another preface for "Book Nine" under duress. I lost a bet at the race track today and also bet upon the New York Giants to win today's game in the World Series. Both errors in judgement being a permanent loss to the family savings-bank account. Hence, the mood for gay frivolity had reverse English on it and sooner than deceive the general reader and pull a mock show of glad tidings, I will simply tell the truth and beseech you to advise your friends to purchase (or steal) all available copies of "this book-formed ash-can", as I am paid for each and every copy reaching the General Public. Thanking you for getting bunked with this particular copy, I am your devoted slave and highwayman, Bud Fisher. P.S. — Follow the green line in passing out and charge your expenses to charity. B. F.'

Contents
Compilation of 46 daily newspaper strips numbered between No. 97 and No. 276, copyrighted 1924 by H.C. ('Bud') Fisher. Strips are arranged one to a page, with an original cover, title page and introduction by the artist. Cardboard covers.

182 Skeezix and Uncle Walt

1924. $1.00. 128 pp. Publisher: Reilly & Lee Co., 536 Lake Shore Drive, Chicago. Artist: Frank King. Syndicate: Chicago Tribune.

Contents
Compilation of daily newspaper strips copyrighted by the *Chicago Tribune* and originally entitled 'Gasoline Alley'. The series began on 23 August 1919. Printed black-and-white with coloured cover specially designed by the artist, Frank King.

183 Barney Google and Spark Plug: Book 3

1925. 25¢. 52 pp. 10×9³/₄. Publisher: Cupples & Leon Co., 443 Fourth Avenue, New York. Artist: Billy De Beck.

Contents
Compilation of daily newspaper strips reprinted in black-and-white and arranged one to the page. Two-colour cover on cardboard, and title page specially drawn by the artist, Billy De Beck.

184 Bringing Up Father: Ninth Series

1925. 25¢. 52 pp. 10×10. Publisher: Cupples & Leon Co., 443 Fourth Avenue, New York. Syndicate: International Feature Service.

Contents
Compilation of 46 daily newspaper strips arranged one to the page, printed black-and-white. Cardboard covers in two colours specially drawn by the artist, George McManus.

185 The Gumps: Book 2

1925. 25¢. 52 pp. 10×9³/₄. Publishers: Cupples & Leon Co., 443 Fourth Avenue, New York. Artist: Sidney Smith. Syndicate: Chicago Tribune.

Contents
Compilation of daily newspaper strips reprinted in black-and-white and arranged one to the page. Cardboard cover in two colours, and title page specially drawn by the artist, Sidney Smith.

186 Home Sweet Home

1925. Publisher: M.S. Publishing Co. Artist: H.J. Tuthill. Syndicate: New York Mail.

Contents
Compilation of daily newspaper strips reprinted in black-and-white, syndicated by the *New York Mail*. The artist, H.J. Tuthill, later transferred his strip to the McNaught Syndicate under the new title of 'The Bungle Family'.

187 Mutt and Jeff: Book 10

1925. 25¢. 52 pp. 10× 9³/₄. Publisher: Cupples & Leon Co., 443 Fourth Avenue, New York. Artist: Bud Fisher. Syndicate H.C. Fisher.

Contents
Compilation of 46 daily newspaper strips copyrighted by H.C. ('Bud') Fisher. Strips are arranged one to a page and printed black-and-white. Coloured cover on cardboard, and title page specially drawn by the artist.

188 Reg'lar Fellers

1925. 48 pp. Publisher: M.S. Publications. Artist: Gene Byrnes.

Contents
Compilation of daily newspaper strips printed black-and-white.

189 Skeezix and Pal

1925. $1.00. 112 pp. Publisher: Reilly & Lee Co., 536 Lake Shore Drive, Chicago. Artist: Frank King. Syndicate: Chicago Tribune.

Contents

Compilation of daily newspaper strips copyrighted by the *Chicago Tribune*. Printed black-and-white with a coloured cover specially drawn by the artist, Frank King. Second in the *Gasoline Alley* series by this publisher.

190 Skippy

1925. 64 pp. 8³/₄×11. Publisher: Greenberg Inc., 112 East 19th Street, New York. Artist: Percy L. Crosby.

Contents

Compilation of weekly strips reprinted from *Life* magazine, printed in colour with a cover specially drawn by the artist, Percy L. Crosby. 'Skippy' started on 22 March 1923, and became a newspaper strip in 1925, syndication being taken over by King Features from 7 October 1926.

191 Tom Sawyer and Huck Finn

1925. 60¢. 52 pp. 10×10³/₄. Publisher: Stoll & Edwards Co., 425 Fourth Avenue, New York. Artist: Clare Dwiggins.

Contents

Compilation of 16 Sunday newspaper supplement strips copyrighted 1923 and 1924, and printed in four colours. Cardboard covers, specially drawn by the artist, Clare Dwiggins ('Dwig'). The characters were based on those created in a series of stories by Mark Twain. The strips are rearranged so that each Sunday page covers three pages, four pictures to the page.

192 All the Funny Folks

1926. 112 pp. 11¹/₂×3¹/₂. Publisher: World Press Today Inc.

Contents

Compilation of newspaper strips reprinted in four colours, including 'Barney Google and Spark Plug' by Billy De Beck, 'The Captain and the Kids' by Rudolph Dirks, 'Happy Hooligan' by Fred Opper, 'Bringing Up Father' by George McManus, 'Toots and Casper' by Jimmy Murphy, 'Tillie the Toiler' by Russ Westover, and others. Hardcover book.

193 Barney Google and Spark Plug: Book 4

1926. 25¢. 52 pp. 10×9³/₄. Publisher: Cupples & Leon Co., 443 Fourth Avenue, New York. Artist: Billy De Beck.

Contents

Compilation of newspaper strips reprinted in black-and-white, arranged one to the page. The two-colour cover on cardboard and the title page were specially drawn by the artist, Billy De Beck.

194 Bringing Up Father Big Book

1926. 75¢. 152 pp. 10×9¾. Publisher: Cupples & Leon Co., 443 Fourth Avenue, New York. Artist: George McManus. Syndicate: International Feature Service.

Contents
Compilation of three earlier editions in the *Bringing Up Father* series of reprint books by this publisher. Contains 138 daily newspaper strips arranged one to a page, printed black-and-white. Bound in boards with three-colour dust-wrapper and title page designed by the artist, George McManus.

195 Bringing Up Father: Tenth Series

1926. 25¢. 52 pp. 10×10. Publisher: Cupples & Leon Co., 443 Fourth Avenue, New York. Artist: George McManus. Syndicate: International Feature Service.

Contents
Compilation of 46 daily newspaper strips arranged one to the page and printed black-and-white. Two-colour cover on cardboard specially drawn by the artist, George McManus.

196 The Gumps: Book 3

1926. 25¢. 52 pp. 10×9¾. Publisher: Cupples & Leon Co., 443 Fourth Avenue, New York. Artist: Sidney Smith. Syndicate: Chicago Tribune.

Contents
Compilation of 46 daily newspaper strips reprinted in black-and-white. Two-colour cover on cardboard, and title page specially drawn by the artist, Sidney Smith.

197 The High-Kicking Kellys

1926. 28 pp. 11×8. Publisher: Vaudeville News Corporation, New York. Artist: Jack Ward.

Introduction
'Here we have the first cartoon book ever published, depicting the humorous side of one of the most fascinating branches of the theatrical profession — Vaudeville. The requirements of a vaudeville artist are many. He is his own author, producer, press agent, sales manager and deliverer. His success depends greatly upon his ability to visualize his own work from every seat in the theatre — in short, he is also his own audience. He must love his audience to love his work. He is a public toy and a very inspiring one. The lure of the footlights attracts a great many well-meaning people who do not qualify for the stage. "The High-Kicking Kellys" are fashioned after this type. Their ambitions exceed their talents, but if they can keep up their courage for the next fifty years, they may become a box-office attraction in some aquarium. Many of the following cartoons depict actual happenings in

Vaudeville. I happen to know, as I am a vaudeville artist by profession and a cartoonist on the make-up shelf only.'

Contents
Compilation of 44 comic strips reprinted from *Vaudeville News and Star*, printed in black-and-white with a two-colour cardboard cover. The artist, Jack Ward, was a partner in the vaudeville act of Northlane and Ward. He has drawn a special cover and title page.

198 Little Orphan Annie

1926. 75¢. 96 pp. 7×8½. Publisher: Cupples & Leon Co., 443 Fourth Avenue, New York. Artist: Harold Gray. Syndicate: Chicago Tribune.

Introduction
'FOREWORD
Ladees an' Gentlemen, and all you young birds out there in front, too: — Un'customed as I am to public 'pearances, and all that alfalfa, I just want to say this bustin' into liter-chure is a big s'prise to me. 'Course I s'pose I ought to be sorta bashful 'bout having a swell pitcher-book like this put out all filled up with nothin' but fancy poses and wise cracks of yours truly. But you don't see me blushin', do you? No sir. Down where I come from you get over bein' bashful young. You gotta toot yer own horn or get run over. See? Nope, I'm not bashful. But honest, folks, I'm proud, I am, that you and your relatives and neighbors, deep down in your hearts, thought enough of me to write in and ask to have a book like this put out. Yessir, folks, it sure makes you feel swell to find out, sorta un's'pectedly, how many real true friends you have. I thank you.'

Contents
Compilation of 86 daily newspaper strips reprinted from 1925, copyrighted by the *Chicago Tribune*. The strips are arranged one to the page, printed black-and-white, with an original cover and title page drawn by the artist, Harold Gray. Cardboard covers printed in three colours. Part of the book was reprinted in 1934 as a 36-page comic book included in *The Treasure Box of Famous Comics* (Cupples & Leon). The book was also reprinted in 1974 by Dover Publications Inc., New York, as part of *Little Orphan Annie and Little Orphan Annie in Cosmic City*. Dover Publications also reprinted it in a changed format, measuring 6×10¼ with 68 pages, as *Little Orphan Annie*.

199 Mutt and Jeff Big Book

1926. 75¢. 152 pp. 10×9¾. Publisher: Cupples & Leon Co., 443 Fourth Avenue, New York. Artist: Bud Fisher. Syndicate: H.C. Fisher.

Contents
Compilation of three earlier editions in the Mutt and Jeff series of reprint books by this publisher. Has 138 daily newspaper strips arranged one to a page, printed black-and-white. Bound in boards with three-colour dust-wrapper and title page drawn by the artist, Bud Fisher.

200 Mutt and Jeff: Book 11

1926. 25¢. 52 pp. 10×9¾. Publisher: Cupples & Leon Co., 443 Fourth Avenue, New York. Artist: Bud Fisher. Syndicate: H.C. Fisher.

Contents
Compilation of 46 daily newspaper strips copyrighted by H.C. ('Bud') Fisher. Strips arranged one to a page, printed black-and-white. Coloured cover on cardboard, and title page specially drawn by the artist.

201 The Newlyweds and Their Baby

1926. 58 pp. 13×10. Publisher: Saalfield & Co., Akron, Ohio. Artist: George McManus.

Contents
Compilation of newspaper strips reprinted from the Sunday supplements, printed in four colours on one side of the page only. This popular strip started in 1904. *Note:* this book is dated 1907 in *The Comic Book Price Guide*, but other reference works give 1926.

202 Skeezix at the Circus

1926. $1.00. 112 pp. Publisher: Reilly & Lee Co., 536 Lake Shore Drive, Chicago. Artist: Frank King. Syndicate: Chicago Tribune.

Contents
Compilation of daily newspaper strips syndicated by the *Chicago Tribune*. Printed black-and-white with special coloured cover drawn by the artist, Frank King. Third in the *Gasoline Alley* series by this publisher.

203 Tillie the Toiler

1926. 25¢. 52 pp. 10×9³/₄. Publisher: Cupples & Leon Co., 443 Fourth Avenue, New York. Artist: Russ Westover. Syndicate: King Features.

Contents
Compilation of the daily newspaper strip copyright King Features Syndicate. Has 46 strips arranged one to a page and printed black-and-white with a cardboard cover. Special cover illustration and title page drawn by the artist, Russ Westover. Tillie the Toiler made her comic strip debut in January 1921.

204 On the Links

December 1926. 48 pp. 9×10. Publisher: Associated Feature Service.

Contents
Compilation of the daily newspaper strip, printed in black-and-white.

205 Barney Google and Spark Plug: Book 5

1927. 25¢. 52 pp. 10×9³/₄. Publisher: Cupples & Leon Co., 443 Fourth Avenue, New York. Artist: Billy De Beck.

Contents
Compilation of 46 newspaper strips reprinted in black-and-white and arranged one to the page. Two-colour cover on cardboard, and title page specially drawn by the artist, Billy De Beck.

206 Bringing Up Father: Series No. 11

1927. 25¢. 52 pp. 10×9³/₄. Publisher: Cupples & Leon Co., 443 Fourth Avenue, New York. Artist: George McManus. Syndicate: International Feature Service.

Contents
Compilation of 46 daily newspaper strips arranged one to the page and printed black-and-white. Two-colour cover on cardboard specially drawn by the artist, George McManus.

207 Bringing Up Father: Series No. 12

1927. 25¢. 52 pp. 10×9³/₄. Publisher: Cupples & Leon Co., 443 Fourth Avenue, New York. Artist: George McManus. Syndicate: International Feature Service.

Contents
Compilation of 46 daily newspaper strips arranged one to a page, printed black-and-white. Two-colour cover on cardboard specially drawn by the artist, George Mcmanus.

208 Felix the Cat

1927. 24 pp. 8×10¹/₄. Publisher: McLoughlin Bros., 74 Park Street, Springfield, Massachusetts. Artist: Otto Messmer. Syndicate: King Features.

Contents
Compilation of newspaper strips reprinted from the Sunday supplements and copyright 1926–1927 by King Features Syndicate. Printed in four colours throughout. *Note:* although the strip is credited to Pat Sullivan, producer of the Felix the Cat cartoon films, the strips are drawn by his chief animator, Otto Messmer.

209 The Gumps: Book 4

1927. 25¢. 52 pp. 10×9³/₄. Publisher: Cupples & Leon Co., 443 Fourth Avenue, New York. Artist: Sidney Smith. Syndicate: Chicago Tribune.

Contents

Compilation of 46 daily newspaper strips reprinted in black-and-white and arranged one strip to the page. Two-colour cover and title page specially drawn by the artist, Sidney Smith. Cardboard covers.

210 Little Orphan Annie in the Circus

1927. 75¢. 96 pp. 7×8³/₄. Publisher: Cupples & Leon Co., 443 Fourth Avenue, New York. Artist: Harold Gray. Syndicate: Chicago Tribune.

Contents

Compilation of daily newspaper strips copyrighted 1926 by the *Chicago Tribune*. The 86 strips are arranged one to a page, printed black-and-white, and bound in a cardboard cover, printed in three colours. The artist, Harold Gray, has drawn the cover and title page. Book No. 2 of the Little Orphan Annie series.

211 Mr. and Mrs.

1927. 25¢. 28 pp. Publisher: Stanton Publishing Co., 2537 South State Street, Chicago. Artist: Clare Briggs. Syndicate: New York Tribune.

Contents

Compilation of strips reprinted from the Sunday edition of the *New York Tribune*. Printed in full colour throughout, the strips are arranged so that one full-page strip covers two pages of the book.

212 Moon Mullins

1927. 25¢. 52 pp. 9³/₄×9³/₄. Publisher: Cupples & Leon Co., 443 Fourth Avenue, New York. Artist: Frank Willard. Syndicate: Chicago Tribune.

Contents

Compilation of 46 daily newspaper strips copyrighted by the *Chicago Tribune*. Strips are arranged one to a page, printed black-and-white. Two-colour cardboard cover and title page designed by the artist, Frank Willard.

213 Mutt and Jeff: Book 12

1927. 25¢. 52 pp. 10×9³/₄. Publisher: Cupples & Leon Co., 443 Fourth Avenue, New York. Syndicate: H.C. Fisher.

Contents

Compilation of 46 daily newspaper strips copyrighted by H.C. Fisher. Strips arranged one to a page and printed black-and-white, with coloured cover and title page specially drawn by the artist.

214 Skeezix and Uncle Walt

1927. Publisher: Reilly & Lee Co., Chicago. Artist: Frank King. Syndicate: Chicago Tribune.

Contents
Compilation of daily newspaper strips copyrighted by the *Chicago Tribune*. Printed black-and-white with a coloured cover specially drawn by the artist, Frank King. No. 4 in the *Gasoline Alley* series by this publisher.

215 Tillie the Toiler Book 2

1927. 25¢. 52 pp. 10×9¾. Publisher: Cupples & Leon Co., 443 Fourth Avenue, New York. Artist: Russ Westover. Syndicate: King Features.

Contents
Compilation of daily newspaper strips copyright by King Features Syndicate. Contains 46 strips, arranged one to a page, printed black-and-white, bound in cardboard covers. Special cover and title page drawn by the artist, Russ Westover.

216 Barney Google and Spark Plug: Book 6

1928. 25¢. 52 pp. 10×9¾. Publisher: Cupples & Leon Co., 443 Fourth Avenue, New York. Artist: Billy De Beck.

Contents
Compilation of 46 daily newspaper strips printed in black-and-white and arranged one to the page. Two-colour cover and title page drawn by the artist, Billy De Beck. Card covers. This is the last in this series.

217 Bringing Up Father: Series No. 13

1928. 25¢. 52 pp. 10×9¾. Publisher: Cupples & Leon Co., 443 Fourth Avenue, New York. Artist: George McManus. Syndicate: International Feature Service.

Contents
Compilation of 46 daily newspaper strips printed in black-and-white and arranged one to a page. Two-colour cover on cardboard specially drawn by the artist, George McManus.

218 Bringing Up Father: Series No. 14

1928. 25¢. 52 pp. 10×9¾. Publisher: Cupples & Leon Co., 443 Fourth Avenue, New York. Artist: George McManus. Syndicate: International Feature Service.

Contents

Compilation of 46 daily newspaper strips printed in black-and-white and arranged one to a page. Two-colour cover on cardboard specially drawn by the artist, George McManus.

219 The Gumps: Book 5

1928. 25¢. 52 pp. 10×9¾. Publisher: Cupples & Leon Co., 443 Fourth Avenue, New York. Artist: Sidney Smith. Syndicate: Chicago Tribune.

Contents

Compilation of 46 daily newspaper strips printed in black-and-white and arranged one to the page. Two-colour cover on cardboard, and title page drawn by the artist, Sidney Smith.

220 Little Orphan Annie and the Haunted House

1928. 60¢. 96 pp. 7×8¾. Publisher: Cupples & Leon Co., 443 Fourth Avenue, New York. Artist: Harold Gray. Syndicate: Chicago Tribune.

Contents

Compilation of daily newspaper strips copyright the *Chicago Tribune*. The 86 strips are arranged one to a page, printed black-and-white. Bound in boards with three-colour dust-wrapper and title page designed by the artist, Harold Gray. No. 3 of the *Little Orphan Annie* series.

221 Moon Mullins: Series 2

1928. 25¢. 52 pp. 9¾×9¾. Publisher: Cupples & Leon Co., 443 Fourth Avenue, New York. Artist: Frank Willard. Syndicate: Chicago Tribune.

Contents

Compilation of 46 daily newspaper strips copyrighted by the *Chicago Tribune*. Strips are arranged one to a page, printed black-and-white. Two-colour cardboard cover and title page specially drawn by the artist, Frank Willard.

222 Mutt and Jeff: Book 13

1928. 25¢. 52 pp. 10×9¾. Publisher: Cupples & Leon Co., 443 Fourth Avenue, New York. Artist: Bud Fisher. Syndicate: H.C. Fisher.

Contents

Compilation of 46 daily newspaper strips copyrighted by the artist, H.C. (Bud) Fisher. Strips arranged one to a page and printed black-and-white. Coloured cover on cardboard and title page specially drawn by the artist.

223 Skeezix Out West

1928. Publisher: Reilly & Lee Co., Chicago. Artist: Frank King. Syndicate: Chicago Tribune.

Contents
Compilation of daily newspaper strips copyrighted by the *Chicago Tribune*. Printed in two colours with a special coloured cover drawn by the artist, Frank King. No. 5 of the Gasoline Alley series by this publisher.

224 'Smatter Pop?

1928. 25¢. 52 pp. 7×8½. Publisher: E.I. Co. (Experimenter Publishing Co.), 230 Fifth Avenue, New York. Artist: C.M. Payne. Syndicate: Bell Syndicate Inc.

Contents
Compilation of 48 daily newspaper strips copyright 1927 the Bell Syndicate Inc. Printed black-and-white in a three-colour card cover, an original drawing by the artist, C.M. Payne. Publication of this book can be dated by the advertisement for *Amazing Stories* Vol. 2, No. 11, which was published in February 1928.

225 Smitty

1928. 96 pp. 7×8¾. Publisher: Cupples & Leon Co., 443 Fourth Avenue, New York. Artist: Walter Berndt. Syndicate: Chicago Tribune.

Introduction
'When a feller busts into public life, like us guys in the newspapers, it's only a matter o' time before some feller is buzzin' around to publish a book about your career. I wouldn't mind that so much . . . all the big guys tell me that they've had it done . . . but I an't so sure that it's becomin' to a feller of my dignity. After all I an't a big guy . . . yet. But they've wrote books about Lindy, and movie stars and such . . . yes, I'm in the movies, too . . . so I suppose I gotta stand for it. Cracked ice. I'm just wonderin' how you folks are going to stand for it! Honest, I hope you won't laugh. It's nothin' to giggle at. Especially when this Berndt fellah grabs all the dough for it. That's what makes me mad. Hoping you are the same, I am, as ever yours, Smitty.'

Contents
Compilation of 86 daily newspaper strips dated from 16 December 1927 to 24 March 1928, copyright the *Chicago Tribune*. Strips are arranged one to a page, printed black-and-white, and bound in cardboard. Cover drawing and title page by the artist, Walter Berndt. Part of this book was reprinted in 1934 as a 36-page comic book included in the same publisher's *Treasure Box of Famous Comics*.

226 Tillie the Toiler Book 3

1928. 25¢. 52 pp. 10×9¾. Publisher: Cupples & Leon Co., 443 Fourth Avenue, New York. Artist: Russ Westover. Syndicate: King Features.

Contents

Compilation of daily newspaper strips copyright by King Features Syndicate. Contains 46 strips arranged one to a page, printed black-and-white and bound in cardboard covers. Special cover and title page drawn by the artist, Russ Westover.

227 Bringing Up Father Big Book No. 2

1929. 75¢. 152 pp. 10×9³/₄. Publisher: Cupples & Leon Co., 470 Fourth Avenue, New York. Artist: George McManus. Syndicate: International Feature Service Inc.

Contents

Compilation of three earlier editions in the Bringing Up Father series of reprint books by this publisher. Contains 138 daily newspaper strips arranged one to a page, printed black-and-white. Bound in boards with a three-colour dust-wrapper and title page designed by the artist, George McManus.

228 Bringing Up Father: Series 15

1929. 25¢. 52 pp. 10×9³/₄. Publisher: Cupples & Leon Co., 470 Fourth Avenue, New York. Artist: George McManus: Syndicate: International Feature Service.

Contents

Compilation of 46 daily newspaper strips reprinted in black-and-white and arranged one to a page. Two-colour cover on cardboard specially drawn by the artist, George McManus.

229 Bringing Up Father: Series 16

1929. 25¢. 52 pp. 10×9³/₄. Publisher: Cupples & Leon Co., 470 Fourth Avenue, New York. Artist: George McManus. Syndicate: International Feature Service.

Contents

Compilation of 46 daily newspaper strips reprinted from dates between August and November 1927, copyright International Feature Service Inc. The strips cover part of a sequence concerning Jiggs' and Maggie's trip around the world. Strips are arranged one to a page, with an original cover, title page, and introduction by the artist. Cardboard covers.

230 Gasoline Alley

1929. 94 pp. 6³/₄×8³/₄. Publisher: Reilly & Lee Co., Chicago. Artist: Frank King. Syndicate: Chicago Tribune.

Introduction
'ABOUT GASOLINE ALLEY

"Did you pick your characters for Gasoline Alley from real life?" The answer is yes and no. And the question, a perennial and a fair one. I did first pounce on Walt, a brother-in-law, for my leading character. Not, however, because he was particularly well fitted for a comedian, but because he was handy and he was good natured. Almost anyone, with a little exaggeration, would make a good comic character. There is no lack of raw material. Not only the woods, but the streets and houses are full of it. I have taken infinite liberties with Walt's physique, his mentality and his daily activities, and I believe that my original guess that he would stand for a lot, has proven correct. I have been nearly as rough with Bill, who started in real life and ended up as one of the Gasoline Alley bunch — the others are gathered bit by bit from human nature — diluted a bit here and there perhaps — flavored to taste and colored so as to be acceptable as the genuine article. Avery, for instance, possesses the economical instincts claimed by the Scotch but by no means peculiar to them. Avery was not taken bodily from real life but is pieced together from many human fragments. I do not agree with some alleged authorities that I furnished most of them myself. No, Avery is synthetic Scotch.

I hope my audience will get a measure of interest and fun out of these pictures. I had pleasure in drawing them. It is a privilege to be the master of destinies, and director of every urge and event in the lives of such a group of folks. They may be dream folks, but the responsibilities are real, because I know these characters are real to many thousands of readers. I have received a myriad of letters that proved it. Personally, I am not convinced they are dream folks. They have furnished me and mine for years with the solid basic materials of life — food, raiment and a tight roof. They have paid my motor license fees and fines and kept me in gasoline. I, for one, know they are real. Friends, meet the Gasoline Alley bunch! Frank King.'

Contents
Compilation of 83 daily newspaper strips copyright the *Chicago Tribune*. Strips are arranged one to a page, and the dates have been removed. Printed black-and-white with a three-colour cover drawn by the artist, Frank King. Cardboard covers. This book reprints strips from the earlier series of Skeezix books by this publisher.

231 The Gumps: Book 6

1929. 25¢. 52 pp. 10×9³/₄. Publisher: Cupples & Leon Co., 470 Fourth Avenue, New York. Artist: Sidney Smith. Syndicate: Chicago Tribune.

Contents
Compilation of 46 daily newspaper strips reprinted in black-and-white, and arranged one to a page. Two-colour cover on cardboard, and title page specially drawn by the artist, Sidney Smith.

232 The Illustrated Tarzan Book

1929. 50¢. 80 pp. 7×9. Publisher: Grosset & Dunlap, 1140 Broadway, New York. Artist: Harold Foster. Syndicate: Metropolitan Newspaper Service.

Contents
Compilation of the daily newspaper strip illustrating Edgar Rice Burroughs' novel, *Tarzan of the Apes*. The first newspaper appearance was on 7 January 1929, drawn by Harold Foster. This hard-cover book with coloured dust-jacket was printed in black-and-white throughout. It was reprinted in

1934 at the reduced price of 25¢. A facsimile edition was published in 1967 by the House of Greystoke as *Burroughs Bibliophile* No. 2, price $5.00.

233 Little Orphan Annie Bucking the World

1929. 60¢. 96 pp. 7×8³/₄. Publisher: Cupples & Leon Co., 470 Fourth Avenue, New York. Artist: Harold Gray. Syndicate: Chicago Tribune.

Contents
Compilation of daily newspaper strips copyright the *Chicago Tribune*. The 86 strips are arranged one to a page, printed black-and-white. Bound in boards with three-colour dust-wrapper and title page specially drawn by the artist, Harold Gray. No. 4 of the *Little Orphan Annie* series.

234 Moon Mullins: Series 3

1929. 25¢. 52 pp. 9³/₄×9¹/₂. Publisher: Cupples & Leon Co., 470 Fourth Avenue, New York. Artist: Frank Willard. Syndicate: Chicago Tribune.

Introduction
'FOREWORD BY MOON MULLINS HIMSELF
Well, folks, here is the third volume of "The Private Life of me and the kid brother, Kayo". Each and every one a education in itself. No home complete without one. Thousands and thousands of people are starting the day right by reading this book while they take their morning shower instead of singing and waking the other boarders up. Famous writers, actors, ball players and chiropodists all agree that this is really the only book they ever enjoyed reading while taking the blindfold test. A prominent physician says that he has found great comfort in these pages (i.e. by tearing them out and putting them under his coat on a cold night.) Mussolini wrote recently to his pal Lowenthal: — "I have just finished the third volume of the life of that great man Moonshine Mullins, it has given me self-confidence at last." There are hundreds of different uses you folks can put this gem of literature and art to, but I'll let you figure them out yourself as it will give zest to any jolly party that is fed up on crossword puzzles and playing post office. Well read 'em and weep. So long folks, I'll see you in the funny papers. Yours truly, Moonshine Mullins, Esq.'

Contents
Compilation of 46 daily newspaper strips copyrighted 1928 by the *Chicago Tribune*. Strips are arranged one to the page, printed black-and-white, with an original cover and title page drawn by the artist, Frank Willard. Cardboard cover. This book was reprinted in 1976 by Dover Publications Inc., New York, as part of *Moon Mullins: Two Adventures*.

235 Mutt and Jeff Big Book No. 2

1929. 75¢. 152 pp. 10×9³/₄. Publisher: Cupples & Leon Co., 470 Fourth Avenue, New York. Artist: Bud Fisher. Syndicate: H.C. Fisher.

Contents

Compilation of three earlier editions of the Mutt and Jeff series of reprint books by this publisher. Contains 138 daily newspaper strips arranged one to a page, printed black-and-white. Bound in boards with three-colour dust-wrapper and title page drawn by the artist, Bud Fisher.

236 Mutt and Jeff: Book 14

1929. 25¢. 52 pp. 10×9³/₄. Publisher: Cupples & Leon Co., 470 Fourth Avenue, New York. Artist: Bud Fisher. Syndicate H.C. Fisher.

Contents

Compilation of 46 daily newspaper strips copyrighted by H.C. ('Bud') Fisher. Strips arranged one to a page, printed black-and-white. Cardboard cover in colours and title page specially drawn by the artist.

237 Reg'lar Fellers

1929. 60¢. 96 pp. 7×8¹/₂. Publisher: Cupples & Leon Co., 470 Fourth Avenue, New York. Artist: Gene Byrnes. Syndicate: Gene Byrnes.

Contents

Compilation of daily newspaper strips printed in black-and-white, one to a page. Board covers with coloured dust-wrapper designed by the artist, Gene Byrnes, who was also his own syndicate. Part of this book was reprinted as a 36-page comic book in coloured cover, included in the packaged set, *Treasure Box of Famous Comics* (1934).

238 Smitty at the Ball Game

1929. 60¢. 96 pp. 7×8³/₄. Publisher: Cupples & Leon Co., 470 Fourth Avenue, New York. Artist: Walter Berndt. Syndicate: Chicago Tribune.

Contents

Compilation of 86 daily newspaper strips copyright the *Chicago Tribune*. Strips are arranged one to the page, printed black-and-white. Bound in boards with coloured dust-wrapper and title page drawn by the artist, Walter Berndt. No. 2 in the *Smitty* series.

239 Tillie the Toiler Book 4

1929. 25¢. 52 pp. 10×9³/₄. Publisher: Cupples & Leon Co., 470 Fourth Avenue, New York. Artist: Russ Westover. Syndicate: King Features.

Contents

Compilation of 46 daily newspaper strips copyright King Features Syndicate. Strips are arranged one to a page, printed black-and-white. Bound in cardboard covers with three-colour cover specially drawn by the artist, Russ Westover.

240 The Funnies

'Flying — Sports — Adventure'

No. 1: 16 January 1929–No. 36: 18 October 1930. 10¢. (1–21); 5¢. (22–36). 24 pp. (1, 2); 32 pp. (3–5); 24 pp. (6–21); 16 pp (22–36). 10½ × 15½. Publisher: Dell Publishing Co. (George T. Delacorte Jr.), 100 Fifth Avenue, New York. Editorial: Harry Steeger (editor); Abril Lamarque (comic art editor); Edythe Seims (assistant editor); George T. Delacorte Jr. (managing editor).

Contents of No. 1

1 Frosty Ayre	Joe Archibald
2 My Big Brudder	Tack Knight
3 Rock Age Roy	Boody Rogers
4 How to Fly	Charles Curtis, Ed Hermes
5 Buck Buford	Howard Williamson (BW)
6 Under Wraps (story)	F. N. Litten (BW)
7 Stubby Shoots the Works (story)	Kenneth Whipple (BW)
8 Pirates Ahoy! (story)	Charles B. Driscoll (BW)
Lucky Duck	Joe Archibald
9 How Can I Become an Explorer (feature, BW)	
Jacky	Sidney Garber
10 Jungle Vengeance (story)	Earle Danesford (BW)
12 Deadwood Gulch	Boody Rogers (BW)
13 Corporal Tim	Hafon (BW)
14 Dare Devil Gazabo	J. Molina (BW)
15 Peaches	Tack Knight (BW)
16 Shylock Bones	Joe Archibald (BW)
17 What's Wrong with These Pictures (BW)	
18 Frank and Ernest	Bencho (BW)
19 Puzzles	Nat (BW)
20 Joe Gum	Gil King (BW)
21 Bug Movies	Stookie Allen
22 Sancho and the Don	Ralph Wolfe
23 Cookie-Pushers	Buford Tune
24 Campus Clowns	Boody Rogers

First Editorial

'WATCH US STEP!

In the next *Funnies* the further adventures of Stubby, the kid cop, in the haunted house! Grease Monkey, a thrilling story of winter sports; Great Snakes, another exciting biography in our explorer series! Corporal Tim, Rock Age Roy, Sancho and the Don, Cookie Pushers, Frosty Ayre — and all the rest — will be with us again. And don't forget! There will be another great flying lesson! Learn to fly with Speed Kelly!'

The Funnies was the first regular comics magazine to be published and sold on newsstands. It was modelled on the British tabloid comic weeklies, crossed with the Sunday newspaper supplements. No. 1 was undated, but entered as Second Class material with the United States Post Office on 27 December 1928. All the strips in No. 1 were the copyright of Film Humor Inc., and were apparently designed to be syndicated to newspapers. The copyright lines were changed to Dell Publishing Co., from No. 2. Only eight pages of the original 24 were in full colour, the rest being in black-and-white. Originally a weekly published every Wednesday, frequency changed to monthly from No. 5, which was dated April 1929. From No. 18 (30 April 1930) publication day became every third Wednesday. Publication became weekly again from No. 22 (12 July), and the price was halved to 5¢, with the page count reduced to 16. New strips were introduced after No. 1, as follows:

No. 2
2 Black Diamonds   Lance Nolley, Hal Stephens
27 Chubby   Frank Reilly
30 Cracks Wise and Otherwise
31 Alec   Sidney Garber
No. 5 Ol' Boy Bigsby   Kenneth Kaufstine
No. 6
2 Bush League Barry   Victoria Pazmino
8 Animal Crackers   Whitby
9 Clancy the Cop   Victoria Pazmino
14 Timmy O'Toole and Peaches   Dunkel
21 Ever Ready Eddie   Moe Leff
24 Jimmy Jams   Victoria Pazmino
No. 7 Colonel Knutt   Dunkel
No. 8
11 Make Believe Mary   Art Helfant
13 Percy and Ferdie   H. A. McGill
15 Sweet Tooth Eddie   Art Helfant
20 Copper Penny   Ted O'Loughlin
   Ingenious Gene   Jeff Haze
No. 9
3 Jonathan, Jazzbo and Jim   Art Helfant
   Archie Bawled   Gosh
22 Ozone Oscar   Dunkel
No. 10
14 Sniffy   Glen Wood
16 Mystic Martin   Dunkel
No. 11
12 Blackstone Magic
No. 12
9 Doctor B. Voltage   Rudy Zamora
No. 13
8 Peter the Pup   Godfrey
18 Jungle Jems   Lane
No. 15
8 Now You Tell One   Dunkel
No. 17   Bunny Schultz
15 Foxy Grandpa
No. 18
12 Vagabond Van   Dunkel
16 Captain Kiddum   Frank Little

No. 25
6 Private Rhodes   Joe Archibald

The Funnies was revived by Dell Publishing in standard comic book format, commencing with a new No. 1 issue dated October 1936.

241 Bringing Up Father: Series No. 17

1930. 25¢. 52 pp. 10×9¾. Publisher: Cupples & Leon Co., 470 Fourth Avenue, New York. Artist: George McManus.

Contents
Compilation of 46 daily newspaper strips printed in black-and-white, arranged one strip to the page. Coloured cover on cardboard, specially designed by the artist, George McManus.

242 Bringing Up Father: Series No. 18

1930. 25¢. 52 pp. 10×9¾. Publisher: Cupples & Leon Co., 470 Fourth Avenue, New York. Artist: George McManus.

Contents
Compilation of 46 daily newspaper strips printed in black-and-white, arranged one strip to the page. Coloured cover on cardboard, specially designed by the artist, George McManus.

243 The Gumps: Book 7

1930. 25¢. 52 pp. 10×9¾. Publisher: Cupples & Leon Co., 470 Fourth Avenue, New York. Artist: Sidney Smith. Syndicate: Chicago Tribune.

Contents
Compilation of 46 daily newspaper strips reprinted in black-and-white, arranged one strip to the page. Colour cover on cardboard, and title page specially drawn by the artist, Sidney Smith. This is the last in *The Gumps* series by this publisher.

244 Little Orphan Annie — Never Say Die

1930. 60¢. 96 pp. 7×8¾. Publisher: Cupples & Leon Co., 470 Fourth Avenue, New York. Artist: Harold Gray. Syndicate: Chicago Tribune.

Contents
Compilation of daily newspaper strips copyright the *Chicago Tribune*. The 86 strips are arranged one to a page, printed black-and-white. Bound in boards with three-colour dust-wrapper and title page designed by the artist, Harold Gray. No. 5 of the *Little Orphan Annie* series.

245 Moon Mullins Big Book

1930. 75¢. 152 pp. 10×9¾. Publisher: Cupples & Leon Co., 470 Fourth Avenue, New York. Artist: Frank Willard. Syndicate: International Feature Service.

Contents
Compilation of three earlier editions in the *Moon Mullins* series of reprint books by this publisher. Contains 138 daily newspaper strips arranged one to a page, printed black-and-white. Bound in boards with three-colour dust-wrapper and title page designed by the artist, Frank Willard.

246 Moon Mullins: Series 4

1930. 25¢. 52 pp. 9¾×9½. Publisher: Cupples & Leon Co., 470 Fourth Avenue, New York. Artist: Frank Willard. Syndicate: Chicago Tribune.

Contents
Compilation of 46 daily newspaper strips copyrighted by the *Chicago Tribune*. Strips are arranged one to the page, printed black-and-white. Coloured cover and title page designed by the artist, Frank Willard.

247 Mutt and Jeff: Book 15

1930. 25¢. 52 pp. 10×9¾. Publisher: Cupples & Leon Co., 470 Fourth Avenue, New York. Artist: Bud Fisher. Syndicate: H.C. Fisher.

Contents
Compilation of 46 daily newspaper strips copyrighted by H.C. ('Bud') Fisher. Strips arranged one to a page and printed black-and-white. Cardboard cover in colours and title page specially drawn by the artist.

248 Smitty the Flying Office Boy

1930. 60¢. 96 pp. 7×8¾. Publisher: Cupples & Leon Co., 470 Fourth Avenue, New York. Artist: Walter Berndt. Syndicate: Chicago Tribune.

Contents
Compilation of daily newspaper strips copyright the *Chicago Tribune*. Contains 86 strips arranged one to a page, printed black-and-white. Bound in boards with coloured dust-wrapper and title page drawn by the artist, Walter Berndt. No. 3 in the *Smitty* series.

249 Tillie the Toiler Book 5

1930. 25¢. 52 pp. 10×9¾. Publisher: Cupples & Leon Co., 470 Fourth Avenue, New York. Artist: Russ Westover. Syndicate: King Features.

Contents

Compilation of daily newspaper strips copyright King Features Syndicate. Contains 46 strips arranged one to a page, printed black-and-white. Bound in cardboard with three-colour cover specially drawn by the artist, Russ Westover.

250 Vignettes of Life

1930. 98 pp. $9 \times 12^{3}/_{4}$. Publisher: Reilly & Lee Co., Chicago. Artist: J. Norman Lynd. Syndicate: Public Ledger.

Contents

Compilation of Sunday supplement pages syndicated by the *Public Ledger*, printed in black-and-white. The original broadsheet pages have been rearranged so that one cartoon covers each double-page spread of the book. Thus 45 weekly cartoons fill 90 pages. There is an introduction by contemporary cartoonist Charles Dana Gibson.

251 Winnie Winkle

1930. 25¢. 52 pp. $10 \times 9^{3}/_{4}$. Publisher: Cupples & Leon Co., 470 Fourth Avenue, New York. Artist: Martin Branner. Syndicate: Chicago Tribune.

Contents

Compilation of the daily newspaper strip copyrighted by the Chicago Tribune Syndicate. Has 46 strips reprinted one to a page in black-and-white, with a three-colour cardboard cover plus title page drawn by the artist, Martin Branner. This strip, originally entitled 'Winnie Winkle the Breadwinner', first appeared on 20 September 1920.

252 Clancy the Cop

No. 1: February 1930–No. 2: 1931. 10¢. 52 pp. 10×10. Publisher: Dell Publishing Co., 100 Fifth Avenue, New York. Artist: Victoria Pazmino.

Advertised for the first time in No. 15 of *The Funnies*, February 1930: *Clancy the Copy First Series*: 'The adventures of the law's most famous and brilliant guardian, gathered together in one book.' Clancy the Cop, evidently designed as a daily newspaper strip, was first introduced in *The Funnies* No. 6, 29 May 1929. This comic book is printed in black-and-white throughout.

253 Bringing Up Father: Series No. 19

1931. 25¢. 52 pp. $10 \times 9^{3}/_{4}$. Publisher: Cupples & Leon Co., 470 Fourth Avenue, New York. Artist: George McManus.

Contents

Compilation of 46 daily newspaper strips reprinted in black-and-white, arranged one strip to the page. Coloured covers on cardboard specially drawn by the artist, George McManus.

254 Bringing Up Father: Series No. 20

1931. 25¢. 52 pp. 10×9¾. Publisher: Cupples & Leon Co., 470 Fourth Avenue, New York. Artist: George McManus.

Contents

Compilation of 46 daily newspaper strips reprinted in black-and-white, arranged one strip to the page. Coloured covers on cardboard specially drawn by the artist, George McManus.

255 Bug Movies

1931. 10¢. 52 pp. 10×10. Publisher: Dell Publishing Co., 100 Fifth Avenue, New York. Artist: Stookie Allen.

Contents

Compilation of strips reprinted from the weekly comic book, *The Funnies*, issued by the same publisher, Dell. 'Bug Movies' started in the first issue of *The Funnies*, 16 January 1929.

256 Deadwood Gulch

1931. 10¢. 52 pp. 10×10. Publisher: Dell Publishing Co., 100 Fifth Avenue, New York. Artist: Gordon Rogers.

Contents

Compilation of strips reprinted from the weekly comic book, *The Funnies*, issued by the same publisher, Dell. 'Deadwood Gulch' started in the first issue of *The Funnies*, 16 January 1929.

257 Felix

1931. 50¢. 32 pp. Publisher: Henry Altemus Co., 1326 Vine Street, Philadelphia. Artist: Pat Sullivan. Syndicate: King Features.

Contents

Compilation of newspaper strips reprinted from Sunday supplements, syndicated by King Features. Printed in four colours with special board covers designed by the artist, Otto Messmer (but signed Pat Sullivan).

258 The Gumps Cartoon Book

1931. 24 pp. 10×14. Publisher: National Art Co., New York. Artist: Sidney Smith. Syndicate: Chicago Tribune.

Contents
Compilation of 20 daily newspaper strips reprinted in black-and-white.

259 Harold Teen

1931. 25¢. 52 pp. 9³/₄×9¹/₂. Publisher: Cupples & Leon Co., 470 Fourth Avenue, New York. Artist: Carl Ed. Syndicate: Chicago Tribune.

Contents
Full title: *The Adventures of Harold Teen and His Old Side-Kick — 'Pop Jenks'*. Compilation of daily newspaper strips, 46 in all, dating between 5 March and 21 April 1930, copyright *Chicago Tribune*. Strips are arranged one to a page, printed black-and-white within a three-colour cover drawn by the original artist, Carl Ed, who also drew a new title page. Part of this book was reprinted in 1934 as a 36-page comic, size 6³/₄×8¹/₂. It was included in the same publisher's *Treasure Box of Famous Comics*.

260 Little Orphan Annie Shipwrecked

1931. 60¢. 96 pp. 7×8³/₄. Publisher: Cupples & Leon Co., 470 Fourth Avenue, New York. Artist: Harold Gray. Syndicate: Chicago Tribune.

Contents
Compilation of daily newspaper strips copyright the *Chicago Tribune*. The 86 strips are arranged one to a page, printed black-and-white. Bound in boards with three-colour dust-wrapper and title page designed by the artist, Harold Gray. No. 6 of the *Little Orphan Annie* series.

261 Mickey Mouse: Series No. 1

1931. 25¢. 52 pp. 10×9³/₄. Publisher: David McKay Co., 604 South Washington Square, Philadelphia.

Contents
Compilation of daily newspaper strips reprinted in black-and-white, arranged one strip to the page. The 'Mickey Mouse' strip started on 13 January 1930, and although usually credited as 'by Walt Disney', the original artist was Ub Iwerks, followed by Win Smith, and continued by Floyd Gottfredson. This was the first book collection of the strip. Cardboard covers.

262 Moon Mullins: Series 5

1931. 25¢. 52 pp. 9³/₄×9¹/₂. Publisher: Cupples & Leon Co., 470 Fourth Avenue, New York. Artist: Frank Willard. Syndicate: Chicago Tribune.

Contents
Compilation of 46 daily newspaper strips copyrighted 1930 by the *Chicago Tribune*. Strips are arranged one to the page, printed black-and-white, with an original cover and title page drawn by the artist, Frank Willard. Cardboard covers. This book was reprinted in 1976 by Dover Publications Inc., New York, as the second part of *Moon Mullins: Two Adventures*.

263 Mutt and Jeff: Book 16

1931. 25¢. 52 pp. 10×9³/₄. Publisher: Cupples & Leon Co., 470 Fourth Avenue, New York. Artist: Bud Fisher. Syndicate: H.C. Fisher.

Contents
Compilation of 46 daily newspaper strips copyrighted by H.C. ('Bud') Fisher. Strips arranged one to a page, printed black-and-white. Cardboard cover in colours and title page specially drawn by the artist.

264 Smitty the Jockey

1931. 60¢. 96 pp. 7×8³/₄. Publisher: Cupples & Leon Co., 470 Fourth Avenue, New York. Artist: Walter Berndt. Syndicate: Chicago Tribune.

Contents
Compilation of 86 daily newspaper strips copyright the *Chicago Tribune*. Strips are arranged one to a page, printed black-and-white. Bound in boards with coloured dust-wrapper and title page drawn by the artist, Walter Berndt. No. 4 in the *Smitty* series.

265 Tailspin Tommy Story and Picture Book

1931 (No. 266). 10¹/₂×10. Publisher: McLoughlin Brothers, 74 Park Street, Springfield, Massachusetts. Artist: Hal Forrest. Syndicate: Bell Syndicate.

Contents
Compilation of newspaper strips reprinted in four colours, copyrighted by the Bell Syndicate. 'Tailspin Tommy' first appeared as a daily strip in April 1928. The book is numbered 266 in this publisher's series.

266 Thimble Theater Starring Popeye

No. 1: 1931–No. 2: 1932. 25¢. 52 pp. 10×10. Publisher: Sonnet Publishing Co., Broadway, New York. Artist: E.C. Segar. Syndicate: King Features.

Contents
Compilation of daily newspaper strips reprinted one to a page. Printed in black-and-white with a coloured cover on cardboard specially drawn by the artist, Elzie Crisler Segar. He also drew a title page and wrote an introduction for each issue. The strips are copyrighted 1931–1932 by King Features Syndicate.

267 Tillie the Toiler Book 6

1931. 25¢. 52 pp. 10×9³/₄. Publisher: Cupples & Leon Co., 470 Fourth Avenue, New York. Artist: Russ Westover. Syndicate: King Features.

Contents

Compilation of 46 daily newspaper strips copyright King Features Syndicate. Strips are arranged one to a page, printed black-and-white. Bound in cardboard with three-colour cover specially drawn by the artist, Russ Westover.

268 Winnie Winkle Book 2

1931. 25¢. 52 pp. 10×9¾. Publisher: Cupples & Leon Co., 470 Fourth Avenue, New York. Artist: Martin Branner. Syndicate: Chicago Tribune.

Contents

Compilation of the daily newspaper strip copyrighted by the Chicago Tribune Syndicate. Contains 46 strips reprinted one to a page in black-and-white, bound in a three-colour cardboard cover plus title page specially drawn by the artist, Martin Branner.

269 Big Little Books

No. 707: 1932–No. 1494: 1938. 10¢. 320; 300; 256; 384; 432 pp. 3¾×4¼. Publisher: Whitman Publishing Co., Racine, Wisconsin.

1932

No. 707	*The Adventures of Dick Tracy, Detective*	Chester Gould

1933

No. 708	*Little Orphan Annie*	Harold Gray
No. 710	*Dick Tracy and Dick Tracy Jr.*	Chester Gould
No. 716	*Little Orphan Annie and Sandy*	Harold Gray
No. 717	*Mickey Mouse*	Walt Disney
No. 723	*Dick Tracy Out West*	Chester Gould
No. 723	*Tom Beatty Ace of the Secret Service*	George Taylor
No. 726	*Mickey Mouse in Blaggard Castle*	Walt Disney
No. 731	*Mickey Mouse the Mail Pilot*	Walt Disney
No. 734	*Chester Gump at Silver Creek Ranch*	Sidney Smith
No. 742	*Buck Rogers in the 25th Century AD*	Dick Calkins
No. 744	*Tarzan of the Apes*	Hal Foster
No. 745	*Smitty: Golden Gloves Tournament*	Walter Berndt
No. 746	*Moon Mullins and Kayo*	Frank Willard
No. 747	*Tailspin Tommy in the Famous Pay-roll Mystery*	Hal Forrest
No. 748	*Little Orphan Annie and Chizzler*	Harold Gray
No. 749	*Dick Tracy from Colorado to Nova Scotia*	Chester Gould
No. 750	*Mickey Mouse Sails for Treasure Island*	Walt Disney

1934

No. 751	*Wash Tubbs in Pandemonia*	Roy Crane
No. 754	*Reg'lar Fellers*	Gene Byrnes
No. 755	*Men of the Mounted*	Ted McCall

77

No. 756 *Mickey Mouse Presents a Walt Disney Silly Symphony*	Walt Disney
No. 760 *Believe It or Not*	Robert Ripley
No. 761 *The Story of Skippy*	Percy L. Crosby
No. 763 *Alley Oop and Dinny*	V.T. Hamlin
No. 765 *Buck Rogers and the City below the Sea*	Dick Calkins
No. 766 *Chester Gump Finds the Hidden Treasure*	Sidney Smith
No. 767 *The Adventures of Tiny Tim*	Stanley Link
No. 772 *Erik Noble and the Forty-Niners*	B. McNaughton
1935	
No. 1101 *Hairbreadth Harry in Department Q.T.*	F.O. Alexander
No. 1103 *Little Orphan Annie with the Circus*	Harold Gray
No. 1105 *Dick Tracy and the Stolen Bonds*	Chester Gould
No. 1106 *Ella Cinders and the Mysterious House*	Charlie Plumb
No. 1107 *Lieutenant Commander Don Winslow, U.S.N.*	Leon Beroth
No. 1109 *Oswald the Lucky Rabbit*	Walter Lantz
No. 1110 *Flash Gordon on the Planet Mongo*	Alex Raymond
No. 1112 *Skeezix in Africa*	Frank King
No. 1116 *Dan Dunn, Secret Operative 48*	Norman Marsh
No. 1119 *Betty Boop in Snow White*	Max Fleischer
No. 1122 *Scrappy*	Charles Mintz
No. 1123 *Joe Palooka the Heavyweight Boxing Champ*	Ham Fisher
No. 1124 *Tailspin Tommy: The Dirigible Flight to the North Pole*	Hal Forrest
No. 1126 *Captain Easy, Soldier of Fortune*	Roy Crane
No. 1133 *Bringing Up Father*	George McManus
No. 1134 *Moon Mullins and the Plushbottom Twins*	Frank Willard
No. 1137 *Dick Tracy Solves the Penfield Mystery*	Chester Gould
No. 1138 *Mickey Mouse the Detective*	Walt Disney
No. 1140 *Little Orphan Annie and the Big Train Robbery*	Harold Gray
No. 1142 *Radio Patrol*	Charlie Schmidt
No. 1143 *Buck Rogers on the Moons of Saturn*	Dick Calkins
No. 1146 *Chester Gump in the City of Gold*	Sidney Smith
No. 1153 *Mickey Mouse and the Bat Bandit*	Walt Disney
No. 1154 *Little Orphan Annie and the Ghost Gang*	Harold Gray
No. 1156 *Terry and the Pirates*	Milton Caniff
No. 1157 *Red Barry, Ace Detective: Hero of the Hour*	Will Gould
No. 1158 *Betty Boop in Miss Gulliver's Travels*	Max Fleischer
No. 1160 *Mickey Mouse and Bobo the Elephant*	Walt Disney
No. 1162 *Little Orphan Annie and Punjab the Wizard*	Harold Gray
No. 1163 *Dick Tracy and the Boris Arson Gang*	Chester Gould
No. 1166 *Flash Gordon and the Monsters of Mongo*	Alex Raymond
No. 1167 *Mandrake the Magician*	Phil Davis
No. 1169 *Buck Rogers and the Depth Men of Jupiter*	Dick Calkins
No. 1170 *Dick Tracy on the Trail of Larceny Lil*	Chester Gould
No. 1171 *Flash Gordon and the Tournaments of Mongo*	Alex Raymond
No. 1172 *Tailspin Tommy Hunting for Pirate Gold*	Hal Forrest
No. 1175 *Frank Buck Presents Ted Towers, Animal Master*	Glen Cravath
No. 1177 *Ace Drummond*	Clayton Knight

No. 1178 *Buck Rogers and the Doom Comet*   Dick Calkins
1936
No. 1185 *Dick Tracy in Chains of Crime* Chester Gould
No. 1186 *Little Orphan Annie and the $1,000,000 Formula*   Harold Gray
No. 1187 *Mickey Mouse and the Sacred Jewel*   Walt Disney
No. 1190 *Flash Gordon and the Witch Queen of Mongo*   Alex Raymond
No. 1197 *Buck Rogers and the Planetoid Plot*   Dick Calkins
No. 1198 *Li'l Abner in New York*   Al Capp
1937
No. 1100 *The Phantom* Ray Moore
No. 1102 *The Return of Tarzan*   Rex Maxon
No. 1103 *King of the Royal Mounted*   Zane Grey
No. 1110 *Tailspin Tommy and the Island in the Sky*   Hal Forrest
No. 1111 *Mickey Mouse Presents Walt Disney's Silly Symphonies Stories*   Walt Disney.
No. 1112 *Dick Tracy and the Racketeer Gang*   Chester Gould
No. 1113 *Mutt and Jeff*   Bud Fisher
No. 1115 *Og, Son of Fire*   Irving Crump
No. 1117 *Little Annie Rooney and the Orphan House*   Brandon Walsh
No. 1118 *G-Man on the Crime Trail*   George Clark
No. 1120 *Little Miss Muffet*   Fanny Cory
No. 1125 *Dan Dunn, Secret Operative 48 on the Trail of the Counterfeiters*   Norman Marsh
No. 1127 *Skyroads with Hurricane Hawk*   Russell Keaton
No. 1128 *Mickey Mouse and Pluto the Racer*   Walt Disney
No. 1129 *Felix the Cat*   Pat Sullivan
No. 1130 *Apple Mary and Dennie Foil the Swindlers*   Martha Orr
No. 1136 *Sombrero Pete*   Morton Cowen
No. 1138 *Jungle Jim*   Alex Raymond
No. 1139 *Jungle Jim and the Vampire Woman*   Alex Raymond
No. 1140 *Tim Tyler's Luck: Adventures in the Ivory Patrol*   Lyman Young
No. 1144 *Secret Agent X9*   Charles Flanders
No. 1147 *G-Man versus the Red X*
No. 1148 *Doctor Doom International Spy Faces Death at Dawn*   Conrad Vane
No. 1152 *Smilin' Jack and the Stratosphere Ascent*   Zack Mosley
No. 1159 *Hall of Fame of the Air*   Clayton Knight
No. 1163 *Popeye Sees the Sea*   E.C. Segar
No. 1164 *Freckles and the Lost Diamond Mine*   Merrill Blosser
No. 1165 *Tom Beatty Ace of the Service Scores Again*   Robert Weisman
No. 1169 *Silly Symphony Featuring Donald Duck*   Walt Disney
No. 1171 *Dan Dunn, Secret Operative 48 and the Crime Master*   Norman Marsh
No. 1172 *Tiny Tim and the Mechanical Men*   Stanley Link
No. 1173 *Radio Patrol Trailing the Safeblowers*   Charlie Schmidt
No. 1179 *King of the Royal Mounted and the Northern Treasure*   Zane Grey
No. 1180 *Kayo in the Land of Sunshine*   Frank Willard
No. 1199 *Perry Winkle and the Rinkeydinks*   Martin Branner
1938
No. 1401 *Just Kids*   Ad Carter
No. 1402 *Chester Gump in the Pole to Pole Flight*   Sidney Smith

No. 1403 *Oswald Rabbit Plays G-Man*	Walt Lantz
No. 1404 *Buck Jones and the Two Gun Kid*	Robert Wiseman
No. 1405 *Popeye and the Jeep*	E.C. Segar
No. 1406 *Little Annie Rooney on the Highway to Adventure*	Darrell McClure
No. 1407 *Flash Gordon in the Water World of Mongo*	Alex Raymond
No. 1408 *Skeezix at the Military Academy*	Frank King
No. 1409 *Mickey Mouse Runs His Own Newspaper*	Walt Disney
No. 1410 *The Beasts of Tarzan*	Rex Maxon
No. 1412 *Terry and the Pirates Shipwrecked on a Desert Island*	Milton Caniff
No. 1415 *Blondie and Baby Dumpling*	Chic Young
No. 1416 Little Orphan Annie in the Movies	Harold Gray
No. 1417 *Bronc Peeler the Lone Cowboy*	Fred Harman
No. 1420 *Dick Tracy and the Hotel Murders*	Chester Gould
No. 1421 *Smokey Stover the Foo Fighter*	Bill Holman
No. 1422 *Junior Nebb on the Diamond Bar Ranch*	Sol Hess
No. 1423 *Tailspin Tommy and the Hooded Flyer*	Hal Forrest
No. 1440 *Tex Thorne Comes Out of the West*	Hal Arbo
No. 1441 *Silly Symphony Featuring Donald Duck*	Walt Disney
No. 1444 *Capt. Frank Hawks, Air Ace, and the League of Twelve*	Irwin Myers
No. 1446 *Dick Tracy and the Spider Gang*	Chester Gould
No. 1448 *Inspector Wade Solves the Mystery of the Red Aces*	Lyman Anderson
No. 1449 *Little Orphan Annie and the Mysterious Shoemaker*	Harold Gray
No. 1550 *Popeye in Quest for His Poopdeck Pappy*	E.C. Segar
No. 1452 *King of the Royal Mounted Gets His Man*	Allen Dean
No. 1454 *Dan Dunn, Secret Operative 48, on the Trail of Wu Fang*	Norman Marsh
No. 1455 *Wash Tubbs and Captain Easy Hunting for Whales*	Roy Crane
No. 1457 *Cowboy Lingo*	Fred Harman
No. 1458 *Wimpy the Hamburger Eater*	E.C. Segar
No. 1459 *Barney Baxter in the Air with the Eagle Squadron*	Frank Miller
No. 1460 *Snow White and the Seven Dwarfs*	Walt Disney
No. 1467 *Pluto the Pup*	Walt Disney
No. 1468 *Brick Bradford with Brocco the Modern Buccaneer*	Clarence Gray
No. 1473 *Alley Oop with Dinny in the Jungles of Moo*	V.T. Hamlin
No. 1476 *Mickey Mouse in a Race for Riches*	Walt Disney
No. 1477 *Smitty in Going Native*	Walter Berndt
No. 1478 *Donald Duck in Hunting for Troubles*	Walt Disney
No. 1491 *Dick Tracy and the Man with No Face*	Chester Gould
No. 1494 *Tailspin Tommy and the Sky Bandits*	Hal Forrest

The *Big Little Books* form a bridge between the outsized cardboard-covered comic books published by Frederick Stokes Co. and the square-shaped comic books of the Cupples & Leon Co. on the one hand, and the 68-page four-colour comic books which evolved in the mid-1930s. Big Little Books were handy-sized, small books, printed black-and-white throughout, with specially-designed board covers in four colours. The majority of Big Little Books were reprints of daily and Sunday newspaper strips, but rearranged so that one picture fell on the right-hand page, while the story was told in textual narrative on the left-hand page. All captions and balloons were removed from the pictures by the publisher's art department. The books were sold at 10¢ in chain-stores such as the F.W. Woolworth Co.

The numbers in the series, as listed here, have jumps in their continuity since titles that do not conform to the comic book format, such as motion picture adaptations using photographs from the films instead of drawings, have been eliminated. From 1939 the series changed its title from *Big Little Books* to *Better Little Books*. See also *Little Big Books* by a rival publisher.

270 Bobby Thatcher and the Treasure Cave

1932. 86 pp. 7×9. Publisher: Henry Altemus Co., 1326 Vine Street, Philadelphia. Artist: George Storm. Syndicate: Bell Syndicate.

Contents
Compilation of daily newspaper strips copyrighted by the Bell Syndicate Inc. Printed black-and-white in a hardcover edition. The strip 'Bobby Thatcher' started in March 1927.

271 Bringing Up Father: Series No. 21

1932. 25¢. 52 pp. 10×9³/₄. Publisher: Cupples & Leon Co., 470 Fourth Avenue, New York. Artist: George McManus.

Contents
Compilation of 46 daily newspaper strips reprinted in black-and-white, arranged one strip to the page. Coloured cover on cardboard specially drawn by the artist, George McManus.

272 Bringing Up Father: Series No. 22

1932. 25¢. 52pp. 10×9³/₄. Publisher: Cupples & Leon Co., 470 Fourth Avenue, New York. Artist: George McManus.

Contents
Compilation of 46 daily newspaper strips reprinted in black-and-white, arranged one strip to the page. Coloured cover on cardboard specially drawn by the artist, George McManus.

273 Clifford McBride's Immortal Napoleon and Uncle Elby

1932. 12×17. Publisher: Castle Press. Artist: Clifford McBride. Syndicate: Arthur J. Lafave.

Contents
Compilation of newspaper strips reprinted from Sunday supplements, and with a special introduction by Don Herold. The Strip 'Napoleon and Uncle Elby' became daily on 6 June 1932, but had been running as a weekly from 5 May 1929.

274 Dolly Dimples and Bobby Bounce

1932. 60¢. 96 pp. 7×8½. Publisher: Cupples & Leon Co., 470 Fourth Avenue, New York. Artist: Grace Drayton.

Contents

Compilation of newspaper strips printed black-and-white, with board covers and coloured dust-wrapper.

275 Just Kids

1932 (No. 283). 16 pp. 9½×12. Publisher: McLoughlin Brothers, 74 Park Street, Springfield, Massachusetts. Artist: Ad Carter. Syndicate: King Features.

Contents

Three-colour reprints of the newspaper strip, with the panels used to illustrate a text story. 'Just Kids' started on 23 July 1923.

276 Little Orphan Annie a Willing Helper

1932. 60¢. 96 pp. 7×8½. Publisher: Cupples & Leon Co., 470 Fourth Avenue, New York. Artist: Harold Gray. Syndicate: Chicago Tribune.

Contents

Compilation of daily newspaper strips copyright by the *Chicago Tribune*. The 86 strips are arranged one to a page, printed black-and-white. Bound in boards with special three-colour dust-wrapper and title page designed by the artist, Harold Gray. No. 7 of the *Little Orphan Annie* series.

277 Mickey Mouse: Book No. 2

1932. 25¢. 52 pp. 10×9¾. Publisher: David McKay Co., 604 South Washington Square, Phildelphia.

Contents

Compilation of the daily newspaper strip, reprinted in black-and-white and arranged one strip to the page. Cardboard covers, with special artwork by the Walt Disney Studio.

278 Moon Mullins: Series 6

1932. 25¢. 52 pp. 9¾×9¾. Publisher: Cupples & Leon Co., 470 Fourth Avenue, New York. Artist: Frank Willard. Syndicate: Chicago Tribune.

Contents

Compilation of 46 daily newspaper strips, copyrighted by the *Chicago Tribune*. Strips are arranged one to a page, printed black-and-white. Coloured covers on cardboard, specially drawn by the artist, Frank Willard.

279 Mutt and Jeff: Book 17

1932. 25¢. 52 pp. 10×10. Publisher: Cupples & Leon Co., 470 Fourth Avenue, New York. Artist: Bud Fisher. Syndicate: H.C. Fisher.

Contents
Compilation of 46 daily newspaper strips dated between 27 April and 26 June 1931, copyright H.C. Fisher. Strips are arranged one to the page, with an original cover, title page and foreword by the artist. Cardboard covers.

280 Smitty in the North Woods

1932. 60¢. 96 pp. 7×8³/₄. Publisher: Cupples & Leon Co., 470 Fourth Avenue, New York. Artist: Walter Berndt. Syndicate: Chicago Tribune.

Contents
Compilation of daily newspaper strips, copyright the *Chicago Tribune* and printed black-and-white. Special cover and title page drawn by the artist, Walter Berndt. No. 5 in the *Smitty* series.

281 The Story of Happy Hooligan

1932 (No. 281). 16 pp. 9¹/₂×12. Publisher: McLoughlin Brothers, 74 Park Street, Springfield, Massachusetts. Artist: Frederick Burr Opper.

Contents
Three-colour reprints of the long-running strip from the Sunday supplements, with the panels used to illustrate a text story. Published in the year that the strip was discontinued.

282 Strange As It Seems

1932. Unpriced. 68 pp. 8×10¹/₂. Publisher: Blue Star Publishing Co., New York. Artist: John Hix. Syndicate: McClure Newspapers.

Compilation one-shot of the syndicated newspaper feature copyright the McClure Newspaper Syndicate Inc. The panels are dated from September 1931 to April 1932, but are not printed in order. The entire book is printed in black-and-white, except for the full-colour cover, which is repeated on the back page.

283 Tailspin Tommy

1932. 100 pp. 7×8³/₄. Publisher: Cupples & Leon Co., 470 Fourth Avenue, New York. Artist: Hal Forrest. Syndicate: Bell Syndicate.

Contents
Compilation of daily newspaper strips, copyright 1930 by Bell Syndicate Inc. Printed black-and-white; hardback, with special cover in colours drawn by the artist, Hal Forrest.

284 Tillie the Toiler Book 7

1932. 25¢. 52 pp. 10×9³/₄. Publisher: Cupples & Leon Co., 470 Fourth Avenue, New York. Artist: Russ Westover. Syndicate: King Features.

Contents
Compilation of daily newspaper strips, copyright King Features Syndicate. Printed black-and-white, one strip to a page. Cardboard cover printed in three colours, specially drawn by the artist, Russ Westover.

285 Winnie Winkle Book 3

1932. 25¢. 52 pp. 10×9³/₄. Publisher: Cupples & Leon Co., 470 Fourth Avenue, New York. Artist: Martin Branner. Syndicate: Chicago Tribune.

Introduction
'Dear Reader: Artistotle or Shakespeare or some one of those smart astrologers I think it was, who once said, somebody's life was like an open book, and I think they must have meant me, because my life is certainly like an open book. Anyway, this is the third time I've been sandwiched in between two covers. It's getting so a girl can't have any privacy at all any more. If I had an inkling (or even a pen and inkling) of what my boss, Mr Branner, was up to when he got together with Mr Cupples and Mr Leon, you can just bet I would have gotten a permanent or at least a finger wave and I would have used some more powder and lipstick, but no, they all just rushed me right into this book, so here I am again. However, I suppose I shouldn't complain about my boss, because he gives me lots of lovely, fashionable dresses to wear. Besides, every girl really likes to be looked at, so here's looking at you, gentle reader, and hoping you'll be looking at me. Sincerely, your working girl friend, Winnie Winkle.'

Contents
Compilation of the daily newspaper strip copyrighted by the Chicago Tribune Syndicate. Contains 46 strips arranged one to a page, printed in black-and-white and bound in a three-colour cover specially drawn by the artist, Martin Branner.

286 Adventures of the Detective

1933. 10¢. 36 pp. 9¹/₂×12. Publisher: Humor Publishing Co. Artist: Martin Nadle.

Contents
This one-shot comic book, printed throughout in black-and-white and bound in a coloured cover, featured original adventures of 'Ace King' by Martin Nadle.

287 Bob Scully, the Two-Fisted Hick Detective

1933. 10¢. 36 pp. 9$^1/_2$×12. Publisher: Humor Publishing Co. Artist: Howard Dell.

Contents
This one-shot comic book printed throughout in black-and-white and bound in a coloured cover, featured original adventures of 'Bob Scully' by Howard Dell.

288 Bringing Up Father: Series No. 23

1933. 25¢. 52 pp. 10×9$^3/_4$. Publisher: Cupples & Leon Co., 470 Fourth Street, New York. Artist: George McManus.

Contents
Compilation of 46 daily newspaper strips reprinted in black-and-white, arranged one strip to the page. Coloured cover on cardboard specially drawn by the artist, George McManus.

289 Bringing Up Father: Series No. 24

1933. 25¢. 52 pp. 10×9$^3/_4$. Publisher: Cupples & Leon Co., 470 Fourth Street, New York. Artist: George McManus.

Contents
Compilation of 46 daily newspaper strips reprinted in black-and-white, arranged one strip to the page. Coloured cover on cardboard specially drawn by the artist, George McManus.

290 Buck Rogers in the 25th Century

1933. Free (promotional). 36 pp. 6×8. Publisher: Kelloggs Co., Battle Creek, Michigan. Artist: Dick Calkins. Syndicate: John F. Dille.

Introduction
'Poor old Jules Verne! He took a look into the future and all he saw was the possibilities of the Airplane and the Submarine. The real facts of science — the tremendous advances in invention which were to include such amazing devices as the jumping belt, interplanetary rocket ships, the rocket pistol, inertron and all the other amazing developments of the twenty-fifth century — which Buck Rogers herein describes —Jules overlooked them all. Now listen to Buck Rogers.'

Contents
Text story adapted by Phil Nowlan from his Sunday supplement newspaper strip syndicated by the John F. Dille Company, with specially drawn cover and illustrations drawn by Dick Calkins, and printed throughout in full colour. Produced as a promotional giveaway to children listening to the 'Buck Rogers' radio serial sponsored by Kelloggs Corn Flakes, Rice Krispies, Pep, All Bran and Whole Wheat Biscuits.

'Buck Rogers' first appeared as a daily newspaper strip on 7 January 1929, with a full-colour Sunday supplement page following on 30 March 1930.

291 Century of Comics

1933. Free (promotional). 100 pp. 7¹/₂ × 10¹/₂. Publisher: Eastern Color Printing Co., 50 Church Street, New York. Editorial: Max C. Gaines.

Compilation of Sunday newspaper supplement strips, printed in four colours and including strips previously reprinted in *Famous Funnies: A Carnival of Comics* and *Funnies On Parade*. Produced by Max Gaines as an advertising premium to promote juvenile interest in Kinney Shoe Stores, Milk-O-Malt, Wanamaker Stores, Wheatena, etc. A mint copy is valued at $2,100 in Overstreet's *Comic Book Price Guide* for 1989.

292 Detective Dan: Secret Operative 48

1933. 10¢. 36 pp. 9¹/₂ × 12. Publisher: Humor Publishing Co. Artist: Norman Marsh.

This one-shot comic book, printed throughout in black-and-white and bound in a coloured cover, featured original adventures of a character who would become better known as 'Dan Dunn: Secret Operative 48'. Artist Norman Marsh began drawing the strip under this title, for Publishers Syndicate, who distributed it daily from 16 October 1933.

293 Dick Tracy and Dick Tracy Jr. and How they Captured Stooge Viller

1933. 96 pp. 7 × 8¹/₂. Publisher: Cupples & Leon Co., 443 Fourth Avenue, New York. Artist: Chester Gould. Syndicate: Chicago Tribune.

Contents
Compilation of daily newspaper strips copyrighted 1932 by the *Chicago Tribune*. The strips are arranged one to the page, printed black-and-white, with an original coloured cover and title page drawn by the artist, Chester Gould. This is the first *Dick Tracy* book. The strip first appeared on 4 October 1931.

294 Funnies on Parade

No. 1 (unnumbered): 1933 (undated). Free (promotional). 36 pp. 7¹/₂ × 10¹/₂. Publisher: Eastern Color Printing Co., 50 Church Street, New York. Editorial: Harry I. Donenfield.

Contents of No. 1
1 Cover

2 (R) Nipper; Footprints on the Sands of Time   Clare Dwiggins
3 (R) Reg'lar Fellers; Draw It Y'self   Gene Byrnes
4 (R) Holly of Hollywood; Keeping Up with the Joneses   Pop Momand
5 (R) Cicero; Mutt and Jeff   Bud Fisher
6 (R) Hairbreadth Harry; High-Gear Homer   F.O. Alexander
7 (R) Fisher's Children's Corner; Joe Palooka   Ham Fisher
8 (R) Blackstone Magic (BW)
10 (R) Little Brother; The Bungle Family   H.J. Tuthill
11 (R) Nipper; Footprints on the Sands of Time   Clare Dwiggins
12 (R) Blackstone Magic (BW)
14 (R) Fisher's True Life Dramas; Joe Palooka   Ham Fisher
15 (R) Hairbreadth Harry; High-Gear Homer   F.O. Alexander
16 (R) Cicero; Mutt and Jeff   Bud Fisher
17 (R) Holly of Hollywood; Keeping Up with the Joneses   Pop Momand
18 (R) Reg'lar Fellers; Draw It Y'self   Gene Byrnes
20 (R) Holly of Hollywood; Keeping Up with the Joneses   Pop Momand
21 (R) Cicero; Mutt and Jeff   Bud Fisher
22 (R) Hairbreadth Harry; High-Gear Homer   F.O. Alexander
23 (R) Fisher's Silly Scoops; Joe Palooka   Ham Fisher
24 (R) Blackstone Magic (BW)
26 (R) Strange As It Seems   John Hix
27 (R) Little Brother; The Bungle Family   H.J. Tuthill
28 (R) Blackstone Magic (BW)
30 (R) Joe Palooka   Ham Fisher
31 (R) Hairbreadth Harry; High-Gear Homer   F.O. Alexander
32 (R) Cicero; Mutt and Jeff   Bud Fisher
33 (R) Holly of Hollywood; Keeping Up with the Joneses   Pop Momand
34 (R) Smatter Pop; Honeybunch's Hubby   C.M. Payne
35 (R) Somebody's Stenog; The Back-Seat Driver   A.E. Hayward
36 Cover (continued)

The father of the modern comic book, this one-shot magazine was created by Harry I. Donenfield, sales manager of the Eastern Color Printing Company, whose colour printing presses in Waterbury, Connecticut, produced comic sections for several Sunday newspapers. The booklet was a casual assembly of currently popular Sunday comic pages, reduced to approximately a quarter of original size and inserted into a specially designed cover. It was produced as a promotional giveaway for Proctor & Gamble. The strips were copyrighted by Associated Newspapers, Gene Byrnes, H.C. Fisher, McNaught Syndicate, Public Ledger, and Bell Syndicate. A mint copy is valued at $1,505 in Overstreet's *Comic Book Price Guide* for 1989.

295 How Dick Tracy and Dick Tracy Jr. Caught the Racketeers

1933. 96 pp. 7×8½. Publisher: Cupples & Leon Co., 443 Fourth Avenue, New York. Artist: Chester Gould. Syndicate: Chicago Tribune.

Contents

Compilation of daily newspaper strips copyrighted by the *Chicago Tribune*. The strips run from 3 August 1933 to 8 November 1933, and are arranged one to the page. Printed black-and-white with an original coloured cover and title page drawn by the artist, Chester Gould. The second *Dick Tracy* book, and the last by this publisher.

296 Joe Palooka

1933. 52 pp. 7×8½. Publisher: Cupples & Leon Co., 443 Fourth Avenue, New York. Artist: Ham Fisher. Syndicate: McNaught Syndicate.

Contents

Compilation of daily newspaper strips copyrighted by the McNaught Syndicate. The strips are arranged one to the page, printed black-and-white, with an original cover and title page drawn by the artist, Ham Fisher. Cardboard covers. The strip started in 1928.

297 No Entry

298 The Little King

1933. $2.00. 8¾×10¼. 80 pp. Publisher: Farrar & Reinhart Inc., 232 Madison Avenue, New York. Artist: Otto Soglow.

Contents

Compilation of strips reprinted from *The New Yorker* magazine. Hardback, with a dust-jacket in colours specially drawn by the artist, Otto Soglow. British edition published in 1933 by Duckworth, 3 Henrietta Street, London, price 7s. 6d., with a cheap edition the following year, price 3s. 6d.

'The Little King', a wordless, purely visual gag strip, originally appeared in *The New Yorker*, a sophisticated weekly magazine. William Randolph Hearst duly secured the character for his newspaper Sunday supplements, and the first four-colour strip was syndicated by King Features on 9 September 1934. These were later reprinted in the monthly comic book, *King Comics*.

299 Little Orphan Annie in Cosmic City

1933. 96 pp. 7×8½. Publisher: Cupples & Leon Co., 443 Fourth Avenue, New York. Artist: Harold Gray. Syndicate: Chicago Tribune.

Contents

Compilation of 86 daily newspaper strips copyrighted by the *Chicago Tribune* and dated from 26 August to 31 December 1932. The strips are arranged one to the page, printed black-and-white, with an original coloured cover and title page drawn by the artist, Harold Gray. Cardboard covers. This book was reprinted in 1974 by Dover Publications Inc., New York, as the second half of a paperback entitled *Little Orphan Annie and Little Orphan Annie in Cosmic City*.

300 Men of Daring

1933. 100 pp. 7×8³/₄. Publisher: Cupples & Leon Co., 443 Fourth Avenue, New York. Artist: Stookie Allen.

Introduction
'INTRODUCTION FOR MEN OF DARING by Lowell Thomas
Confucius, or perhaps it was one of the other Chinese sages, said: "One picture is worth a thousand words." No one has capitalized on this fact better than Stookie Allen in his hundreds of drawings of men of daring. It was a source of some pleasure to me to learn that this interesting series has finally been gathered together between the covers of a book and here they are, 45 of them, rogues and heroes, scoundrels and soldiers of fortune, but every one of them (with one exception) a fascinating, interesting study on the things that so many of us wish we had the nerve to do. For some of his subjects Stookie Allen has gone back a few hundred years to the days when men seemed to be bolder than they are today, but don't let anybody get the idea that adventure is dead. He has only to look at some of the present-day men of daring and their interesting histories to know that there is plenty of excitement in the world for those who want to go out and find it. It was Theodore Roosevelt who took for his motto: "Only those are fit to live who do not fear to die." I presume there isn't a human soul who does not wish that he might have the opportunity to go out into the wide world and make his fortune among the physical dangers of strange lands and stranger people. But don't get the idea that there may not be plenty of adventure right in your own back yard so to speak. The most interesting things about all these lives and images of men who have made and are making history is their likeness mentally. They have thrived on danger and offered inspiration to millions of youths. Good luck to Stookie Allen and his men of daring. Lowell Thomas.'

Contents
Forty-five factual cartoons featuring 300 pictures of such heroes as Buffalo Bill, Charles Lindbergh, William Beebe, and Count Felix Von Luckner. The format follows the familiar 'Believe It or Not' newspaper strips by Robert L. Ripley. Printed black-and-white throughout with a cardboard cover in red and black.

301 Mickey Mouse: Book No. 3

1933. 52 pp. 10×9³/₄. Publisher: David McKay Co., 604 South Washington Square, Philadelphia.

Contents
Compilation of Sunday supplement strips reprinted in four colours. Cardboard covers, specially designed by the Walt Disney Studio. This is the first Mickey Mouse strip book in full colour. This book was reprinted (in part: 30 pages) by the Whitman Publishing Co. as *Mickey Mouse*, numbered 948 in their children's book series (1935).

302 Moon Mullins: Book No. 7

1933. 25¢. 52 pp. 9³/₄×9¹/₂. Publisher: Cupples & Leon Co., 470 Fourth Avenue, New York. Artist: Frank Willard. Syndicate: Chicago Tribune.

Introduction

'Dear Reader: Although my dear Nephew's Name appears on the cover of this biography, and his life may point out a great moral lesson to the youth and beauty of our nation, where, may I ask, whould he be today if it wasn't for his Uncle William? Would he be fast, loose and fancy free to play pool, have those wonderful romantic adventures and come in at any hour of the night without getting a third degree and maybe his block knocked off it it wasn't for me? No! Through my trials and tribulations he has learnt a very valuable lesson and avoided the marriage department of the license bureau in his shopping tours. And so like the great man, Alfie Loewenthal, one of nature's funniest noblemen, my nephew continues to hang around the drug store corner and holler "Oh you Kiddo" at the ladies that look lonesome. So perhaps my life will be a lesson to you dear reader, if it's not too late for you to learn lessons. And make a bigger and better man or woman. So hoping that all your folks are well and with kindest regards to yourself, I remain yours truly, William P. Mullins.'

Contents

Compilation of 46 daily newspaper strips reprinted from dates between July and September 1932, copyright the *Chicago Tribune*. Strips are arranged one to the page, with an original cover, title page and introduction by the artist. Cardboard covers.

303 Mutt and Jeff: Book 18

1933. 25¢. 52 pp. 10×9³/₄. Publisher: Cupples & Leon Co., 470 Fourth Avenue, New York. Artist: Bud Fisher. Syndicate: H.C. Fisher.

Contents

Compilation of 46 daily newspaper strips copyrighted by H.C. ('Bud') Fisher. Strips arranged one to the page, printed in black-and-white. Cardboard cover in three colours and title page specially drawn by the artist.

304 Smitty at Military School

1933. 60¢. 96 pp. 7×8³/₄. Publisher: Cupples & Leon Co., 443 Fourth Avenue, New York. Artist: Walter Berndt. Syndicate: Chicago Tribune.

Contents

Compilation of daily newspaper strips, copyrighted by the *Chicago Tribune* and printed in black-and-white. Special cover and title page drawn by the artist, Walter Berndt. No. 6 in the *Smitty* series, and the last by this publisher.

305 Tarzan of the Apes to Color

1933. 24 pp. 10³/₄×15¹/₄. Publisher: Saalfield Publishing Co., Akron, Ohio. Artist: Hal Foster. Syndicate: United Features.

Contents

Compilation of daily newspaper strips copyrighted 1929, arranged as two enlarged panels to each page for children to colour with paints or crayons. Printed 16 pages in black-and-white, 8 pages in full colour.

306 Tillie the Toiler Book 8

1933. 25¢. 52 pp. 10×9³/₄ Publisher: Cupples & Leon Co., 443 Fourth Avenue, New York. Artist: Russ Westover. Sydnicate: King Features.

Contents
Compilation of daily newspaper strips copyrighted by King Features Syndicate and printed in black-and-white. Forty-six strips arranged one to a page and bound in a cardboard cover specially drawn by the artist, Russ Westover. Last in this series.

307 Winnie Winkle Book 4

1933. 25¢. 52 pp. 10×9³/₄. Publisher: Cupples & Leon Co., 443 Fourth Avenue, New York. Artist: Martin Branner. Syndicate: Chicago Tribune.

Contents
Compilation of the daily newspaper strip copyrighted by the *Chicago Tribune* Syndicate. Forty-six strips arranged one to a page and printed black-and-white, bound in a cardboard cover printed in three colours. Cover and title page specially drawn by the artist, Martin Branner. Last in the *Winnie Winkle* series.

308 Mickey Mouse Magazine

No. 1: January 1933–No. 9: September 1933. 5¢. 5¹/₄times 7¹/₄. Publisher: Kamen-Blair Co. (Kay Kamen). Editorial: Kay Kamen (editor).

Contents
Monthly magazine containing jokes, cartoons, stories, puzzles, games, features, editorials, readers' letters, and other magazine-style features, all highly illustrated with characters from the Walt Disney cartoon films specially drawn for the magazine, but no comic strips. Although the first two issues were priced at 5¢ the magazine was given away free as promotional material by cinemas showing the Disney cartoon films, and by stores selling Disney toys and merchandise.
Although this series cannot be considered a comic book, it is important as the first official and regular Disney character publication, which eventually led to the Disney comic books. It was followed by a second series of *Mickey Mouse Magazine* beginning November 1933.

309 Gulf Comic Weekly

No. 1–No. 4 (April–May 1933). Free (promotional). 4 pp. 10¹/₂×15. Publisher: Gulf Refining Co., Pittsburgh. From No. 5, title changed to *Gulf Funny Weekly*.

Contents of No. 1
1 The Uncovered Wagon   Stan Schendel

2 Curly and the Kids	Victor
3 Smileage	Svess

Advertisements
Gulf Gasoline.

The first giveaway comic to use all-original strips created for the comic. Full-colour tabloid, with advertising confined to the back page. A new issue was given away every week to customers of Gulf service stations. The comic was also the first to be nationally advertised over the radio. The original commercial, broadcast on 30 April 1933, was as follows: 'In addition you can have, free for the asking, a copy of Gulf's new *Comic Weekly*, a regular four-page, full-colour funny paper. Don't miss it!'

310 Gulf Funny Weekly

No. 5: June 1933–No. 422: 23 May 1941. Free (promotional). 4 pp. $10^1/_2 \times 15$ (5–302); $7^1/_4 \times 10^1/_4$ (303–422). Publisher: Gulf Refining Co., Pittsburgh. Advertisement.

Contents of No. 5 (first issue)
1 The Uncovered Wagon	Stan Schendel
2 Curly and the Kids	Victor
3 Smileage	Svess

Advertisements
Gulf Gasoline.

Continuation of *Gulf Comic Weekly*, given away free each week at Gulf service stations. Full-colour tabloid, reducing to comic book size from No. 303 (10 February 1939). The stars of the Gulf radio show appeared as a front-page strip from 1935: 'The Adventures of Phil Baker, Bottle and Beetle' by Stan Schendel. An adventure serial strip, 'Wings Winfair and His Round the World Flight' by Lyndell, commenced in No. 197 (29 January 1937).

311 Famous Funnies

'A Carnival of Comics'
No. 1 (unnumbered): September 1933 (undated). Free (promotional). 36 pp. $7^1/_2 \times 10^1/_2$. Publisher: Eastern Color Printing Co., 50 Church Street, New York. Editorial: Max C. Gaines.

Contents of No. 1
1 Cover	
2 (R) Hairbreadth Harry; High-Gear Homer	F.O. Alexander
3 (R) Good Deed Dotty; Dixie Dugan	J.P. McEvoy, J.H. Striebel
4 (R) Reg'lar Fellers; Draw It Y'self	Gene Byrnes
5 (R) Fisher's Boxing History; Joe Palooka	Ham Fisher
6 (R) Cicero; Mutt and Jeff	Bud Fisher

7 (R) Nipper; Footprints on the Sands of Time	Clare Dwiggins
8 (R) Magic Tricks	
9 (R) Puzzles	
10 (R) Holly of Hollywood; Keeping up with the Joneses	Pop Momand
12 (R) Puzzles	
13 (R) Magic Tricks	
14 (R) Somebody's Stenog; The Back-Seat Driver	A.E. Hayward
15 (R) Strange As It Seems	John Hix
16 (R) Little Brother; The Bungle Family	H.J. Tuthill
17 (R) Simp O'Dill; The Nebbs	Sol Hess, W.A. Carlson
18 (R) Hairbreadth Harry; High-Gear Homer	F.O. Alexander
20 (R) Reg'lar Fellers; Draw It Y'self	Gene Byrnes
21 (R) Fisher's Foolish History; Joe Palooka	Ham Fisher
22 (R) Smatter Pop; Honeybunch's Hubby	C.M. Payne
23 (R) Somebody's Stenog; The Back-Seat Driver	A.E. Hayward
24 (R) Magic Tricks	
25 (R) Puzzles	
26 (R) Smatter Pop; Honeybunch's Hubby	C.M. Payne
27 (R) Cicero; Mutt and Jeff	Bud Fisher
28 (R) Magic Tricks	Clare Dwiggins
30 (R) Nipper; Footprints on the Sands of Time	
31 (R) Cicero; Mutt and Jeff	Bud Fisher
32 (R) Fisher's History of Boxing; Joe Palooka	Ham Fisher
33 (R) Reg'lar Fellers; Draw It Y'self	Gene Byrnes
34 (R) Little Brother; The Bungle Family	H.J. Tuthill
35 (R) Connie; The Wet Blanket	Frank Godwin
36 Cover (continued)	

Advertisement

'Free! *Famous Funnies*! A book of popular comics. Boys and Girls — here's a book you'll all like. 32 pages including Mutt and Jeff, Hairbreadth Harry, Joe Palooka, Reg'lar Fellers and a lot more. It's full of puzzles, jokes, magic tricks — all sorts of things. You can get a copy of this book free. Just fill out the coupon and mail it to us with the top cut from a package of Wheatena. If you haven't a Wheatena package in your home, ask mother to get you one from her grocer the first thing tomorrow morning!'

The above advertisement for *Famous Funnies* appeared on the back page of the *Chicago Sunday Tribune* comic supplement on 1 October 1933, thus providing a publication date for this otherwise undated comic book. It was not sold on the newsstands, but given away free through the mail in return for the top of a Wheatena cereal package. The book itself is entirely free from advertising and, indeed, origin identification. The contents were entirely reduced-size reprints from Sunday comic pages copyrighted by several syndicates: McNaught, Public Ledger, Associated Newspapers, McClure, Bell, H.O. Fisher, Gene Byrnes, and the Dell Publishing Co. (puzzles and magic features). The only original artwork was the wrap-around cover, a panoramic view of the famous comic strip characters at a funfair, riding a merry-go-round. A mint copy is valued at $1,575 in Overstreet's *Comic Book Price Guide* for 1989.

312 Mickey Mouse Magazine

Vol. 1, No. 1: November 1933–Vol. 2, No. 12 (24): October 1935. Free (promotional). 16 pp. 5¼×7¼. Publisher: Kay Kamen. Editor: Hal Horne.

Contents of No. 1

1 Cartoon of Mickey and Minnie
2 An Important Message to Parents
3 With Mickey Mouse to the North Pole (serial)
7 I Tackle West Point by Mickey Mouse
10 Cartoons
11 The Steeple-Chase by Walt Disney
15 Minnie Mouse Recipes
16 Advertisement: Dairy

First editorial

'An Important Message to Parents from Mickey Mouse.

Milk is the most important food in the growing child's diet, but few children drink all the milk they need. Parents at times find it difficult to educate their children to the importance of milk so that the child will really desire it and voluntarily drink its requirements. Each growing child requires a minimum of one quart or four full glasses of milk every day. This amount is needed in the forming of straight rugged bones and strong sound teeth. And one quart of milk should be in the daily diet of every child until past the adolescent period. This little magazine is published for the sole purpose of assisting parents in getting these facts before their children in an attractive way. It will be delivered to your home monthly by your milkman and with my compliments. We hope your children will enjoy it. If your little ones are too young to read it themselves please read it to them. And do give them my love. Mickey Mouse.'

Although this series cannot be considered a comic book, it forms the link between the first series of *Mickey Mouse Magazine* (No. 1, January 1933) and the third series (No. 1, Summer 1935), which evolved into a comic book. Confusingly, both the first series and second series of *Mickey Mouse Magazine* begin with Vol. No. 1. The second series runs to 24 issues in all, as two volumes of 12 issues each. This series was published as a promotional premium only, and was given away by a number of American dairies whose names were overprinted on the front page. They included Ann Arbor Dairy, Arctic Dairy, Bryant & Chapman, Belle Vernon, Cream Crest, Detroit Creamery, Ewing–Von Allamen, Fairfield Western Maryland, Frechtling's, Grand Rapids Creamery, Hoffman's, Ohio Cloverleaf, Rieck's, Sanitary Dairies, and Southern Dairies.

312a Highlights of History

1933–1934. 10¢. 288 pp. 4×4½. Publisher: World Syndicate Publishing Co., Cleveland, Ohio. Artist: J. Carroll Mansfield. Syndicate: World Syndicate.

(1) *Pioneers of the Old West*
(2) *Kit Carson*
(3) *Buffalo Bill*

Contents
Compilation of daily newspaper strips syndicated by World Syndicate and written and illustrated by
J. Carroll Mansfield. Reprinted as one picture to the page, in black-and-white, with full colour covers
specially drawn by the artist.
Published in the popular *Big Little Book* format, but presented as 'All in Pictures'. i.e., without
additional text. Series of three unnumbered books, the first two copyrighted/published in 1933, the
third in 1934, as 'Highlights of History Series', the title of the daily newspaper strip.

313 All Star Comic Paint Book

1934 (No. 684). 10¢. 336 pp. 8½×3¾. Publisher: Whitman Publishing Co., Racine, Wisconsin.

Contents
Compilation of pictures reprinted from daily newspaper strips, printed black-and-white and suitable
for colouring by paint or crayon. Strips include 'Barney Google' by Billy De Beck. 'The Katzenjammer
Kids' by Harold Knerr, and 'Little Annie Roonie' by Brandon Walsh. Oblong book with semi-stiff
cover in full colour.

314 Big Big Books

1934–1938. 320 pp. 7¼×9½. Publisher: Whitman Publishing Co., Racine, Wisconsin.

No. 4054 *The Story of Little Orphan Annie*	Harold Gray
No. 4055 *The Adventures of Dick Tracy*	Chester Gould
No. 4056 *The Story of Skippy*	Percy L. Crosby
No. 4057 *The Adventures of Buck Rogers*	Dick Calkins
No. 4062 *The Story of Mickey Mouse and the Smugglers*	Walt Disney
No. 4063 *Thimble Theatre Starring Popeye*	E.C. Segar
No. 4071 *Dick Tracy and the Mystery of the Purple Cross*	Chester Gould
No. 4073 *The Adventures of Terry and the Pirates*	Milton Caniff

Series of large-format hardback books based on the popular newspaper strips. Arranged one
picture to each spread, with story text on the left-hand page. Printed black-and-white with full-colour
covers. These books were original material based on the famous characters: 'New Stories — New
Pictures'. Several of the books were reprinted in new editions, with newly designed covers
replacing the originals. There were other titles in the *Big Big Books* series but these were not comics-
oriented.

315 Bringing Up Father: Series No. 25

1934. 25¢. 52 pp. 10×9¾. Publisher: Cupples & Leon Co., 470 Fourth Avenue, New York. Artist:
George McManus.

Contents
Compilation of daily newspaper strips reprinted in black-and-white, arranged one strip to a page.
Three-colour cover on cardboard, specially drawn by the artist, George McManus.

316 Bringing Up Father: Series No. 26

1934. 25¢. 52 pp. 10×9³/₄. Publisher: Cupples & Leon Co., 470 Fourth Avenue, New York. Artist: George McManus.

Contents
Compilation of daily newspaper strips reprinted in black-and-white, arranged one strip to a page. Three-colour cover on cardboard, specially drawn by the artist. The last in this series by this publisher.

317 Buck Jones Big Thrill Library

1934. Free (with gum). 8 pp. 2×3. Publisher: Goudey Gum Co., Boston, Massachusetts.

Contents
Set of six unnumbered booklets given away inside each 1¢ package of Big Thrill chewing gum. Printed black-and-white with full colour on front and back pages, and centre spreads. Pictures combined with text.

318 Buck Rogers Big Thrill Library

1934. Free (with gum). 8 pp. 2×3. Publisher: Goudey Gum Co., Boston, Massachusetts. Artist: Dick Calkins. Syndicate: John F. Dille Co.

(1) *Buck Rogers Thwarting Ancient Demons*
(2) *Buck Rogers: An Aerial Conflict*
(3) *Buck Rogers: The Fight beneath the Sea*
(4) *Buck Rogers: A Handful of Trouble*
(5) *Buck Rogers: Collecting Human Specimens*
(6) *Buck Rogers: A One Man Army*

Contents
Set of six unnumbered booklets given away inside each 1¢ package of Big Thrill chewing gum. Printed black-and-white with full colour on front and back pages, and centre spreads. Pictures from the newspaper strip were combined with text.

319 Cartoon Story Books/Fast Action Story Books

1934 (No. 6833). 15¢; 10¢. 240 pp. 4×5¹/₄. Publisher: Dell Publishing Co. (George T. Delacorte), 149 Madison Avenue, New York.

No. 1 *Dick Tracy, Detective and Federal Agent*   Chester Gould
No. 2 *Flash Gordon vs. the Emperor of Mongo*   Alex Raymond

No. 3 *G-Man on Lightning Island*   Henry Vallely
No. 4 *Tom Mix in the Riding Avenger*   Hal Arbo

Series of four small books modelled on Whitman's *Big Little Books*. Each book is numbered 6833. The first two books reprint pictures from the newspaper strips 'Dick Tracy' by Chester Gould and 'Flash Gordon' by Alex Raymond. The second two books contain all original material. All books follow the pattern of text on the left-hand page, one single picture on the right. The *Cartoon Story Books* series has hard covers in full colour and sold at 15¢. The *Fast Action Story Books* are paperback editions and sold at 10¢.

320 Dick Tracy Big Thrill Library

1934. Free (with gum). 8 pp. 2×3. Publisher: Goudey Gum Co., Boston, Massachusetts. Artist: Chester Gould. Syndicate: Chicago Tribune.

Contents
Set of six unnumbered booklets given away inside each 1¢ package of Big Thrill chewing gum. Printed black-and-white with full colour on front and back pages, and centre spreads. Pictures from the newspaper strip were combined with text.

321 Famous Comics

1934 (No. 684). 96 pp. 8½×3½. Publisher: Whitman Publishing Co., Racine, Wisconsin.

Contents
No. 1 Little Jimmy   James Swinnerton
The Katzenjammer Kids   Harold Knerr
Barney Google   Billy De Beck
No. 2 Polly and Her Pals   Cliff Sterrett
Little Jimmy   James Swinnerton
The Katzenjammer Kids   Harold Knerr
No. 3 Little Annie Rooney   Brandon Walsh
Polly and Her Pals   Cliff Sterrett
The Katzenjammer Kids   Harold Knerr

Series of three small-size booklets in paper covers, that came in a special presentation box. Each booklet is a compilation of daily newspaper strips copyrighted by King Features Syndicate. Printed black-and-white with coloured covers.

322 Famous Comics Cartoon Books

1934. 68 pp. 7¼×8. Publisher: Whitman Publishing Co., Racine, Wisconsin.

No. 1202 *Captain Easy and Wash Tubbs*   Roy Crane
No. 1204 *Freckles and His Friends*   Merrill Blosser

Series of two hardcover books reprinting daily newspaper strips in black-and-white, with full-colour covers. See also *Famous Funnies Cartoon Books*.

323 Famous Funnies Cartoon Books

1934. 68 pp. 7¹/₄×8. Publisher: Whitman Publishing Co., Racine, Wisconsin.

No. 1200 *The Captain and the Kids*   Bernard Dibble
No. 1203 *Ella Cinders*   Bill Conselman, Charlie Plumb

Series of two hardcover books reprinting daily newspaper strips in black-and-white, with full-colour covers. See also *Famous Comics Cartoon Books*.

324 Famous Funnies: Series 1

1934. 10¢. 68 pp. 7¹/₂×10¹/₂. Publisher: Dell Publishing Co. (George T. Delacorte Jr.), 149 Madison Avenue, New York. Editor: Max C. Gaines. Eastern Color Printing Co., 50 Church Street, New York.

This was the first comic book to be published for sale to the public, instead of as a promotional giveaway. It was assembled from pages already published in the two previous giveaway comic books, *Funnies on Parade* and *Famous Funnies: A Carnival of Comics*, which in their turn were reprints of comic pages from Sunday newspaper supplements. There was a print run of 35,000 copies, which were sold through chain stores at 10¢ a copy. Successful sales led to the publication of *Famous Funnies* as a regular title for newsstand distributon, commencing with a new No. 1 issue dated July 1934. A mint copy of this comic book is valued at $3,000 in Overstreet's *Comic Book Price Guide* for 1989.

325 Karmetz Premium Comicbooks

1934. Free (promotional). 48 pp. 5¹/₂×4¹/₄. Publisher: Whitman Publishing Co./Karmetz.

No. 1 *The Adventures of Dick Tracy, Detective*   Chester Gould
No. 2 *The Adventures of Dick Tracy and Dick Tracy Jr.*   Chester Gould
No. 3 *Chester Gump at Silver Creek Ranch*   Sidney Smith
No. 4 *Chester Gump Finds the Hidden Treasure*   Sidney Smith
No. 5 *Little Orphan Annie*   Harold Gray
No. 6 *Little Orphan Annie and Sandy*   Harold Gray
No. 7 *Wash Tubbs*   Roy Crane

Series of eight (one was not a comic strip book) small oblong books reprinting pictures from daily newspaper strips with additional text on the left-hand pages. Printed black-and-white with soft covers in full colour. *Note:* these books are abridgements of previously published *Big Little Books* by the same publisher, Whitman. They were produced for Karmetz, a promotional agency, who supplied them to sundry companies and stores as giveaways for children.

326 Little Big Books

No. 1051: 1934–No. 1117: 1936. 15¢ (10¢ soft cover). 160 pp. $7^3/_4 \times 3^1/_2$; $4 \times 5^3/_4$; $6 \times 4^1/_2$; $4^3/_4 \times 5^1/_4$. Publisher: Saalfield Publishing Co., Akron, Ohio. Syndicate: King Features.

No. 1051 1934 *Popeye*	E.C. Segar
No. 1052 1934 *Just Kids*	Ad Carter
No. 1053 1934 *Adventures of Tim Tyler*	Lyman Young
No. 1054 1934 *Little Annie Rooney*	Brandon Walsh
No. 1055 1934 *Katzenjammer Kids in the Mountains*	Harold Knerr
No. 1056 1934 *Krazy Kat and Ignatz Mouse in Koko Land*	George Herriman
No. 1059 1934 *Brick Bradford and the City beneath the Sea*	William Ritt
No. 1060 1934 *Polly and Her Pals*	Cliff Sterrett
No. 1081 1935 *Elmer and His Dog Spot*	Doc Winner
No. 1082 1935 *The Adventures of Pete the Tramp*	C.D. Russell
No. 1083 1935 *Barney Google*	Billy De Beck
No. 1087 1935 *Little Jimmy's Gold Hunt*	James Swinnerton
No. 1088 1935 *Popeye in Puddleburg*	E.C. Segar
No. 1094 1935 *Just Kids and the Mysterious Stranger*	Ad Carter
No. 1113 1936 *Popeye in Choose Your Weppins*	Max Fleischer
No. 1117 1936 *Popeye's Ark*	E.C. Segar

Contents
Series of small books of four variant shapes reprinting daily newspaper strips copyrighted by King Features Syndicate. Each has two editions, both with full-colour covers, but one in hardback (selling at 15¢) and one in softback (selling at 10¢). Printed black-and-white throughout.
The Saalfield Publishing Company's answer to Whitman's *Big Little Books* was the *Little Big Books*. The size varied, but the pattern was similar: pictures from the original comic strips are used to illustrate the story, which is told in text. All speech balloons were removed from the pictures. Other titles in this series were original illustrated stories, or adaptations from current films. *Note:* the book *Popeye in Choose Your Weppins* is adapted from the Paramount cartoon film, not from the Segar comic strip.

327 Little Orphan Annie Adventure Books

1934. Free (promotional). 40 pp. $3^1/_4 \times 3^1/_2$. Publisher: Whitman Publishing Co., Racine, Wisconsin. Artist: Harold Gray. Syndicate: Chicago Tribune.

No. 1 *Little Orphan Annie and the Pinchpennys*
No. 2 *Little Orphan Annie and the Lucky Knife*

No. 3 *Little Orphan Annie and Daddy Warbucks*
No. 4 *Little Orphan Annie at Happy Home*
No. 5 *Little Orphan Annie and Her Dog Sandy*
No. 6 *Little Orphan Annie Finds Mickey*

Set of six small booklets reprinting pictures from the daily newspaper strip by Harold Gray, syndicated by the *Chicago Tribune*. The stories are told in text on the left-hand pages, in the style of *Big Little Books*. Printed black-and-white with full-colour covers. Produced by Whitman for Ovaltine, who gave them away in return for the aluminium seal found in the top of each Ovaltine can.

328 Little Orphan Annie and Uncle Dan

1934. 60¢. 96 pp. 7×8³/₄. Publisher: Cupples & Leon Co., 443 Fourth Avenue, New York. Artist: Harold Gray. Syndicate: Chicago Tribune.

Contents
Compilation of daily newspaper strips copyright by the *Chicago Tribune*. The 86 strips are arranged one to a page, printed in black-and-white. Bound in boards with a three-colour dust-wrapper and title page designed by the artist, Harold Gray. No. 9 of the *Little Orphan Annie* series, and the last by this publisher.

329 Mickey Mouse: Book No. 4

1934. 25¢. 52 pp. 10×9³/₄. Publisher: David McKay Co., 604 South Washington Square, Philadelphia.

Contents
Compilation of daily newspaper strips reprinted in black-and-white and arranged one strip to the page. Cardboard covers in two colours, specially drawn by the Walt Disney Studio. The last in this publisher's series of *Mickey Mouse* comic books.

330 Popeye Cartoon Book

1934 (No. 2095). 40 pp. 8¹/₂×13. Publisher: Saalfield Publishing Co., Akron, Ohio. Artist: E.C. Segar. Syndicate: King Features.

Contents
Compilation of Sunday newspaper supplement strips copyrighted 1933 by King Features Syndicate and reprinted in full colour throughout. The strips are arranged one half to each page: the book has to be turned sideways to be read. Cardboard covers.

331 Secret Agent X-9: Book One

1934. 84 pp. 8×7¹/₂. Publisher: David McKay Co., 604 Washington Square, Philadelphia. Artist: Alex Raymond. Syndicate: King Features.

Contents
Compilation of 78 daily newspaper strips dated from January to April 1934, copyright King Features Syndicate Inc. Written by Dashiell Hammett and illustrated by Alex Raymond. Strips are arranged one to the page. Printed black-and-white within two-colour cardboard covers, which are not drawn by the original artist.

332 Secret Agent X-9: Book Two

1934. 124 pp. 8×7½. Publisher: David McKay Co., 604 Washington Square, Philadelphia. Artist: Alex Raymond. Syndicate: King Features.

Contents
Compilation of 118 daily newspaper strips dating from April 1934, copyright King Features Syndicate Inc. Written by Dashiell Hammett and illustrated by Alex Raymond. Strips are arranged one to the page. Printed black-and-white within coloured cardboard covers, which are not drawn by the original artist.

333 Skippy's Own Book of Comics

1934. Free (promotional). 52 pp. Publisher: Eastern Color Printing Co. (for Phillips Dental Magnesia), 50 Church Street, New York. Editorial: Max C. Gaines. Artist: Percy L. Crosby. Syndicate: King Features.

Contents
Compilation of Sunday supplement strips reprinted in four colours. This comic book was published and distributed as an advertising premium for Phillips Dental Magnesia toothpaste, who sponsored the 'Skippy' radio show. It was the first reprint comic book devoted to strips of one single character.

334 Tailspin Tommy Big Thrill Library

1934. Free (with gum). 8 pp. 2×3. Publisher: Goudey Gum Co., Boston, Massachusetts. Artist: Hal Forrest.

Contents
Set of six unnumbered booklets given away inside each 1¢ package of Big Thrill chewing gum. Printed black-and-white with full colour on front and back pages, and centre spreads. Pictures from the newspaper strip were combined with text.

335 Tales of Demon Dick and Bunker Bill

1934 (No. 793). 80 pp. 10½×5. Publisher: Whitman Publishing Co., Racine, Wisconsin. Artist: Dick Spencer.

Contents
Humorous story for children told completely in comic strip form, in five chapters. Oblong book printed in black-and-white throughout, with hard covers in full colour. No. 793 in the Whitman Books series.

336 Tim McCoy: Police Car 17

1934 (No. 674). 36 pp. 11×14³/₄. Publisher: Whitman Publishing Co., Racine, Wisconsin.

Contents
The story of a film, *Police Car 17*, adapted into comic strip format. Printed black-and-white throughout, with full-colour cover. No. 674 in the Whitman Books series.

337 Treasure Box of Famous Comics

1934. 36 (× 5) pp. 6³/₄×8¹/₂. Publisher: Cupples & Leon Co., 470 Fourth Avenue, New York.

(1) *Little Orphan Annie*	Hrold Gray
(2) *Smitty*	Walter Berndt
(3) *Reg'lar Fellers*	Gene Byrnes
(4) *Harold Teen*	Carl Ed
(5) *Dick Tracy and Dick Tracy Jr.*	Chester Gould

This is a set of five small-sized comic books, each containing 32 pages of daily newspaper strips of the title character, bound in three-colour card covers. Each book is an abridgement of the earlier cardboard-covered editions, as listed in this Catalogue. The books were contained in a special box.

338 Wee Little Books

1934 (No. 512). 40 pp. 3¹/₄×3¹/₂. Publisher: Whitman Publishing Co., Racine, Wisconsin. Artist: Floyd Gottfredson.

No. 1 *Mickey Mouse at the Carnival*
No. 2 *Mickey Mouse and Tanglefoot*
No. 3 *Mickey Mouse's Up Hill Fight*
No. 4 *Mickey Mouse's Misfortune*
No. 5 *Mickey Mouse Will Not Quit*
No. 6 *Mickey Mouse·Wins the Race*

Set of six small booklets reprinting pictures from the daily newspaper strip 'Mickey Mouse' by Floyd Gottfredson (credited to Walt Disney). The sequence covered by the six books ran from 17 June to 3 October 1933. The stories are told in text on the left-hand pages, in the style of *Big Little Books*. Sold as a set of six in a special box, given the publisher's number 512. The books are printed in black-and-white with full-colour covers. *Note:* four other sets of *Wee Little Books* were published, but were not comics-related material.

339 Comic Cuts

No. 1: 19 May 1934–No. 9: 28 July 1934. 5¢. 24 pp. 10½×15½. Publisher: H.L. Baker Co. Inc.

Weekly comic in tabloid format, modelled on the British style but printed in four colours throughout. Frequency changed to fortnightly after No. 7 (30 June 1934), but to little avail as the publication was discontinued after No. 9. Little is known of the contents, which may have included strips reprinted from the British comic of the same title.

340 Famous Funnies

'The Nation's Comic Monthly'
No. 1: July 1934–No. 218: July 1955. 10¢. 68 pp. 7½×10¼. Publisher: Eastern Color Printing Co. (William J. Pape), 50 Church Street, New York. Editorial: Harold A. Moore (editor); Stephen Douglas (art editor).

Contents of No. 1

1 Cover	Jon Mayes
2 (R) Toonerville Folks; Little Stanley	Fontaine Fox
3 (R) Amaze a Minute	Arnold
4 (R) Little Brother; The Bungle Family	H.J. Tuthill
5 (R) Tailspin Tommy	Hal Forrest, Glen Chaffin
6 (R) Somebody's Stenog; The Back-Seat Driver	A.E. Hayward
7 (R) Hairbreadth Harry; High-Gear Homer	F.O. Alexander
8 (R) Good Deed Dotty; Dixie Dugan	J.P. McEvoy, J.H. Striebel
9 (R) Cicero; Mutt and Jeff	Bud Fisher
10 (R) Pam; Donald Dare	A.W. Brewerton
11 (R) Simp O'Dill; The Nebbs	Sol Hess, W.A. Carlson
12 (R) Smatter Pop; Honeybunch's Hubby	C.M. Payne
13 (R) Nipper; Footprints on the Sands of Time	Clare Dwiggins
14 (R) Connie; The Wet Blanket	Frank Godwin
15 (R) Jolly Geography; High Lights of History	J. Carroll Mansfield
16 (R) Ben Webster's Page	Edwin Alger
17 (R) Toonerville Folks; Little Stanley	Fontaine Fox
18 (R) Puzzles	A.W. Nugent
20 (R) Toonerville Folks; Little Stanley	Fontaine Fox
21 (R) Ben Webster's Page	Edwin Alger
22 (R) Jolly Geography; High Lights of History	J. Carroll Mansfield
23 (R) Connie; The Wet Blanket	Frank Godwin
24 (R) Nipper; Footprints on the Sands of Time	Clare Dwiggins
25 (R) Smatter Pop; Honeybunch's Hubby	C.M. Payne

26 (R) Simp O'Dill; The Nebbs	Sol Hess, W.A. Carlson
27 (R) Pam; Donald Dare	A.W. Brewerton
28 (R) Cicero; Mutt and Jeff	Bud Fisher
29 (R) Good Deed Dotty; Dixie Dugan	J.P. McEvoy, J.H. Striebel
30 (R) Hairbreadth Harry; High Gear Homer	F.O. Alexander
31 (R) Somebody's Stenog; The Back-Seat Driver	A.E. Hayward
32 (R) Tailspin Tommy	Hal Forrest, Glen Chaffin
33 (R) Little Brother; The Bungle Family	H.J. Tuthill
34 Dick Whittington Went to London (story)	Jane Corby
36 (R) Little Brother; The Bungle Family	H.J. Tuthill
37 (R) Tailspin Tommy	Hal Forrest, Glen Chaffin
38 (R) Somebody's Stenog; The Back-Seat Driver	A.E. Hayward
39 (R) Hairbreadth Harry; High-Gear Homer	F.O. Alexander
40 (R) Good Deed Dotty; Dixie Dugan	J.P. McEvoy, J.H. Striebel
41 (R) Cicero; Mutt and Jeff	Bud Fisher
42 (R) Pam; Donald Dare	A.W. Brewerton
43 (R) Simp O'Dill; The Nebbs	Sol Hess, W.A. Carlson
44 (R) Smatter Pop; Honeybunch's Hubby	C.M. Payne
45 (R) Nipper; Footprints on the Sands of Time	Clare Dwiggins
46 (R) Connie; The Wet Blanket	Frank Godwin
47 (R) Jolly Geography; High Lights of History	J. Carroll Mansfield
48 (R) Been Webster's Page	Edwin Alger
49 (R) Toonerville Folks; Little Stanley	Fontaine Fox
50 (R) Puzzles	A.W. Nugent
52 (R) Toonerville Folks; Little Stanley	Fontaine Fox
53 (R) Ben Webster's Page	Edwin Alger
54 (R) Jolly Geography; High Lights of History	J. Carroll Mansfield
55 (R) Connie; The Wet Blanket	Frank Godwin
56 (R) Nipper; Footprints on the Sands of Time	Clare Dwiggins
57 (R) Smatter Pop; Honeybunch's Hubby	C.M. Payne
58 (R) Simp O'Dill; The Nebbs	Sol Hess, W.A. Carlson
59 (R) Pam; Donald Dare	A.W. Brewerton
60 (R) Cicero; Mutt and Jeff	Bud Fisher
61 (R) Good Deed Dotty; Dixie Dugan	J.P. McEvoy, J.H. Striebel
62 (R) Hairbreadth Harry, High-Gear Homer	F.O. Alexander
63 (R) Somebody's Stenog; The Back-Seat Driver	A.E. Hayward
64 (R) Tailspin Tommy	Hal Forrest, Glen Chaffin
65 (R) Little Brother; The Bungle Family	H.J. Tuthill
66 (R) Screen Oddities	Roscoe Fawcett, Thompson
67 (R) Cicero; Mutt and Jeff	Bud Fisher
68 Cover (continued)	Jon Mayes

Advertising

None in the early issues, but by No. 9 full pages for Buck Rogers 25th Century Caster (Rapaport Brothers) and Buck Jones 60 Shot Repeater Rifle (Daisy Manufacturing Co.), plus Iver Johnson Bicycles.

The true father of all American comic books, *Famous Funnies* fulfils all the classic requirements: size ($7^1/_2 \times 10^1/_4$), page count (64 plus cover), colour (full four-colour printing throughout), paper (low-quality newsprint for interior pages, higher-quality coated stock for cover), price (10¢), publication frequency (monthly), even the short text story to satisfy the requirements of the United States Post Office for registration as second-class matter to qualify for lower postal rates. The only thing lacking was an original comic strip character specifically created for the comic book, although this would soon be rectified with the introduciton of 'Seaweed Sam the Rhyming Rover' by Victoria Pazmino. There was a minimum of original artwork in No. 1: the wrap-around cover by Jon Mayes, which featured some of the inside characters watching Augustus Mutt playing golf. The contents were compiled from Sunday supplement pages copyrighted by the Bell Syndicate, Public Ledger Inc., the McNaught Syndicate, H.C. Fisher, J. Carroll Mansfield, and Jay Jerome Williams, dated 1932–1934. Other characters introduced during the run included: Jane Arden and Lena Pry by Monte Barrett and Jack McGuire (No. 2); Flying to Fame or Slim and Tubby by Russell Ross and John Welch (No. 2); Ned Brant at Carter by Bob Zuppke and B.W. Depew (No. 2); Buck Rogers in the 25th Century by Phil Nowlan and Dick Calkins (No. 3); Dan Dunn by Norman Marsh (No. 5); Olly of the Movies by Julian Ollendorff (No. 5); Babe Bunting by Roy Williams (No. 18); no fewer than ten new strips began in No. 19, including Our Boarding House, Out Our Way, Boots, Alley Oop, Captain Easy, and Freckles and His Friends; Apple Mary (No. 20); Dickie Dare by Milton Caniff, Scorchy Smith by Noel Sickles and Oaky Doaks by R.B. Fuller (No. 25). Even this stalwart reprint comic book succumbed to the superhero craze by introducing 'Fearless Flint the Flint Man' by H.G. Peter, in No. 89 (December 1941). A mint copy of No. 1 is valued at $2,100 in Overstreet's *Comic Book Price Guide* for 1989.

341 Mickey Mouse and Minnie at Macy's

December 1934. Free (promotional). 144 pp. $3^1/_4 \times 3^1/_2$. Publisher: Whitman Publishing Co., Racine, Wisconsin.

Contents
Small comic book with text in the style of the *Big Little Books* but with a soft cover. Printed black-and-white with covers in full colour. Produced as a promotion for Macy's Toyland.

342 Xmas Funnies

December 1934. Free (promotional). 36 pp. $7^1/_4 \times 10^1/_4$. Publisher: Eastern Color Printing Co., 40 Church Street, New York.

Contents
Reprints of selected pages from *Famous Funnies*, including 'Mutt and Jeff' by Bud Fisher, etc. Published as a promotional giveaway for Kinney's Shoe Stores.

343 Big Thrill Library

1935. Free (with gum). 8 pp. 2×3. Publisher: Goudey Gum Co., Boston, Massachusetts.

(1) *Crafty Keen the Detective*
(2) *Hal Hunter among the Savages*
(3) *Mirtho the Clown*
(4) *Operator 7 of the Secret Service*
(5) *Reckless Steele, Soldier of Fortune*
(6) *Yip Roper the Young Cowboy*

Contents
Series of six unnumbered booklets given away inside 1¢ packages of Big Thrill chewing gum. Printed black-and-white with full colour on front, back and centre spreads. Pictures combined with text. This series followed on the 1934 *Big Thrill Library* of Buck Jones, Buck Rogers, Dick Tracy and Tailspin Tommy, introducing all original comic strip characters designed for the booklets. Artists unknown.

344 Chip Collins' Adventures on Bat Island

1935 (No. L 14). 15¢. 94 pp. 5×7$^1/_2$. Publisher: Lynn Publishing Co., New York. Artist: Jack Wilhelm.

Contents
Small book reprinting panels from the newspaper strip 'Chip Collins, Adventurer' by William Ritt, drawn by Jack Wilhelm. The story is told in text printed on the left-hand pages, written by Gerald Breitigam. Printed black-and-white with board covers in full colour.

345 Cocomalt Premium Comicbooks

1935. Free (promotional). 256; 200 pp. 3$^1/_2$×4$^1/_2$. Publisher: Whitman Publishing Co., Racine, Wisconsin.

No. 1 *Alley Oop in the Invasion of Moo*	V.T. Hamlin
No. 3 *Buck Rogers in the City of Floating Globes*	Dick Calkins
No. 4 *Buck Rogers in the 25th Century A.D.*	Dick Calkins
No. 6 *Captain Easy and Wash Tubbs*	Roy Crane
No. 7 *Chester Gump at Silver Creek Ranch*	Sidney Smith
No. 8 *King of the Royal Mounted*	Zane Grey
No. 9 *Men of the Mounted*	Ted McCall
No. 10 *Moon Mullins and Kayo*	Frank Willard
No. 11 *Reg'lar Fellers*	Gene Byrnes
No. 12 *Smitty: Golden Gloves Tournament*	Walter Berndt
No. 13 *Tailspin Tommy: Wings Over the Arctic*	Hal Forrest

Series of 14 small comic books in the *Big Little Book* format: single pictures reprinted from daily newspaper strips illustrating a text story which is printed on the left-hand page of each spread. Some of these are shortened versions of previously published *Big Little Books*, others are original for the series (No. 1, No. 3). Produced by Whitman for the R.B. Davis Company, makers of Cocomalt chocolate drink. Printed in black-and-white with soft covers in full colour. *Note:* only those books adapted from comic strips are included in the above list.

346 Curley Harper at Lakespur

1935 (No. L 19). 15¢. 192 pp. $4^1/_2 \times 5^3/_4$. Publisher: Lynn Publishing Co., New York. Artist: Lyman Young.

Contents
Small book reprinting panels from the newspaper strip drawn by Lyman Young. The story is told in text printed on the left-hand pages, written by Gerald Breitigam. Printed black-and-white with board covers in full colour.

347 Donnie and the Pirates

1935 (No. L 13). 15¢. 192 pp. $4^1/_2 \times 5^3/_4$. Publisher: Lynn Publishing Co., New York. Artist: Darrell McClure.

Contents
Small book reprinting panels from the newspaper strip 'Donnie' drawn by Darrell McClure. The story is told in text written by George Gerry and printed on the left-hand pages. Printed black-and-white with board covers in full colour. *Note:* a sequel book, *Donnie and Vulture Varn*, is advertised but may not have been published.

348 Famous Comics

1935. Free (promotional). 24 pp. $7^1/_2 \times 10^1/_4$. Publisher: Zain-Eppy.

Contents
Compilation of Sunday newspaper supplement strips previously published in *Famous Funnies*. The strips are dated 1934 and include Joe Palooka by Ham Fisher, Hairbreadth Harry by F.O. Alexander, Napoleon by Clifford McBride, and The Nebbs by Sol Hess and W.A. Carlson. Given away free as an advertising premium.

349 Favorite Comics

No. 1–No. 3: 1935. Free (promotional). 68 pp. $7^1/_2 \times 10^1/_4$. Publisher: Dif Corporation, Garwood, New Jersey.

Contents of No. 1
1 Cover   Victoria Pazmino

3 (R) Joe Palooka; Fisher's Nursery Rhymes	Ham Fisher
4 (R) Hairbreadth Harry; High-Gear Homer	F.O. Alexander
5 (R) Connie; The Wet Blanket	Frank Godwin
6 (R) Jolly Geography; Highlights of History	J. Carroll Mansfield
7 (R) Magic Made Easy	
8 (R) Buck Rogers	Phil Nowlan, Dick Calkins
12 (R) Somebody's Stenog; The Back Seat Driver	A.E. Hayward
13 (R) Strange As It Seems	John Hix
14 (R) Napoleon	Clifford McBride
15 Dip & Duck	M.E. Brady
16 (R) Ben Webster's Page	Edwin Alger
17 (R) Good Deed Dotty; Dixie Dugan	J.P. McEvoy, J.H. Striebel
18 (R) Flying to Fame	Russell Ross, John Welch
20 (R) Puzzles	A.W. Nugent
21 (R) Hairbreadth Harry; High-Gear Homer	F.O. Alexander
22 (R) Joe Palooka; Fisher's Loony Legends	Ham Fisher
23 (R) Strange As It Seems	John Hix
24 (R) Nipper; Footprints on the Sands of Time	Clare Dwiggins
25 (R) Good Deed Dotty; Dixie Dugan	J.P. McEvoy, J.H. Striebel
26 (R) Smatter Pop; Honeybunch's Hubby	C.M. Payne
27 (R) Simp O'Dill; The Nebbs	Sol Hess, W.A. Carlson
28 (R) The Bungle Family; Little Brother	H.J. Tuthill
29 (R) Joe Palooka; Fisher's Dizzy Dramas	Ham Fisher
30 (R) Napoleon	Clifford McBride
31 (R) Vignettes of Life	J. Norman Lynd
32 (R) Jolly Geography; Highlights of History	J. Carroll Mansfield
33 (R) Little Brother; The Bungle Family	H.J. Tuthill
34 (R) Simp O'Dill; The Nebbs	Sol Hess, W.A. Carlson
35 (R) Smatter Pop; Honeybunch's Hubby	C.M. Payne
36 (R) Lena Pry; Jane Arden	Monte Barrett, Jack McGuire
40 (R) Somebody's Stenog; The Back-Seat Driver	A.E. Hayward
41 (R) Puzzles	A.W. Nugent
42 (R) The Frog Pond Ferry; Buttons & Fatty	M.E. Brady
44 (R) Simp O'Dill; The Nebbs	Sol Hess, W.A. Carlson
45 (R) Jolly Geography; Highlights of History	J. Carroll Mansfield
46 Tim McKee's Stratosphere Adventure (story)	Ralph Daigh
48 (R) Strange As It Seems	John Hix
49 (R) Good Deed Dotty; Dixie Dugan	J.P. McEvoy, J.H. Striebel
50 (R) Ben Webster's Page	Edwin Alger
51 (R) Little Brother; The Bungle Family	H.J. Tuthill
52 (R) Ned Brant at Carter	Bob Zuppke, B.W. Depew
54 (R) Hairbreadth Harry; High-Gear Homer	F.O. Alexander
55 Dip & Duck	M.E. Brady
56 (R) Magic Made Easy	
57 (R) Adventures of Jabby	
(R) Alec and Itchy	George Mulholland
58 (R) Little Brother; The Bungle Family	H.J. Tuthill

108

59 (R) Holly of Hollywood; Keeping Up with the Joneses	Pop Momand
60 (R) Napoleon	Clifford McBride
61 (R) Simp O'Dill; The Nebbs	Sol Hess, W.A. Carlson
62 (R) Connie; The Wet Blanket	Frank Godwin
63 (R) Hairbreadth Harry; High-Gear Homer	F.O. Alexander
64 (R) Joe Palooka; Fisher's Silly Scoops	Ham Fisher
65 (R) Good Deed Dotty; Dixie Dugan	J.P. McEvoy, J.H. Striebel
66 (R) Jolly Geography; Highlights of History	J. Carroll Mansfield

Advertisements
Dif Household Cleaner; Dif Hand Cleaner.

Back issues of *Famous Funnies* with their covers removed, bound into specially designed four-colour covers as a 'new' comic book to advertise Dif. A set of three comic books, each with the same cover design but with different backing colours: No. 1 is blue, No. 2 is yellow, No. 3 is green. Book No.1 contains *Famous Funnies* No. 4. Each comic book was given free with the purchase of two boxes of Dif the Different Cleaner: Softens the Hardest Water.

350 Henry

1935. 25¢. 52 pp. Publisher: David McKay Co., 604 South Washington Square, Philadelphia. Artist: Carl Anderson. Syndicate: King Features.

Contents
Compilation of daily newspaper strips copyrighted by King Features Syndicate, and printed black-and-white in a full-colour cover. 'Henry' first appeared as a weekly cartoon panel in *The Saturday Evening Post* on 19 March 1932, and became a daily comic strip from 17 December 1934.

351 Jimmy and the Tiger

1935 (No. L 15). 15¢. 192 pp. 4^1/$_2$×5^3/$_4$. Publisher: Lynn Publishing Co., New York. Artist: Vic Forsythe.

Contents
Small book reprinting panels from the newspaper strip 'Joe Jinks' drawn by Vic Forsythe. The story is told in text written by George Gerry and printed on the left-hand pages. Printed black-and-white with board covers in full colour.

352 Little Annie Rooney

1935. 25¢. 52 pp. Publisher: David McKay Co., 604 South Washington Square, Philadelphia. Artist: Darrell McClure. Syndicate: King Features.

Contents
Compilation of daily newspaper strips copyrighted by King Features Syndicate, and printed black-and-white in a full-colour cover. 'Little Annie Rooney', created by writer Brandon Walsh, first appeared on 10 January 1929.

353 Mickey Mouse Sails for Treasure Island

1935. Free (promotional). 192 pp. 3½×4½. Publisher: Whitman Publishing Co., Racine, Wisconsin.

Contents
Small-size comic book in *Big Little Book* format, abridged from the original *Big Little Book* edition and issued as a premium by Kolynos Dental Cream. Reprints pictures from the daily newspaper strip drawn by Floyd Gottfredson, with the story in text on the left-hand pages. Black-and-white with a soft cover in four colours.

354 Mickey Mouse the Mail Pilot

1935. Free (promotional). 288 pp. 4×4. Publisher: Whitman Publishing Co., Racine, Wisconsin.

Contents
Special edition of the *Big Little Book* of the same title, issued as a premium by the American Gas Company. Abridged; printed black-and-white with a soft cover in four colours. Reprinted from the daily newspaper strip drawn by Floyd Gottfredson.

355 Perkins Premium Comicbooks

1935. Free (promotional). 48 pp. 5¾×3½. Publisher: Whitman Publishing Co./Perkins.

No. 1 *Chester Gump Finds the Hidden Treasure*	Sidney Smith
No. 2 *Dick Tracy the Detective and Dick Tracy Jr.*	Chester Gould
No. 3 *Ella Cinders and the Mysterious House*	Charlie Plumb
No. 4 *Men of the Mounted*	Ted McCall
No. 5 *Tailspin Tommy and the Pay-roll Mystery*	Hal Forrest
No. 6 *Tarzan of the Apes*	Harold Foster
No. 7 *The Tarzan Twins*	Edgar Rice Burroughs
No. 8 *Terry and the Pirates*	Milton Caniff

Series of eight small oblong books reprinting pictures from daily newspaper strips with additional text on the left-hand pages. Printed black-and-white with soft covers in full colour. *Note:* these books are abridgements of previously published *Big Little Books* by the same publisher, Whitman. They were produced for Perkins, a promotional agency, who supplied them to sundry companies and stores as giveaways for children. The main distributor was Kool-Aid (Lemix-Korlix Corporation).

356 Popeye: Book No. 1: The Gold Mine Thieves

1935. 25¢. 52 pp. 10×9¾. Publisher: David McKay Co., 604 Washington Square, Philadelphia. Artist: Elzie Crisler Segar. Syndicate: King Features.

Contents
Compilation of daily newspaper strips of 'Thimble Theatre Starring Popeye', reprinting the serial adventure 'Popeye in Black Valley', dated 5 November 1934 to 12 January 1935. The 46 strips are arranged one to the page, with an original cover (not drawn by the original artist, Segar) which is

reprinted as a title page. Cardboard covers. The book is modelled closely on the successful format for comic strip reprints published by Cupples & Leon.

357 Popeye: Book No. 2

1935. 25¢. 52 pp. 10×9³/₄. Publisher: David McKay Co., 604 Washington Square, Philadelphia. Artist: Elzie Crisler Segar. Syndicate: King Features.

Contents
Compilation of daily newspaper strips of 'Thimble Theatre Starring Popeye'. The 46 strips are arranged one to the page, with an original cover that is reprinted as a title page. Black-and-white in cardboard covers.

358 The Story of Skippy

1935. Free (promotional). 200 pp. 3¹/₂×4¹/₂. Publisher: Whitman Publishing Co., Racine, Wisconsin. Artist: Percy L. Crosby.

Contents
Special edition of the *Big Little Book* of the same title, issued as a premium by Phillips Toothpaste, sponsors of the 'Skippy' radio programme. Reprints pictures from the daily strip by Percy L. Crosby, with the story in text on the left-hand pages. Black-and-white with a soft cover in four colours.

359 Top-Line Comics

1935. 160 pp. 3³/₄×4. Publisher: Whitman Publishing Co., Racine, Wisconsin.

Set No. 1 (No. 540)
No. 1 *Bobby Thatcher and the Samarang Emerald*	George Storm
No. 2 *Broncho Bill in Suicide Canyon*	Harry O'Neill
No. 3 *Freckles and his Friends in the North Woods*	Merrill Blosser

Set No. 2 (No. 541)
No. 1 *Little Joe and the City Gangsters*	Ed Leffingwell
No. 2 *Smilin' Jack and His Flivver Plane*	Zack Mosley
No. 3 *Streaky and the Football Signals*	Gus Edson

Set No. 3 (No. 542)
No. 1 *Dinglehoofer und His Dog*	Doc Winner
No. 2 *Jungle Jim*	Alex Raymond
No. 3 *Sappo*	Elzie Segar

Set No. 4 (No. 543)

No. 1 *Alexander Smart Esq.*	Doc Winner
No. 2 *Bunky*	Billy De Beck
No. 3 *Nicodemus O'Malley*	Ad Carter

Series of twelve small comic books in special boxes, packed three to a boxed set. Reprints of pictures from daily and Sunday newspaper strips, with the story told in text printed on the left-hand pages in the style of *Big Little Books*. Printed black-and-white with four-colour covers.

360 New Fun

'The Big Comic Magazine'
No. 1: February 1935–No. 6: October 1935. 10¢. 36 pp. 10¼×15. Publisher: National Allied Publications Inc. (Malcolm Wheeler-Nicholson), 49 West 45th Street, New York. Editorial: 49 West 45th Street, New York; Lloyd Jacquet (editor); Dick Loederer (art editor); Sheldon H. Stark (cartoon editor); H.D. Cushing (advertising manager).

Title changed to *More Fun* from No. 7.

Contents of No. 1

1 Jack Woods	Lyman Anderson
2 Editorial: 'Hello Everybody'	Lloyd Jacquet
3 Sandra of the Secret Service Oswald the Rabbit	John Lindermayer
4 Jigger and Ginger	Schus
5 Barry O'Neill	Lawrence Lariar
6 The Magic Crystal of History	Adolphe Barreaux
7 Wing Brady, Soldier of Fortune	De Kerosett
8 Ivanhoe by Sir Walter Scott	Charles Fianders
9 Judge Perkins	Bert Whitman
10 Don Drake on the Planet Saro	Clemens Gretter
11 Loco Luke	Jack Warren
12 Spook Ranch (story)	Roger Furlong
14 Scrub Hardy	Joe Archibald
15 Jack Andrews, All-American Boy	Lyman Anderson
16 Bathysphere, a Martian Dream (feature)	
17 Sports (feature)	Joe Archibald
18 On the Radio (feature)	
19 In the Movies (feature)	
20 Model Aircraft (feature)	
21 Aviation (feature)	
22 How to Build a Model of Hendrik Hudson's Half Moon (feature)	
24 Cap'n Erik	Bob Weinstein
25 Buckskin Jim the Trail Blazer	
26 Popular Science (feature)	
27 Stamps and Coins (feature)	
28 Young Homemakers (feature)	

Advertisements
International Correspondence Schools; Charles Atlas; Jowett Institute of Physical Culture; Midwest Radio Corp; U.S. School of Music; Gillette Proback Junior; Model Airplane News; Weil Company; Shav-Easy Gem Razor; Coyne Electrical School; B. Max Mehl; Cloverine Salve; Ideal Aeroplane Supply Co.; Tom Mix Ralston Purina.

First editorial
'HELLO EVERYBODY
Here's the New Magazine You've Been Waiting For! Fun speaking — stand by! all stations! I'm bringing you this first issue of *Fun* Magazine — to be followed by more and more — carrying with every issue a new cargo of mystery and thrills — come with me and I'll lead you all over the world — under the sea and up into the sky — we'll fight Indians on the Western plains — we'll strive at football and baseball and basket ball — we'll ride above the burning Sahara desert with Wing Brady — we'll follow Sandra in her courageous battles against the secret activities of sinister enemies, we'll don armor and take lance in hand and ride beside Ivanhoe through the tournaments and under the castle walls of old England, we'll jump into the Magic Crystal with Bobby and Binks and see ancient Egypt and Babylonia, hear the thunder of the tread of Alexander's marching phalanxes, see the Roman legions battling against the barbarians — we'll come back and ride the waves in Cap'n Erik's good ship — we'll dive under the sea with the Super Police — we'll flash through space with Don Drake and see strange planets and weird people — folks! — we'll go places and do things — and we'll chuckle at Judge Perkins and Loco Luke and the rest of the cock-eyed crew of cuckoo birds.
Now hear ye! Hear ye! Hear ye! I, Fun, known as Fun the Fantastic — do hereby make, appoint and commission each and every one of you as assistant editors of this reckless, rollicking and revivifying magazine — and do hereby command you to get on the job and write me telling me how you like it and vicey-versey — and telling moreover the good ideas you have and the good jokes that the rest of us might enjoy and sending in the funny drawings that we might laugh at — don't be a tightwad and keep good things to yourselves — and I, Fun, known as Fun the Fantastic, do hereby promise that each and every issue of this magazine will be bigger and better and more chockful of fun — and if you do your share and tell your friends about *Fun* — I'll promise — *muy pronto* — as Loco Luke would say — to bring you a new *Fun* every week instead of one a month! What do you think of that?'

This monthly tabloid-size comic book is credited with being the founding father of the National Comics–Superman D.C. line of comic books, which continues to be a leading comic book company to this day. It was created by Major Malcolm Wheeler-Nicholson, an ex-officer of the U.S. Cavalry turned pulp magazine fiction writer. His original intention was to form a syndicate of new serial and series strips for Sunday newspaper syndication, but finding this scheme too expensive to mount successfully, Wheeler-Nicholson collated the material into a regular comic book. After six issues had used up the tabloid-designed material, Wheeler-Nicholson relaunched the comic in a smaller format under the new title of *More Fun*. A mint copy of No. 1 is valued at $5,600 in the Overstreet *Comic Book Price Guide* for 1989.

361 Gilmore Cub

No. 1: April 1935. Free (promotional). 8 pp. 15½×21½. Publisher: Gilmore Oil Co., Los Angeles.

Contents of No. 1
1 (R) Strange As It Seems	John Hix
2 Coloring Contest	
3 (R) Strange As It Seems	John Hix
4 The Gilmore Red Lion Circus	John Hix
6 Gilmore's Puzzle Page	John Hix
7 (R) Famous People John Hix	
8 (R) Record Breakers	John HIx

Advertisements
Gilmore Red Lion Gasoline; Lion Head Motor Oil.

First editorial
'JOHN HIX SAYS LEARN TO DRAW
Boys and girls — learn to draw! Everybody should know how. It's great fun learning, too. Just to help you I've started color drawings of the Gilmore Lion and the Lion Head Motor Oil Can — but they aren't done yet. You have to finish them by coloring them the way you think best. Use crayon or water colors — it doesn't make any difference. Just be careful not to make the colors too heavy, or let them run over the edges where you don't want them. Then mail completed sketch to me in care of the Gilmore Oil Company, Los Angeles — and if it's one of the winners you'll get your award right away. The names and addresses of all the boys and girls who win awards will be published in a future issue of the *Gilmore Cub*. Watch for them.'

Broadsheet-size comic published to promote the use of Gilmore Oil, mostly compiled from the Sunday feature pages drawn by John Hix, syndicated by the McNaught Syndicate, but with some special material by the artist. Full colour on pages 1, 3, 4, 5 only, the rest being black-and-white.

362 The Big Book of Fun Comics

October 1935. 10¢. 52 pp. 10¼×15. Publisher: National Allied Publications (Malcolm Wheeler-Nicholson); 49 West 45th Street, New York. Editor: Lloyd Jacquet.

Contents
Compilation of strips reprinted from the first four issues of *New Fun*. As such it is considered to be the first comic book 'annual', and the first in the D.C. Comics canon. Cardboard covers with specially drawn cover in four colours, printed on front and back; blank inside covers (no advertisements). Not priced on cover, but sold at 10¢ in F.W. Woolworth stores, rather than on newsstands. Numbered 'Series 1' but no further editions published.

363 Mickey Mouse and Minnie March to Macy's

December 1935. Free (promotional). 144 pp. 3¼×3½. Publisher: Whitman Publishing Co., Racine, Wisconsin.

Contents
Small comic book with text in the style of the *Big Little Books*, but with a soft cover. Printed black-and-white with covers in full colour. Produced as a promotion for Macy's Toyland.

364 Mickey Mouse and the Magic Carpet

December 1935. Free (promotional). 144 pp. 3½×4. Publisher: Kay Kamen/Whitman Publishing Co., Racine, Wisconsin.

Contents
Small comic book with text in the style of the *Big Little Books*, but with a soft cover. Printed black-and-white with covers in full colour. Produced as a promotion for Stewart's Toyland.

365 New Comics

'The International Picture Story Magazine'
No. 1: December 1935–No. 11: December 1936. 10¢. 84 pp. (1–5); 68 pp. (6–11). Publisher: National Allied Newspaper Syndicate Inc. (Malcolm Wheeler-Nicholson), 420 De Soto Avenue, St. Louis, Missouri. Editorial: 373 Fourth Avenue, New York; Malcolm Wheeler-Nicholson (editor); Vincent A. Sullivan (assistant); William H. Cook (managing); John F. Mahon (business manager).

Title changed to *New Adventure Comics* from No. 12.

Contents of No. 1

1 Cover	Vincent Sullivan
3 Editorial: 'Salute!'	
4 Now When I Was a Boy	Leo O'Mealia
6 Sir Loin of Beef	R.G. Leffingwell
8 Billy the Kid	Whitney Ellsworth
10 Sagebrush 'n' Cactus	R.G. Leffingwell
14 The Vikings	Rolland Livingstone
16 J. Worthington Blimp Esq.	Sheldon Mayer
20 The Tinker Twins at Penn Point	Joe Archibald (BW)
22 Sawbones C.O.D. (story)	Joe Archibald (BW)
27 It's Magic (feature)	Andrini the Great (BW)
28 Petey the Pup (story)	Constance Naar (BW)
30 Needles	Al Stahl
32 Dizzy and Daffy (jokes)	Bo Brown
33 17–20 in the Black	Tom Cooper, Billy Weston (BW)
36 Just Suppose	H.C. Kiefer, A.D. Kiefer (BW)
38 Cartoon Corner: Pen Lines	Stanley (BW)
39 The Pixie Puzzle Adventures	Matt Curzon (BW)
40 Chikko Chakko	Ellis Edwards (BW)

115

42 Gulliver's Travels	Walter Kelly
44 Freddie Bell, He Means Well	Matt Curzon (BW)
46 Sister and Brother	Emma C. McKean (BW)
47 Bunco Bear	Dave Ruth (BW)
48 The Travel Twins (cut-out)	Emma C. McKean (BW)
49 Fun for All: A Test for Eye and Wit	Emma C. McKean (BW)
50 Wing Walker	Thor (BW)
54 Cap'n Spinniker	Tom Cooper
56 Stamps and Coins (feature) (BW)	
58 Hobbies (feature)	Danny Ryan (BW)
60 Sports (feature)	Joe Archibald (BW)
61 They Started Young	Joe Archibald (BW)
62 Worthwhile Films to Watch For (feature)	Josephine Craig (BW)
63 The Book Shelf (feature)	Constance Naar (BW)
64 Captain Quick	John Elby (BW)
66 Jibby Jones	Vincent Sullivan
68 The Strange Adventures of Mr. Weed	Sheldon Mayer
72 Ray and Gail	Clemens Gretter
74 Allan de Beaufort	Rafael Astarita
78 Dickie Duck	Matt Curzon
80 Peter and Ho-lah-an	Rolland Livingstone
82 It's a Dern Lie	R.G. Leffingwell

Advertisements
Gilbert Sets; Meccano Sets; Little Miss Muffet Sets; Shirley Temple Doll (all Pastime Novelty Co., 373 Fourth Avenue, New York).

First editorial
'SALUTE!
Hello! Here we are with the first number of *New Comics* — the International Picture Story Magazine. Here's something you have always wanted — eighty pages packed and jammed with new comic features, written and drawn especially for *New Comics* — never printed before anywhere. Here is a magazine of picturized stories chock full of laughter and thrills, comic characters of every hue, knights and Vikings of ancient days, adventuring heroes, detectives, aviator daredevils of today and hero supermen of the days to come! We know that your eyes won't suffer from strain while you enjoy these clearly drawn pictures and the large readable text, but we can't guarantee that you won't strain your ribs from laughter at the antics of these comic characters. Also, we'll guarantee that no matter how wise you are, there are heaps of things you will learn about this wide world and its people and their histories every time you read through a copy of *New Comics Magazine*. So climb aboard and rise with us every month through Eighty Pages of wit and humor, drama and thrills. Laughter is the universal antidote for the blues. Be a *New Comics* booster. Yours in command, The Editors.'

New Comics No. 1 was the first American comic book proper in that it followed the format pioneered by *Famous Funnies* with a page size of $7\frac{1}{4}$ inches by 10, but introduced all-original comic strips especially drawn for the magazine. Certain refinements remained: its cover was on the same newsprint paper stock as the inside pages until No. 7 (August 1936), and the page count did not become the regular 68 until No. 6 (July 1936). Regular characters introduced in later issues include

The Federal Men by Jerome Siegel and Joe Shuster (No. 2), A Tale of Two Cities by Merna Gamble (No. 4), Maginnis of the Mounties by J.C. Leonard (No. 4), Dale Daring by Ryan (No. 4), Captain Bill of the Texas Rangers by Homer Fleming (No. 4), Steve Conrad on Dolorosa Isle by Creig Flessel (No. 5) Sandor and the Lost Civilization by Homer Fleming (No. 5), She by H. Rider Haggard and Sven Elven (No. 6), The Golden Dragon by Tom Hickey (No. 6), and The Blood Pearls by Malcolm Wheeler-Nicholson and Munson Paddock (No. 8). The increase in adventure strip content over comic strip content is reflected in the change of title to *New Adventure Comics* from No. 12. A mint copy of No. 1 is valued at $2,625 in Overstreet's 1989 *Comic Book Price Guide*.

366 Mickey Mouse Magazine

Vol. 1, No. 1: Summer 1935–Vol. 5, No. 12: September 1940. 25¢; 10¢. 44 pp. 36 pp. 10×13; 8^1/$_4$×11^1/$_2$; 7^1/$_2$×10^1/$_4$ (Vol. 5, No. 9–No. 12). Publisher: Hal Horne Inc., 551 Fifth Avenue, New York. Editorial: Hal Horne (editor); Irving Brecher, A. Lipscott (associate editors).

Title changed to *Walt Disney's Comics and Stories* from October 1940.

Contents of No. 1
 1 Cover
 2 Table of Contents
 3 Jokes
 4 'Sno Use
 5 Dot's Dot
 6 Professor Goof's Useful Inventions
 7 Mickey and the Corn Storks (story)
10 Didja Ever Try; Didja Ever See
11 Color Up This Page
12 All Us in Blunderland
14 Now for School
16 Crossword Puzzle
17 Around the Clock with Mickey
18 Mimickey Mickey
19 Let's Draw Minnie
20 Taking the Blunders Out of Blunderland
21 A Good Sport
22 The Fun Book Frolics
24 Donald Duck's Bootblock-Heads
25 Lost by a Hare (story)
28 Over the Mickeyphone
29 Jest Jingles
30 Side Show
32 Treasure Smile-Land (story)
35 Do You Know
36 Pluto the Pup's Barkin' Counter
38 Horacescope
40 Hi Diddle Diddle

117

Advertisements
Kolynos Dental Cream; Mickey Mouse Ties (D.H. Neumann Co.); Junior Literary Guild; Mickey Mouse Hand Car (Lionel Corporation); Post Toasties (General Foods).

'A Fun-Book for Boys and Girls to Read to Grown-ups', this was the third series to bear the title *Mickey Mouse Magazine*. It was certainly more a magazine for children than a comic book, although the first issue was printed throughout in full colour. No. 1 was also listed as a quarterly publication, dated Summer (June–August) 1935, but an editorial announcement stated that the magazine would be going monthly from the second issue (subscription $2.50 for 12 issues). The page size was also reduced from 10×13 inches to 8¼×11½, the page count from 44 to 36, and interior printing reduced from four colours to two (red/black, green/black, blue/black). The publisher changed from Hal Horne Inc. to Kay Kamen Ltd., with offices shifted from 551 Fifth Avenue to 1270 Sixth Avenue, New York City. Reprints of the Sunday supplement strip of Mickey Mouse (drawn by Floyd Gottfredson) began in Vol. 2, No. 1, going into full colour from No. 10, when alternate interior pages began to be printed in four colours. The magazine reduced to regular comic book proportions (7½×10¼) from Vol. 5, No. 9 (June 1940) and was so successful that after three more issues *Mickey Mouse Magazine* was discontinued and a new series begun, *Walt Disney's Comics and Stories*, Vol. 2, No. 1 (October 1940). An 'autographed first edition' of *Mickey Mouse Magazine* No. 1 was given away to all 1936 subscribers. A mint copy of No. 1 is valued at $980 in Overstreet's 1989 *Comic Book Price Guide*.

367 Blondie and Dagwood

1936 (No. L 21). 15¢. 94 pp. 5×7½. Publisher: Lynn Publishing Co., New York. Artist: Chic Young. Syndicate: King Features.

Contents
Small book reprinting the Sunday supplement strip 'Blondie' by Chic Young, with additional narrative. Pictures are arranged one to a page and printed in full colour throughout. Board covers in full colour.

368 Butterfly Comics

'8 Pages of Leading Comics'
No. 1–No. 4 (1936). Free (promotional). 8 pp. 7½×10¼. Publisher: Butterfly Bread. Editorial: Dell Publishing Company, 149 Madison Avenue, New York.

Contents of No. 1

1 (R) Spooky		Bill Holman
2 (R) The Gumps		Sidney Smith
3 (R) Lovey Dovey; Texas Slim		Fred Johnson
4 (R) Ella and Her Fella; Jinglet		Al Posen
5 (R) Mort Green & Wife; Zipper		Gaar Williams
6 (R) Red Magic		A.W. Nugent
8 (R) Smokey Stover		Bill Holman

Advertisement
Butterfly Bread

Promotional comic given away at stores stocking Butterfly Bread, compiled from reprinted Sunday newspaper strips, already reprinted in earlier editions of *Popular Comics*. No editorial, but carries the message '8 pages of leading comics. Read them in your favorite newspaper and in *Popular Comics*, America's Favorite Comic Magazine.'

369 Buttons and Fatty in the Funnies

No. 1 (W 936): 1936. Unpriced. 28 pp. $10^1/_4 \times 15^1/_2$. Publisher: Whitman Publishing Co., Racine, Wisconsin.

Contents of No. 1
1–28 (R) Buttons and Fatty   M.E. Brady

Compilation of Sunday supplement strips copyrighted by the *Brooklyn Daily Eagle*. Undated, but with the same production number as *Lily of the Alley in the Funnies*: W 936.

370 Dick Tracy the Detective

1936. 10¢. 100 pp. $8^1/_2 \times 11^1/_2$. Publisher: David McKay Co., 604 Washington Avenue, Philadelphia. Artist: Chester Gould. Syndicate: Chicago Tribune–New York News.

Contents
Compilation of daily newspaper strips, printed in black-and-white and arranged one and a half strips to the page. The strips are copyright 1935 by the Chicago Tribune–N.Y. News Syndicate. When the publishers, David McKay, introduced their *Feature Book* series of monthly comic books in May 1937, *Dick Tracy the Detective* was reprinted as No. 4, with a different cover drawing (not by the artist, Chester Gould). The book was also reprinted as a limited facsimile edition by Tony Raiola in 1982.

371 Dumb Dora and Bing Brown

1936 (No. L 24). 15¢. 94 pp. $5 \times 7^1/_2$. Publisher: Lynn Publishing Co., New York. Artist: Bill Dwyer. Syndicate: King Features.

Contents
Small book reprinting the Sunday supplement strip 'Dumb Dora' by Bill Dwyer, with additional text narrative by Gerald Breitigam. Pictures are arranged one to a page and printed in full colour throughout. Board covers in full colour.

372 Forty Big Pages of Mickey Mouse

1936 (No. 945). 44 pp. $10^1/_4 \times 12^1/_2$. Publisher: Whitman Publishing Co., Racine, Wisconsin.

Contents
Reprint of No. 1 of *Mickey Mouse Magazine*, excluding its original cover and advertisement pages, and bound in specially drawn cardboard covers.

373 Krim-Ko Comics

No. 1: 1936–No. 184: 1939. Free (promotional). 4 pp. Publisher: Krim-Ko Inc.

Contents
Promotional comic published to encourage children to drink Krim-Ko Chocolate Drink. A new edition was given away every week. This four-page comic featured original strips specially drawn by various artists, and included 'Lola, Secret Agent' among the characters.

374 Lilly of the Alley in the Funnies

No. 1 (W 936): 1936. Unpriced. 28 pp. 10¼×15½. Publisher: Whitman Publishing Co., Racine, Wisconsin.

Contents of No. 1
1–28 (R) Lilly of the Alley   T. Burke

Compilation of Sunday supplement strips, lacking syndication information. Undated, but with the same production number as *Buttons and Fatty in the Funnies*: W 936. The strips may date from the 1920s as there is internal reference to 'Lindy' (Lindbergh).

375 Popeye and the Jeep

1936. 10¢. 100 pp. 8½×11½. Publisher: David McKay Co., 604 Washington Avenue, Philadelphia. Artist: E.C. Segar. Syndicate: King Features.

Contents
Compilation of daily newspaper strips, printed in black-and-white and arranged one and a half strips to the page. The strips are copyright 1936 by King Features Syndicate. When the publishers, David McKay, introduced their *Feature Book* series of monthly comic books in May 1937, *Popeye and the Jeep* was reprinted as No. 3, with a different cover drawing (not by the artist, Elzie Segar). The book was also reprinted as a limited facsimile edition by Tony Raiola in 1982.

376 Pure Oil Comics

1936. Free (promotional). 24 pp. 7½×10¼. Publisher: Eastern Color Printing Co., 40 Church Street, New York.

Contents
Reprint of selected pages from *Famous Funnies*, including 'Buck Rogers' by Dick Calkins, 'Hairbreadth Harry' by F.O. Alexander, 'Napoleon' by Clifford McBride, 'Olly of the Movies' by Julian Ollendorff, etc. Produced as a promotional giveaway for the Pure Oil Company.

377 Salerno Carnival of Comics

1936. Free (promotional). 16 pp. $7^{1}/_{2} \times 10^{1}/_{4}$. Publisher: Eastern Color Printing Co., 40 Church Street, New York.

Contents
Reprint of selected pages from *Famous Funnies*, including 'Buck Rogers' by Dick Calkins. Produced as a promotional giveaway for the Salerno Cookie Company.

378 Strange As It Seems

1936. Free (promotional). 24 pp. 5×7. Publisher: Ex-Lax Co. Artist: John Hix. Syndicate: McNaught.

Contents
Compilation of the Sunday newspaper feature, reprinted in black-and-white. Published as a promotional giveaway by Ex-Lax laxative chocolate.

379 Tarzan Ice Cream Premium Comicbooks (Series One)

1936. Free (promotional). 128 pp. $3^{3}/_{4} \times 3^{1}/_{2}$. Publisher: Whitman Publishing Co., Racine, Wisconsin.

No. 1 *Tarzan and His Jungle Friends*	Edgar Rice Burroughs
No. 2 *Smitty and Herby*	Walter Berndt
No. 3 *Dick Tracy Meets a New Gang*	Chester Gould
No. 5 *Chester Gump and His Friends*	Sidney Smith
No. 6 *Wash Tubbs' Foreign Travels*	Roy Crane
No. 7 *Tailspin Tommy's Perilous Adventure*	Hal Forrest
No. 8 *Little Mary Mixup Wins a Prize*	Robert Brinkerhoff
No. 9 *Dan Dunn's Mysterious Ride*	Norman Marsh
No. 10 *Terry and the Pirates Meet Again*	Milton Caniff
No. 11 *Ella Cinders' Exciting Experience*	Charlie Plumb

Series of twelve small comic books reprinting pictures from daily newspaper strips. Soft covers in full colour, black-and-white interiors. The stories are told in text on the left-hand pages in the style of *Big Little Books*. Produced by Whitman for the Lily-Tulip Corporation, who gave them away in return for twelve cup lids from their Tarzan ice-cream. A second series was published in 1938. *Note:* only those books adapted from comics have been included in the above list.

380 Vicks Comics

1936. Free (promotional). 68 pp. $7^{1}/_{2} \times 10^{1}/_{4}$. Publisher: Eastern Color Printing Co., 40 Church Street, New York.

Contents
Reprint of selected pages from *Famous Funnies* Nos. 15 and 16, including 'Buck Rogers' by Dick Calkins. Produced as a promotional giveaway for the Vicks Chemical Company.

381 Your Favorite Comics

No. 1: 1936–. 10¢. 68 pp. $7^1/_2 \times 10^1/_4$.

Contents of No. 1

1 Cover	
3 (R) Little Orphan Annie; Maw Green	Harold Gray
7 (R) Dick Tracy	Chester Gould
9 (R) Believe It or Not	Robert L. Ripley
10 (R) Gasoline Alley	Frank King
11 (R) Nugent's Original Puzzles	A.W. Nugent
12 (R) Believe It or Not	Robert L. Ripley
13 (R) Bronc Peeler; On the Range	Fred Harman
14 (R) Terry and the Pirates	Milton Caniff
15 (R) Tom Mix the Fighting Cowboy	
16 The Popular Stamp Club (feature)	Montgomery Mulford
17 (R) Winnie Winkle; Looie	Martin Branner
18 (R) Ginger (Meggs)	James Bancks
19 (R) Spooky	Bill Holman
20 (R) The Gumps	Sidney Smith
21 (R) Lovey Dovey; Texas Slim	Fred Johnson
22 (R) Ella and Her Fella; Jinglet	Al Posen
23 (R) Zipper	Bill Holman
24 (R) Don Winslow; Bos'n Hal	Frank Martinek, Leon Beroth
25 (R) Tailspin Tommy; How to Fly	Hal Forrest
27 (R) Spooky	Bill Holman
28 (R) Little Orphan Annie; Maw Green	Harold Gray
29 (R) Winnie Winkle; Looie	Martin Branner
30 (R) The Gumps	Sidney Smith
31 (R) Jinglet	Al Posen
32 (R) Dick Tracy	Chester Gould
33 (R) The Gumps	Sidney Smith
34 (R) Don Winslow; Bos'n Hal	Frank Martinek, Leon Beroth
35 (R) Harold Teen	Carl Ed
36 (R) Little Joe	Ed Leffingwell
37 (R) Little Folks	Tack Knight
38 (R) Gasoline Alley	Frank King
39 (R) Little Joe	Ed Leffingwell
40 (R) Winnie Winkle; Looie	Martin Branner
41 (R) Pam	Brewerton
43 (R) Smitty; Herby	Walter Berndt
44 (R) Moon Mullins; Kitty Higgins	Frank Willard

45 (R) Gasoline Alley	Frank King
46 (R) Bronc Peeler; On the Range	Fred Harman
47 (R) Mort Green & Wife	Gaar Williams
48 (R) Red Magic	A.W. Nugent
50 (R) Smokey Stover	Bill Holman
51 (R) Life's Little Tragedies	Frank Beck
52 Bertie at the Banquet (story)	Chet Grant
54 (R) Streaky	Gus Edson
55 (R) Don Winslow; Bos'n Hal	Frank Martinek, Leon Beroth
57 (R) Believe It or Not	Robert L. Ripley
58 (R) Real Magic	A.W. Nugent
59 (R) Little Joe	Ed Leffingwell
60 (R) Believe It or Not	Robert L. Ripley
61 (R) Little Folks	Tack Knight
62 (R) Harold Teen	Carl Ed
63 (R) Sweeney & Son; Jinglet	Al Posen
64 (R) Major Cosmo Strange DSO	George Baker
66 (R) Mort Green & Wife	Gaar Williams

This unnumbered, undated, and uncredited (to a publisher) comic book consists of a miscellany of reprint pages bound into a crudely drawn cover printed in two colours, red and black. The legend at the bottom reads: 'Compiled of Previously Published Comics Recovered'. The contents are 32 pages of material from No. 4 of *Popular Comics* (May 1936) plus 32 pages consisting of issues numbered 1 to 4 of *Butterfly Comics*, a giveaway promotional comic for Butterfly Bread.

382 More Fun (formerly New Fun)

'The National Comics Magazine'
No. 7: January 1936–No. 127: November 1947. 10¢. 44 pp. (7; 8); 68 pp. (9–). $9^3/_4 \times 11^1/_2$ (7; 8); $7^1/_4 \times 10$ (9–). Publisher: More Fun Magazine Inc. (Malcolm Wheeler-Nicholson), 420 De Soto Avenue, St. Louis, Missouri. Editorial: 373 Fourth Avenue, New York; Malcolm Wheeler-Nicholson (editor); William H. Cook (managing); Vincent A. Sullivan (assistant); John F. Mahon (business manager).

Contents of No. 7 (first issue)

1 Little Linda	Whitney Ellsworth
3 Sandra of the Secret Service	C. Brigham
4 Brad Hardy	C. Brigham
5 Don Drake on the Planet Saro	Clemens Gretter
6 In the Wake of the Wanderer	MacFergus
7 Barry O'Neill	Leo E. O'Mealia
8 Bob Merritt	Leo E. O'Mealia
9 Ivanhoe	Sir Walter Scott
10 Famous Flights	Thor
11 Shavetail (story)	Malcolm Wheeler-Nicholson (BW)
12 Movies (feature) (BW)	
13 Oswald the Rabbit	Al Stahl (BW)

14 Stamps and Coins (feature); Fanny — Vincent Sullivan (BW)
15 Fun Mail (feature) (BW)
16 Skipper Hicks — John Patterson (BW)
17 Sports (feature) — Joe Archibald (BW)
18 Buckskin Jim — Tom Cooper (BW)
19 Slim Pickins — Stan Randall (BW)
20 The Professor — E.F. Koscik (BW)
21 Along the Main Line — Tom Cooper (BW)
22 Charley Fish — Vincent Sullivan (BW)
23 Down by the Old Mill Stream — Walt Kelly (BW)
24 Wing Brady — Henry Kiefer (BW)
25 Henri Duval — Jerome Siegel, Joe Shuster (BW)
26 More Fun and Magic — Dick Loederer (BW)
27 Books; Learn to Be a Cartoonist — Charles Shows (BW)
28 Shavetail (continued) (BW)
29 Doctor Occult the Ghost Detective — Jerome Siegel, Joe Shuster (BW)
30 Join the Treasure Hunt Contest — C. Brigham (BW)
31 Rambler Jim — Stan Randall (BW)
32 Puzzle Page — Matt Curzon (BW)
33 Junior Funsters (feature) — Connie Naar (BW)
34 Oscar (BW)
35 Jack Woods — C. Brigham
36 Magic Crystal of History — Ray Wardel
37 Treasure Island — Charles Flanders
38 Spike Spalding — Vincent Sullivan
39 Little Linda — Whitney Ellsworth
40 Midshipman Dewey — Tom Cooper
41 Pelion and Ossa — Al Stahl
42 2023 Super Police — Clemens Gretter

Advertisements
Meccano; Gilbert Chemistry Sets; Steen's Magic Factory; Remington Noiseless Portable Typewriter.

First editorial (No. 7)
'FUN MAIL
Here comes your magazine in a slightly different shape — but with all the old favorites in new and even more exciting adventures. Don't you like this size better? And isn't it easier to handle? No more will it slip awkwardly out of your hands like an overgrown puppy. Each month, you see, we are trying to improve *Fun*, for "Bigger and Better *Fun*" is our motto. And that we're succeeding in making it the "best magazine ever" seems to be the decision of our readers. You should see the bundles and bundles of letters the postmen bring us. Why, there are so many that if we sat down and answered every one we would have to work day and night. And then where would *Fun* be? Let's see what a few of them say. But first for an important announcement, especially for searchers in the Treasure Hunt. In the October copy of *Fun* the coupon for Cartoons 10–12 read: "Mail this coupon not later than September 30." Well, that was a mistake in the composing room. It should have said not later than October 30, for how in the world could we expect your cartoons and coupon before some of you even got the magazine? So-O-o-O-o-O. as the Fire Chief would say, if any of you boys and girls failed to

send in your fourth set of cartoons in the Treasure Hunt because you thought you were no longer in line for a prize, send them in with your fifth set, printed in this issue, and they'll be accepted.

And now for some of your letters. E.E. Wandry, of Minneapolis, Minnesota, writes: "Would you please send me a copy of your publication, *Fun*, Vo. 1 No. 1, to enable me to keep a complete set? Your publication is a splendid one and merits its weight in gold. I hope you will have great success." These are certainly welcome words, and we only wish we could find a single copy of that first issue. But it was entirely sold out, and we haven't even a torn copy to send you. All of which means that the wise reader of *Fun* will subscribe to it, so that even if the newsdealers sell every copy they have on the very first day — as many of them do — you'll have your copy anyway. Nothing like being prepared . . . Your pal, Fun.'

The change of title from *New Fun* to *More Fun*, and the reduction in page size from $10^1/_4 \times 15$ to $9^3/_4 \times 11^1/_2$, was followed by a further size reduction to $7^1/_4 \times 10$, with issue No. 9 dated March–April 1936. This brought the comic book into line with Major Wheeler-Nicholson's more successful *New Comics*, and to mark the change of format, the following editorial was printed:

'HELLO AGAIN!

Here's the very latest issue of your old friend, *More Fun*, doing business at the same old stands, and just as chock full of comics, thrills and adventures as ever! Notice anything different about us? Yessir, we've had our face lifted. So many people wrote in asking for *More Fun* in a smaller, handier size that we all had to go into a huddle and admit that they were right, as the customer always is. This issue is our answer; smaller on the outside, but bigger than ever inside. Everything between these two covers is brand new, never before published. All the pictures, type and lettering are clear and legible — no eye-strain reading about the adventures of the heroes that flash across the pages of *More Fun*. We know you're going to enjoy these pages, crammed with the kind of brand new features that have made *More Fun* such a sensational favorite, so don't let us keep you. Thanks for listening! Yours, The Editors.'

With this ninth issue the title on the cover became *More Fun Comics*, but the book continued to be printed on newsprint paper throughout, a brighter, slick paper cover not being introduced until No. 12 (August 1936). Among the regular characters introduced during the comic book's long run are:

No. 11 The Three Musketeers	Sven Elven
No. 11 Calling All Cars (Radio Squad)	Jerome Siegel, Joe Shuster
No. 12 Pep Morgan at Riverdale	Creig Flessel
No. 12 Pirate Gold	Sven Elven
No. 14 The Bradley Boys in the Wilderness	Creig Flessel
No. 13 Mark Marson of the Interplanetary Police	Tom Hickey
Johnnie Law	Will Ely
No. 30 Hope Hazard	Alexander Nickitin
No. 30 Hooves of the Tarter Horde	
No. 32 Marg'ry Daw	Stan Asch
No. 32 The Buccaneer	Bernard Baily
No. 32 Cap'n Jerry and the New Guinea Cannibals	R.A. Burley
No. 32 Ginger Snap	Bob Kane
No. 36 The Masked Ranger	Jim Chambers
Detective Sergeant Carey	Joe Donohoe

Gary Hawkes	Rob Jenney
No. 40 Rex Darrell (The Flying Fox)	Terry Gilkison
Red Coat Patrol	John W. Hampton
No. 45 Cal an' Alec	Fred Schwab
No. 46 Lieut. Bob Neal in Peril	B. Hirsch, R. Lehman
No. 52 The Specter	Bernard Baily
No. 55 Doctor Fate	Howard Sherman
No. 56 Congo Bill	
No. 68 Clip Carson	
No. 71 Johnny Quick	Mort Morton Jr.
No. 73 Aquaman	Paul Norris
No. 73 Green Arrow and Speedy	George Papp
No. 101 Superboy	
No. 108 Genius Jones	Stan Kaye
No. 121 Jimminy and the Magic Book	Howard Post

Major Malcolm Wheeler-Nicholson lost control of his comic book publishing empire after the publication of No. 29 dated February 1938. There was a month's delay, then No. 30 came out dated March–April with the changed indicia: 'Published by A.I. Menon, Receiver Nicholson Publishing Co. Inc.'. By the June issue (No. 32) the new indicia read: 'Published by Detective Comics Inc., 420 De Soto Avenue, St. Louis, Missouri'. This was the same address as Nicholson's, but the editorial offices were now given as 480 Lexington Avenue, New York. Vincent A. Sullivan was named as editor.

383 Popular Comics

'America's Favorite Funnies'
No. 1: February 1936–No. 145: July 1948. 10¢. 68 pp. 7½×10¼. Publisher: Dell Publishing Co. (George T. Delacorte Jr.), 149 Madison Avenue, New York. Editorial: Max C. Gaines (editor); Sheldon Mayer (art editor).

Contents of No. 1

1 Cover	
(R) Always Belittlin'; Skippy	Percy Crosby
(R) Reg'lar Fellers; Daisybelle	Gene Byrnes
(R) Little Orphan Annie: Maw Green	Harold Gray
(R) Smilin' Jack	Zack Mosley
(R) Moon Mullins; Kitty Higgins	Frank Willard
(R) Dick Tracy	Chester Gould
(R) Believe It or Not	Robert L. Ripley
(R) Gasoline Alley	Frank King
(R) Real Magic	A.W. Nugent
(R) The Gumps	Sidney Smith
(R) Bronc Peeler; On the Range	Fred Harman
(R) Terry and the Pirates	Milton Caniff
(R) Harold Teen	Carl Ed
(R) Winnie Winkle; Looie	Martin Branner

(R) Ella and her Fella; Jinglet	Al Posen
(R) Lovey Dovey; Texas Slim	Fred Johnson
(R) Streaky	Gus Edson
(R) Ben Webster's Page	Edwin Alger
(R) Don Winslow U.S.N.; Bosun Hal	Frank Martinek, Leon Beroth
(R) A Strain on the Family Tie	Gaar Williams
(R) Little Joe	Ed Leffingwell
(R) Little Folks; Baby Sister	Tack Knight
(R) Smokey Stover	Bill Holman
(R) Smitty; Herby	Walter Berndt
(R) Skull Valley	Garrett Price
(R) Mort Green & Wife; Zipper	Gaar Williams

First editorial (No. 4)
'A WORD TO OUR READERS
With this issue, *Popular Comics*, America's newest and funniest magazine, becomes the most popular and fastest growing magazine in America! No wonder! All your favorite comic characters that you have known for years — in one big book that you can keep forever and enjoy over and over again. And we bring you lots of new ones, too — Tom Mix the fighting cowboy — Major Cosomo Strange, the scientific detective — Life's Little Tragedies — Ginger (Meggs) from far-off Australia — the Popular Stamp Club — and lots of others. Be sure to tell your dealer to reserve the next issue for you!'

Advertisements
Remington Rand Typewriters; Landon School of Cartooning; Slingo Corp. Repeating Slingshot; Packard Knee Action Bicycle (No. 4).

Compilation of newspaper strips reprinted from Sunday supplements, copyrighted by the Chicago Tribune–New York News Syndicate, King Features, Bell Syndicate, Gene Byrnes, Jay Jerome Williams. Characters introduced later in the run include Scribbly by Sheldon Mayer, Don Dixon and the Hidden Empire by Bob Moore and Carl Pfeufer (No. 7), The Nebbs and Simp O'Dill by Sol Hess and W.A. Carlson, Apple Mary and Dennis by Martha Orr, Sister Susie by Alice Harvey, Sweeney & Son by Al Posen, Herky by Clyde Lewis, Toonerville Folks by Fontaine Fox, The Mountain Boys by Paul Webb, Tailspin Tommy by Hal Forrest, Mutt and Jeff by Bud Fisher. Original strips began in 1938 and included: Shark Egan, Toby by Stan Randall, Ted Starr — Racket Buster, G-Men by Jim Gary, Zane Grey's Tex Thorne, Gang Busters, The Hurricane Kids, Ben-Hur, The Masked Pilot by Bob Jenney, Martan the Marvel Man (No. 46), The Voice (No. 51), Professor Supermind and Son (No. 60), The Owl (No. 72), and Captain Midnight (No. 76). Most of the original strips were copyrighted by either Stephen Slesinger or R.S. Callender. There were also strip adaptations of movies, including Jack Randall in 'Man's Country' (No. 34), Tex Ritter in 'Starlight over Texas' (No. 35), and Boris Karloff in 'Mr. Wong, Detective' (No. 42).

384 King Comics

No. 1: April 1936–No. 159: February 1952. 10¢. 68 pp. $7^{1}/_{2} \times 10^{1}/_{4}$. Publisher: David McKay Co., 604 South Washington Square, Philadelphia. Editorial: Ruth Plumly Thompson (editor). Distributor: International Circulation Co. Inc., 57th Street/8th Avenue, New York.

Contents of No. 1

1 Cover	Joe Musial
3 (R) Brick Bradford	William Ritt, Clarence Gray
7 (R) Bunky; Barney Google	Billy De Beck
11 (R) Solve a Jigglette	Harte
12 (R) Ming Foo; Little Annie Rooney	Brandon Walsh, Nicholas Afonsky
16 (R) Henry	Carl Anderson
18 (R) Sports Features	Jack Burnley
19 (R) Scott's Scrapbook	R.J. Scott
20 (R) Henry	Carl Anderson
22 (R) Radio Patrol	Eddie Sullivan, Charlie Schmidt
26 (R) Scott's Scrapbook	R.J. Scott
27 (R) Mandrake the Magician	Lee Falk, Phil Davis
31 (R) Curley Harper; Tim Tyler's Luck	Lyman Young
35 (R) Sappo; Thimble Theatre	Elzie Segar
39 (R) Jungle Jim; Flash Gordon	Alex Raymond
43 (R) Sport Features	Jack Burnley
44 (R) The G-Man	George Clarke, Lou Hanlon
48 (R) Rosie's Beau; Bringing Up Father	George McManus
50 (R) Scott's Scrapbook	R.J. Scott
51 (R) Sport Features	Jack Burnley
52 (R) Rosie's Beau; Bringing Up Father	George McManus
59 (R) Ted Towers, Animal Master	Frank Buck, Glen Cravath
63 (R) King of the Royal Mounted	Zane Grey, Allen Dean

First editorial (No. 4)

'Hello and Aho My Hearties! Ever had a letter from a King before? Well, get set, for here it comes and the Old King of *King Comics* who's writing this one — is looking straight at you and hoping you'll write to him. Hah — "Dear King — " I can almost see myself reading those letters — "Dear King — " though most of my friends call me Jo. For I am Jo King and I'm not joking and you'll have to figure out that one for yourself. But if you think being a King isn't fun, you should spend your days as I do with all these merry rascals down here. If you want to go up, I step into a plane and travel with Ace Drummond; if I want to go down, Brick Bradford's my man. If I feel like big game hunting, there's Ted Towers and Jungle Jim, or if sleuthing is the program for the day, there's King of the Mounties and the Radio Patrol. I have a High Horse to take me about, but often he's balky. Then I ride out with the Little King and that's bound to be comical. After a lively visit with Mandrake or Flash, just for a change I take Henry and Little Annie Rooney to the zoo. The last time I did, Henry tied two monkeys' tails together and I had to give the Guard my crown before we could get away. Still, it's things like this that keep a King young and cheerful. Sometimes when the Royal Cook is in a huff, I have to lunch with Maggie and Father or drop in at Wimpy's to talk to Pop-Eye. The Sailor Man and I are great chums. I've even named my dog Pop-Eye, the little beggar's so fond of spinach it seemed the only name for him. Tell me about your dog when you write. That's the kind of news I like to hear and tell me which of the King Comics you enjoy most. And next to the comics, what do you like best, more stories — science — puzzles — sports? Just tell the Old King and he'll see that you get it — but hello — there's Flash calling for advice on his campaign against Ming of Mongo — I'll have to run — but not before I wish you thirty days of good weather and Fun. In a hurry — but — Merrily Me, Jo King.'

128

Monthly compilation of Sunday supplement strips copyrighted by King Features Syndicate. The only original artwork was by Joe Musial, the King staff artist responsible for the covers. By No. 4 a text story was introduced, written by Ruth Plumly Thompson, famous as the authoress who continued L. Frank Baum's *Wizard of Oz* series. These were illustrated by Marge Henderson Buell, later the creator of 'Little Lulu'. The two also produced a series of full-page illustrations for the comic entitled 'Sis Sez'. Other strips introduced later include 'Barney Baxter in the Air' by Frank Miller (No. 43), 'The Lone Ranger' by Fran Striker (No. 50), and 'The Phantom' by Lee Falk and Ray Moore (No. 61). Unsold copies of the early issues had their dated covers removed, and were recovered in exceedingly cheap and ill-drawn covers, unnumbered and undated, for resale as remainders and as export editions.

385 Tip Top Comics

'Over 100 Funnies'
No. 1: April 1936–No. 225: May 1961. 10¢. 68 pp. Publisher: United Feature Syndicate Inc., 220 East 42nd Street, New York. Editorial: William Laas (editor); Harold Corbin (managing editor).

Contents of No. 1

1 Cover	Mo Leff
2 (R) Tarzan	Hal Foster
3 (R) Li'l Abner; Washable Jones	Al Capp
7 (R) Tarzan	Hal Foster
10 (R) Grin and Bear It	George Lichty
11 (R) Chris Crusty; Ella Cinders	Bill Conselman, Charlie Plumb
14 (R) How it Began; Of All Things	Paul Berdanier
15 (R) Broncho Bill; Bumps	Harry O'Neill
19 (R) Hawkshaw; The Captain and the Kids	Bernard Dibble
22 Join the Tip Top Cartoonists Club (feature)	
24 (R) Phil Fumble; Fritzi Ritz	Ernie Bushmiller
26 (R) Grin and Bear It	George Lichty
27 (R) Looy Dot Dope; Colonel Wowser	Johnny Devlin
30 (R) Freddie & Fritz; For Junior Readers	Dudley T. Fisher Jr.
31 (R) All in the Family; Little Mary Mixup	Robert Brinkerhoff
34 The Boys of Wynnecastle (story)	Dan Chadwick; Melvin Hodla
36 (R) Divot Diggers; Joe Jinks	Vic Forsythe
39 (R) Hawkshaw; The Captain and the Kids	Bernard Dibble
40 (R) Cynical Susie	Becky Sharp, LaVerne Harding
43 (R) Danny Dingle; Dub Dabs	Bernard Dibble
46 Make Your Own Movies (feature)	
48 (R) Peter Pat; Percy Penguin	Mo Leff
50 (R) How It Began; Of All Things	Paul Berdanier
51 (R) Billy Make Believe; How To Make It	H.E. Homan
54 How To Draw Comics (feature)	Robert Brinkerhoff
56 (R) Grin and Bear It	George Lichty
57 (R) Bucky & His Pals; Mr. & Mrs. Beans	Robert L. Dickey
60 (R) Freddie & Fritz; For Junior Readers	Dudley T. Fisher Jr.

61 (R) Alice in Wonderland; Knurl the Gnome   Olive Scott, Ed Keukes
64 (R) Opportunity Knox; Benny; Cat Tales   J. Carver Pusey
67 (R) Grin and Bear It   George Lichty
68 (R) Chris Crusty; Ella Cinders   Bill Conselman, Charlie Plumb

Advertisements
None in the early issues; Johnson Smith & Co. (No. 4); Daisy Air Rifles (No. 5).

The first comic book to be published by United Feature Syndicate, compiled from their own strips as originally published in Sunday newspaper supplements. Later issues introduced Frankie Doodle by Ben Batsford (No. 3); The Boomers by Dick Richards (No. 4); and Jim Hardy by Dick Moores. The first original strips were introduced in No. 54 (February 1941), 'Mirror Man' and 'The Triple Terror'. Unsold issues of *Tip Top Comics* were bound up into annual volumes with special coloured board covers. Three such volumes containing numbers 1–12; 13–24; 25–36 were sold at the 1939 New York World's Fair.

386 The Comics Magazine

No. 1: May 1936. 10¢. 68 pp. Publisher: Comics Magazine Co. Inc., 1723 West 74th Street, Chicago. Editorial: 11 West 42nd Street, New York.

Title changed to *Funny Pages* from No. 2.

Contents of No. 1
1 Cover
3 Editorial: 'The Funny Pages'
4 Chikko Chakko   Ellis Edwards
6 Dr. Mystic the Occult Detective   Jerome Siegel, Joe Shuster (BW)
8 Koko   M. MacIntyre
10 Dickie Duck   Matt Curzon
12 Skinny Shaner   Tom McNamara
14 Big Sid   Stan Randall (BW)
16 Captain Bill of the Rangers   W.M. Allison
20 Behind the Curtain (story)   Wallace Kirk (BW)
24 Cap'n Tripe   Tom Cooper (BW)
26 Porkchops 'n' Gravy   Al Stahl
28 My Grandpa by Lefty Peters   Tom McNamara (BW)
30 T'aint So!   R.G. Leffingwell (BW)
31 Stamp Collecting (feature)   Prof. Phillip S. Pace (BW)
32 Junior Library (feature)   Frances Hope (BW)
34 Ridin' Point   W.M. Allison
36 The Magic Hand (feature)   Presto Merritt (BW)
38 Major Lord   Palmer (BW)
40 Skipper Ham Shanks   John Patterson (BW)
42 Evidence   R.G. Leffingwell
44 Alfy Elephant   Stan Randall (BW)

45 Shocky Plus Gus	Stan Randall (BW)
46 Learn Cartooning	John Patterson (BW)
47 Crossword Puzzle	Stanley Ashworth (BW)
48 Aeronautical Advisory Service (feature)	Raymond Clark (BW)
50 The Black Lagoon	Tom Cooper
54 Stubbie	Clyde Don (BW)
56 Strange Adventures of Mr. Weed	Sheldon Mayer
58 Freddie Bell, He Means Well	Matt Curzon
60 Spunk Hazard	Stan Randall
62 J. Worthington Blimp Esq.	Sheldon Mayer (BW)
64 Prof. Nertz	John Patterson
66 Cannonball Jones	Walt Kelly
Time Waits for No Man	Stan Randall

Advertisements
Science & Mechanics Magazine; Remington Noiseless Portable Typewriter.

First Editorial
'THE FUNNY PAGES
Presented in this magazine are all original and every one of them NEW. The creators of the features in this issue have established themselves with fans in all parts of the world. In *The Comics Magazine* we bring you, in each issue, a brand new batch of splendid adventures and screamingly humorous features. The book is brilliant with four-color reproduction and clean, sharp black-and-white. There are departments that will give you real enjoyment for your evenings. The publishers promise you that they will strive to make this the finest magazine of its kind, and they will welcome comments, criticism or praise. Write your letters to, Yours cordially, The Editors.'

For notes see following entry.

387 Funny Pages (formerly The Comics Magazine)

'The Comics Magazine'
No. 2: June 1936–No. 42: October 1940. 10¢. 68 pp. (1–21); 52 pp. (22–42). 7¼×10½. Publisher: Comics Magazine Co. Inc., 1723 West 74th Street, Chicago. Editorial: 11 West 42nd Street, New York.

Contents of No. 2 (first issue)

1 Cover	Sheldon Mayer
3 Editorial: The Funny Pages	
4 The Further Adventures of Jane and Johnny	W.M. Allison
6 Freddie Bell, He Means Well	Matt Curzon (BW)
8 Skinny Shaner	Tom McNamara
10 Koko	M. MacIntyre
12 Porkchops 'n' Gravy	Al Stahl
14 Capt. Tripe	Tom Cooper (BW)
16 Federal Agent	Jerome Siegel, Joe Shuster
20 The Son of a Gun Comes Through (story)	Wallace Kirk (BW)

23 Alfy Elephant	Stan Randall (BW)
24 T'aint So!	R.G. Leffingwell (BW)
25 The Golden Idol	Tom Cooper
33 Stamp Collectors (feature)	Phillip Pace (BW)
34 The Round-Up	W.M. Allison
36 Junior Library (feature)	Frances Hope (BW)
37 Shocky	Stan Randall (BW)
39 The Magic Hand (feature)	Presto Merritt (BW)
40 Major Frederick Lord	Palmer (BW)
42 Freaks of Luck	Livingstone
44 Big Sid	Stan Randall (BW)
46 Learn Cartooning	John Patterson (BW)
47 Crossword Puzzle	Stanley Ashworth (BW)
48 Aeronautical Advisory Service (feature)	Raymond Clark (BW)
50 The Black Lagoon	Tom Cooper
54 My Grandpa by Lefty Peters	Tom McNamara (BW)
56 Skipper Ham Shanks	John Patterson (BW)
58 Dickie Duck	Matt Curzon
60 Spunk Hazard	Stan Randall
62 Loony Louie the Fire Chief	John Patterson
64 Evidence Eddy	R.G. Leffingwell
66 Cannonball Jones	Walt Kelly

Advertisements
Crowell Publishing Co; *Science and Mechanics* Magazine; Remington Noiseless Portable Typewriter.

First editorial
'THE FUNNY PAGES
. . . in this magazine are all original, all new. They are from the pick of the country's funniest and cleverest free-lance artists. Here you will find comics and thrilling narrative stories done in pictures; bright, clean departments and features designed to please the entire family. The publishers will welcome your comments. Why not write us a letter and air your views? Why not subscribe and be sure you get your copy every month? No dollar ever brought more enjoyment.'

Continuation of *The Comics Magazine*: this title remainded as a subtitle until No. 5 (September 1936). The publisher changed to Ultem Publications Inc. of Mount Morris, Illinois, with effect from September 1937, when the numbering system changed to Vol. 2, No. 1. Harry A. Chesler became the editor, operating from 276 Fifth Avenue, New York. A third publisher came in from March 1938 (Vol. 2, No. 6), namely Centaur Publications Inc. of 420 De Soto Avenue, St. Louis, Missouri (Joseph J. Hardie). The editor was now Lloyd Jacquet at 461 Eighth Avenue, New York. Regular characters made their first appearances as follows:

No. 3 The Sapphire Eye of Sehkmet	Kenneth Ernst
No. 3 The Age of Stone	Victor Dowling
No. 3 The Red Avenger	Ellis Edwards
No. 4 Hezzy of the Hills	Joe Buresch

No. 4 Stubbie
No. 6 The Clock Strikes   Clyde Don
No. 8 Jerry Frost, Sea Scout   George Brenner
No. 9 Doc's Little Big Show   Steve Jussen
V.2 No. 1 Missing Links   Doc Hoag
V.2 No. 1 Block and Fall   Dick Ryan
V.2 No. 1 Smart Alex   Bob Wood
V.2 No. 1 Little Mary of the Circus (Circus Days)   Charles Biro
V.2 No. 2 His Highness   Claire S. Moe
V.2 No. 2 The Great Boodini   John Lindermayer
V.2 No. 3 Abdallah   Fred Schwab
V.2 No. 6 The Master Mind   Craig Fox
V.2 No. 10 The Arrow   George Merkle
V.2 No. 12 Skid Davis, Flyer of Fortune   Paul Gustavson
V.3 No. 1 The Booby Hatch   Al McWilliams
V.3 No. 8 Diana Deane in Hollywood   Fred Schwab
V.4 No. 1 Mantoka, Maker of Magic   Tarpe Mills
V.4 No. 1 The Owl   Richard Bruce
No. 35 Pluton the Great   Martin Filchock
No. 35 The Mad Ming
No. 36 The Incredible Sinister Air Ranger   Harold Delay
No. 38 (R) Gordon Fife and the Boy King
No. 38 Red Man of the Rockies   Bob Moore, Carl Pfeufer
No. 40 Kid Kopper   Art Pinajian
No. 40 Randall Ross the Master Sleuth   Ed Moline
                                  Steve Dahlman

388 Wow

'What a Magazine!'
No. 1: July 1936–No. 4: November 1936. 48 pp. 9½ × 11¼. Publisher: Henle Publications (John Henle), 1 Sherman Avenue, Jersey City, New Jersey. Editorial: 41 Main Street, Flushing, New York; Samuel Iger (editor); Cecil Thayer (associate editor).

Contents of No. 1
Cover
(R) Peewee   Sam Iger
Tom Sherrill   Don De Conn
Tom Tinker   Sam Iger
(R) Dr. Fu Manchu   Leo O'Mealia
S'Fact   Dic
Bully Hayes the Black Pirate   Will Eisner
Space Limited   Serene Summerfield
The Flame   Will Eisner
Smoothie   Bernard Baily
Larry and Tessie   Louis Ferstadt
Make Your Own Cartoons   Wesley Hills

Little Augie
Jocko and His Car
Phoney Philms
Stars on Parade
The Phantom Rider (story)

Bob Smart
Sam Iger
Ed Webster
Bernard Baily

First Editorial
'THE EDITOR TALKS
Fellows! We're going to give you a magazine like this every month — stories, adventure, comics, stamps, aviation, puzzles, radio and movies. I'm sure you'll have as much fun reading it as I had editing it for you. Watch every issue — lots of new fun and thrills. You can help me by getting *Wow* every month and writing me how you enjoy it, sending in suggestions of what new stories and features you would like to read about. I'll read every letter carefully and pay one dollar each for the best letters sent in.'

Advertisements
Martin-Cole Company; Charles Atlas.

Compilation of original strips and text features, mostly packaged by S.M. Iger's Universal Phoenix Features Syndicate. Later issues included King Features Syndicate strips reprinted as promotional material: Flash Gordon by Alex Raymond; Thimble Theatre by E.C. Segar; The Little King by Otto Soglow; Mandrake the Magician by Lee Falk and Phil Davis; Believe It Or Not by Robert L. Ripley; and Tillie the Toiler by Russ Westover. Original strips included Harry Carey (later changed to Harry Karry to avoid trouble with the film star of the same name) by Will Eisner (No. 2); Hiram Hick in New York by Bob Kane (No. 2); Captain Scott Dalton by Will Eisner (No. 3); The Hunchback of Notre Dame by Dick Briefer (No. 3); Buddy Wilbert by Joe Renschel (No. 3); Battle Fleet by Ed Webster (No. 4); Biff and His Pals by George Brenner (No. 4); Sir Hokus Pokus by Louis Ferstadt (No. 4). To reflect the increased strip content the title was changed from *Wow: What a Magazine!* to *Wow Comic Magazine* from No. 3. Interior pages were mostly printed in black-and-white, some with added red; covers in three colours.

389 Famous Favorite Comics

'America's Favorite Funnies'
No. 1: August (1936). 10¢. 68 pp. $7^{1}/_{2} \times 10^{1}/_{4}$.

Contents of No. 1
1 Cover
3 (R) Dick Tracy
7 (R) Mutt and Jeff; Cicero's Cat
8 (R) Moon Mullins; Kitty Higgins
9 (R) Little Joe
10 (R) Little Orphan Annie; Maw Green
12 (R) Always Belittlin'; Skippy
13 (R) Believe It or Not
14 (R) Tippie

Chester Gould
Bud Fisher
Frank Willard
Ed Leffingwell
Harold Gray
Percy Crosby
Robert L. Ripley
Edwina Dumm

15 (R) Life's Little Tragedies	Beck
16 (R) Smitty; Herby	Walter Berndt
17 (R) Bronc Peeler; On the Range	Fred Harman
18 (R) Nugent's Original Puzzles	A.W. Nugent
19 (R) Ella and Her Fella; Jinglet	Al Posen
20 (R) Terry and the Pirates	Milton Caniff
23 (R) Scribbly	Sheldon Mayer
24 (R) Let's Draw Cartoons	Dic
25 (R) Always Belittlin'; Skippy	Percy Crosby
26 (R) Tailspin Tommy	Hal Forrest
28 (R) Tad of the Tanbark; Don Dixon	Bob Moore, Carl Pfeufer
30 (R) Reg'lar Fellers; Daisybelle	Gene Byrnes
31 (R) A Strain on the Family Tie	Gaar Williams
32 Bertie's Picnic (story)	Chet Grant
34 (R) The Gumps	Sidney Smith
36 (R) Harold Teen	Carl Ed
37 (R) Gasoline Alley	Frank King
38 (R) Moon Mullins; Kitty Higgins	Frank Willard
39 (R) Tom Mix the Fighting Cowboy	
40 (R) Major Cosmo Strange DSO	George Baker
42 (R) Real Magic	A.W. Nugent
43 (R) Reg'lar Fellers; Daisybelle	Gene Byrnes
44 (R) Always Belittlin'; Skippy	Percy Crosby
45 (R) Let's Draw Cartoons	Dic
46 (R) Don Winslow; Bos'n Hal	Frank Martinek, Leon Beroth
48 (R) Skull Valley	Garrett Price
49 (R) Little Folks; Baby Sister	Tack Knight
50 (R) Gasoline Alley	Frank King
51 (R) Nugent's Original Puzzles	A.W. Nugent
52 (R) Bronc Peeler; On the Range	Fred Harman
53 (R) Winnie Winkle; Looie	Martin Branner
54 (R) Ben Webster's Page	Edwin Alger
56 (R) Believe It or Not	Robert L. Ripley
57 (R) Always Belittlin'; Skippy	Percy Crosby
58 (R) Tippie	Edwina Dumm
59 Popular Stamp Club (feature)	Montgomery Mulford
60 (R) Smilin' Jack	Zack Mosley
61 (R) Tiny Tim	Stanley Link
62 (R) Mort Green & Wife; Zipper	Gaar Williams
63 (R) Lovey Dovey	Fred Johnson
64 (R) Sweeney & Son	Al Posen
65 (R) Streaky	Gus Edson
66 (R) Gasoline Alley	Frank King

This comic book consists of a complete copy of No. 8 of Dell's *Popular Comics* for September 1936, but without its original cover. It is bound into a blue paper cover which is printed in black ink only on the front, the rest being blank. There is no publisher imprint. Evidently it is an unsold issue returned

135

to the publisher without a cover (standard practice among U.S. newsstand distributors), and remaindered to a small-time wholesaler who has re-covered the comic and given it a new title. The cover drawing is exceptionally crude.

390 The Funnies

'Over 100 Comics'
No. 1: October 1936–No. 64: May 1942. 10¢. 68 pp. $7^{1}/_{2} \times 10^{1}/_{4}$. Publisher: Dell Publishing Co. (George T. Delacorte Jr.), 149 Madison Avenue, New York. Editorial: Helen Meyer (editor); Max C. Gaines. Sheldon Mayer.

Title changed to 'The New Funnies from No. 65.

Contents of No. 1

1 Cover	
2 (R) The Worry Wart	J.R. Williams
3 (R) Dan Dunn, Secret Operative 48	Norman Marsh
7 (R) Mutt & Jeff/Cicero's Cat	Bud Fisher
8 (R) Reg'lar Fellers/Daisybelle	Gene Byrnes
9 (R) This Curious World	William Ferguson
10 (R) Home Magic	A.W. Nugent
11 (R) Boots	Edgar Martin
15 (R) Tailspin Tommy	Hal Forrest
19 (R) Flapper Fanny	Gladys Parker
(R) Salesman Sam	Small
20 (R) Our Boarding House/The Nut Bros.	Bill Freyse
21 (R) Bronc Peeler/On The Range	Fred Harman
22 (R) Myra North, Special Nurse	Ray Thompson, Charles Coll
24 (R) Reg'lar Fellers/Daisybelle	Gene Byrnes
25 (R) Our Boarding House/The Nut Bros.	Bill Freyse
26 (R) Otto Honk	Bill Zaboly
(R) Out Our Way: The Willets	J.R. Williams
27 (R) The Tiny Mites	Hal Cochran, George Scarbo
28 (R) Stranger Than Fiction	Richard Thomas, Walter Galli
29 (R) Captain Easy, Soldier of Fortune	Roy Crane
33 (R) Flapper Fanny	Gladys Parker
Salesman Sam	Small
34 (R) Mutt & Jeff/Cicero's Cat	Bud Fisher
35 (R) Alley Oop	V.T. Hamlin
39 (R) Freckles and his Friends	Merrill Blosser
41 (R) Stranger Than Fiction	Richard Thomas, Walter Galli
42 (R) The Tiny Mites	Hal Cochran, George Scarbo
43 (R) Herky	Clyde Lewis
44 (R) Otto Honk	Bill Zaboly
(R) Out Our Way: The Willets	J.R. Williams
45 (R) A Dog's Life	

46 (R) Major Cosmo Strange DSO	George Baker
48 (R) Ben Webster's Page	Edwin Alger
51 (R) Tad of the Tanbark/Don Dixon	Bob Moore, Carl Pfeufer
54 Happy Mulligan	
56 Spargus 'n' Chubby	
58 (R) Herky	Clyde Lewis
59 (R) Everybody's Playmate	A.W. Nugent
60 (R) This Curious World	William Ferguson
61 (R) Mutt & Jeff/Cicero's Cat	Bud Fisher
62 (R) Reg'lar Fellers/Daisybelle	Gene Byrnes
63 (R) Our Boarding House/The Nut Bros.	Bill Freyse
64 (R) Stories in Stamps (feature)	I.S. Klein
65 (R) Bronc Peeler	Fred Harman
66 (R) Salesman Sam	Small

Advertisements
Johnson Smith & Co.; *Popular Comics*; *The Funnies*.

Dell Publishing revived the title of their early, unsuccessful tabloid comic weekly, and in the new comic book monthly format it became a great success, with a total run (partly as *New Funnies*) of 288 issues, ending in March 1962. It began as a compilation of Sunday newspaper supplement strips copyrighted by Publishers Syndicate, N.E.A. Service, Bell Syndicate, H.C. Fisher and Gene Byrnes, with a small quota of original strips: Sheldon Mayer's Scribbly began in No. 2, Irving Crump's Og, Son of Fire and Milt Youngren's G-Men on the Job in No. 4. The Crime Busters by Al McWilliams started in 1938, as did a series of strip adaptations from western movies, such as Bob Baker in 'Border Wolves' (No. 25). A 1932 strip syndicated by Reilly & Lee based on L. Frank Baum's 'The Wonderland of Oz' and drawn by Walt Spouse was reprinted in 1938. Edgar Rice Burroughs' story 'John Carter of Mars' began in No. 30, and the superhero era was reflected by such new characters as Phantasmo (No. 45), The Black Knight (No. 46), Captain Midnight (No. 57). A strip based on Walter Lantz's animated cartoon character, Andy Panda. started in No. 61, and the whole comic book converted to animated cartoon characters from No. 64: Oswald the Rabbit, Li'l Eight Ball, Felix the Cat, etc. This change of style led to a change of title with the next issue to *The New Funnies*.

391 Funny Picture Stories

'The All-Picture Magazine in Colors'
No. 1: November 1936–Vol. 3, No. 3: May 1939. 10¢. 64 pp. (1–Vol. 2, No. 9); 48 pp (Vol. 2, No. 10–Vol. 3, No. 3). 7¼×10½. Publisher: Comics Magazine Co. Inc., 420 De Soto Avenue, St. Louis, Missouri. Editorial: 11 West 42nd Street, New York.

Title changed to *Comic Pages* from Vol. 3, No. 4: July 1939.

Contents of No. 1

1 Cover: 'Alias the Clock'	George Brenner
3 Contents	
4 Alias the Clock	George Brenner

11 The Border War	Ed McD. Moore Jr.
18 Red Dolan, the Young News Hawk	Joe Campbell Jr.
24 The Floating City: Dick Kent	Art Pinajian
32 Mountain Murder	Joe E. Buresch
40 Shanghaied	John Patterson
48 Wild Horse	W.M. Allison, Buck Ringoe
50 The Spinner: The Case of the Broken Skull	Bert Christman
58 The Sacred White Elephant	Victor J. Dowling

Advertisements
Johnson Smith; Crowell Publishing Co.; Remington Noiseless Portable Typewriter

First editorial
'ACTION! IN PICTURES AND COLORS!
Stories that Live and Breathe. *Funny Picture Stories Magazine* is not all humor by any means. This is the magazine that readers of the popular *Funny Pages* have asked for. Magazine fans the world over have waited for this — Stories Complete in Pictures. And now you can read and see the action, the drama, the thrilling clashes of the hero who fights his way to glory in the tropics, the frozen north, the great west. *Funny Picture Stories* is a monthly magazine. Your news dealer should have it. If you'd rather receive it by mail each month, fill out the coupon below and enclose one dollar — Now —.'

The first comic book devoted to adventure strips, despite the title, which might make a prospective reader think otherwise. Strips and series of interest in later issues include:

No. 2 The Monster Man	Art Pinajian
No. 3 The Newsreel Men	Frank Frollo
No. 4 The Brothers Three	Will Eisner
No. 4 Rockey Baird	Paul J. Lauretta
No. 5 Jay Douglas in a Prehistoric World	Robert Golden
No. 6 Dangerous Documents: Terry Taylor	Robert Wood
No. 6 Bob Steele MD: Between Two Planets	George Brenner
No. 7 In Quest of the Zozosaurus	Eugene Koscik
V.2 No. 1 Jack Strand	Frank Frollo
V.2 No. 1 Lucky Coyne	Creig Flessel
V.2 No. 2 Cutter Carson	Creig Flessel
V.2 No. 3 Gil Calen, G-Man	Craig Fox
V.2 No. 4 Phony Crimes	Paul Gustavson
V.2 No. 5 The Mad One	Frank Frollo
V.2 No. 6 Detective Schultz	Gill Fox
V.2 No. 6 His Highness	Claire S. Moe
V2. No. 8 The Secret Tunnel	Maurice Kashuba
V.2 No. 10 Fadeaway Farr	Jack Binder
V.2 No. 10 How to Draw Funnies	Chuck Thorndike
V.2 No. 11 Fury of the Foreign Legion	Lawrence Spivack
V3. No. 2 Knickerbocker Knights	Malcolm Kildale
V3. No. 3 Lucifer the White Devil	Frank Frollo
V.3 No. 3 Skip Austin	Robert Jenney

The publisher changed to Ultem Publications Inc. of Mount Morris, Illinois, from September 1937; the tenth issue became Vol. 2, No. 1. Harry A. Chesler was made editor, with offices at 276 Fifth Avenue, New York; Kenneth Fitch was managing editor. Ultem was a name coined to cover the partnership of I.W. Ulman and Frank Z. Temerson, of 404 Fourth Avenue, New York. The publisher changed again from March 1938 (Vol. 2, No. 6), becoming Centaur Publications Inc. (Joseph J. Hardie) of 420 De Soto Avenue, St. Louis, Missouri, with editorial offices at 461 Eighth Avenue, New York. After the publication of Vol. 3, No. 3 (May 1939) the title was changed to the more modern *Comic Pages*.

392 Daisy Comics

No. 1 (unnumbered): December 1936. Free (promotional). 36 pp. $5^1/_4 \times 7^1/_2$. Publisher: Daisy Manufacturing Co., 720 Union Street, Plymouth, Michigan. Editorial: Eastern Color Printing Co., 50 Church Street, New York.

Contents of No. 1

1 Cover	
3 Editorial: Howdy Kids	
4 (R) Joe Palooka	Ham Fisher
8 (R) Hairbreadth Harry	F.O. Alexander
10 Colonel Tim McCoy (photo)	
12 (R) Butty and Fatty	Meb
14 (R) Napoleon	Clifford McBride
15 (R) The Frog Pond Ferry	Meb
16 (R) Ned Bryant of Carter	Bob Zuppke, B.W. Depew
20 (R) Flying to Fame	Russell Ross, John Welch
22 (R) Seaweed Sam the Rhyming Rover	Victoria Pazmino
24 (R) Buck Rogers	Phil Nowlan, Dick Calkins
27 Buck Jones Round-Up	
30 (R) Nipper	Clare Dwiggins

Advertisements
Daisy Pump Gun; Daisy Single Shot; Daisy Golden Eagle; Buck Rogers Water Pistol; Bulls Eye Shot.

First editorial
'HOWDY KIDS
You're right, fellows, this is not a Christmas book . . . it's a comic book. But I just want to step in here for a couple of minutes to wish you a Merry Christmas and get a few things off my chest. First . . . about this swell little book, *Daisy Comics*. It's a brand new idea . . . this is the first edition . . . and I sure hope you get some real fun out of it. It's published by Daisy Manufacturing Company for you and your family and friends. Pass it around . . . let the kids in your neighborhood read it . . . show it to your mother and dad. If everybody likes it, the second edition will be out soon . . .'

This givaway comic book in pocket size was packaged for Daisy, the air rifle company, by the publishers of *Famous Funnies*, and consisted entirely of reprints of Sunday newspaper strips which had previously been reprinted in *Famous Funnies*, interspersed with advertisements for Daisy products.

393 Detective Picture Stories

No. 1: December 1936–No. 7: 1937. 10¢. 68 pp. 7¼×10¼. Publisher: Comics Magazine Co. Inc., 11 West 42nd Street, New York. Editorial: 11 West 42nd Street, New York.

Title changed to *Keen Detective Funnies* from No. 8: July 1938.

Contents of No. 1

1 Cover	W.M. Allison
4 The Diamond Dick	W.M. Allison, Wallace Kirk
11 Spurlock & Watkins: Murder in the Blue Room	John Patterson
18 Police Patrol	Ed McD. Moore Jr.
26 The Phantom Killer	George E. Brenner (BW)
34 Sapphire Seas (story)	C.W. Scott, W.M. Allison
36 Wings of Crime	Victor J. Dowling (BW)
44 Roadhouse Racket	Joe E. Buresch (BW)
51 The Spinner: The Tale of Timothy O'Toole	Bert Christman
61 Thurston Hunt: Bogus Bills	Art Pinajian

Advertisements

Johnson Smith; Remington Noiseless Portable Typewriter.

First editorial

'BE A DETECTIVE

Learn how to track the criminal and bring him back alive. Learn the tricks of the ace sleuths, the famous G-men and the clever private detectives. You can do it in twelve easy lessons — and you don't need a tommy-gun or a flashlight. All you need is a dollar. We do the rest. One dollar will bring you twelve issues of the fascinating magazine *Detective Picture Stories*. Read the thrilling stories of the lawbreakers brought to justice, see with your own eyes how the detective gets his man. Here is a magazine crammed full of color, action, plot and punch. You'll see why crime does not pay, why the police always put the finger on the criminal. Mail this coupon today and pin a dollar to it. It will bring you a heap of joy and real thrills.'

The first comic book devoted to a single theme: crime and detection. The second issue introduced 'The Clock' in a case entitled 'Baffled by a Flower', by George E. Brenner. Most of the strips were complete in themselves, such as 'Muss 'Em Up' by Will Eisner (No. 4) and 'The Case of the Missing Heir' by Bob Kane (No. 5). Many strips were later reprinted in Centaur's continuation of this comic book under the title *Keen Detective Funnies*.

394 The John Hix Scrapbook

No. 1: December 1936. 10¢. 68 pp. 7½×10. Publisher: Eastern Color Printing Co., 61 Leavenworth Street, Waterbury, Connecticut. Artist: John Hix. Syndicate: McNaught.

Title changed to *The Second Strange As It Seems Scrapbook*.

Contents of No. 1

1 Cover

Advertisements
Johnson Smith.

First editorial
'WE SALUTE YOU!
With this No. 1 issue of *The John Hix Scrapbook* we introduce a most entertaining and instructive periodical. It will be issued twice a year, every six months. We trust that you have enjoyed this first issue and found it amusing as well as a source of all kinds of valuable information. If you like the facts which John Hix has gathered for you from all sections of the world, we know you will enjoy his fascinating feature 'Strange As It Seems' which appears every month in *Famous Funnies*. This monthly magazine of comics and various other features appears on the newsstands on the 15th of

every month. If you are not now a reader of *Famous Funnies*, we suggest that you get a copy at your nearest newsstand. It costs only 10 cents a copy and gives you hours of thrills, mystery and humor. Try it! Announcement will be made in *Famous Funnies* telling you when issue No. 2 of *The John Hix Scrapbook* will be for sale on the newsstands. Watch for this important announcement in *Famous Funnies*.'

Compilation reprinting the Sunday newspaper feature 'Strange As It Seems', syndicated by the McNaught Syndicate Inc.

395 Famous Cartoon Books

1937 (No. 1010). 5¢. 64 pp. 5¹/₂ × 7¹/₂. Publisher: Whitman Publishing Co., Racine, Wisconsin.

No. 1 *Dan Dunn and the Gangsters' Frame-Up*	Norman Marsh
No. 2 *King of the Royal Mounted in Arctic Law*	Zane Grey
No. 3 *Little Orphan Annie and the Big Town Gunman*	Harold Gray
No. 4 *Smokey Stover, Firefighter of Foo*	Bill Holman

Series of four small comic books reprinting daily newspaper strips in black-and-white, with full-colour covers (hardback). Each book has the same publisher's number: 1010.

396 The Gumps in Radio Land *aka*: Andy Gump and the Chest of Gold

1937. Free (promotional). 100 pp. 3³/₄ × 5¹/₂. Publisher: Lehn & Fink Products Corp. Artist: Gus Edson. Syndicate: Chicago Tribune.

Contents
Premium given away by Pebeco Tooth Past and Tooth Powder in connection with 'The Gumps' radio serial, broadcast five times a week on the Columbia Broadcasting System. Text story illustrated with pictures from the daily newspaper strip syndicated by the *Chicago Tribune*. Printed black-and-white with a four-colour cover specially drawn by the current artist, Gus Edson, who had taken over the strip on the death of creator Sidney Smith.
This book is a reprint of *Chester Gump Finds the Hidden Treasure*, published as Big Little Book No. 766 (1934). To confuse things further, the cover title is *The Gumps in Radio Land*, while the title page reads *Andy Gump and the Chest of Gold*. Exclusive to this edition is a four-page 'Synopsis of the Further Adventures of the Gumps in Radio Land'.

397 Mammoth Comics

No. 1 (unnumbered): 1937 (undated). Unpriced. 84 pp. 8¹/₂ × 10¹/₄. Publisher: Whitman Publishing Co., Racine, Wisconsin; Poughkeepsie, New York.

Contents of No. 1

1 Cover	
4 (R) Tailspin Tommy	Hal Forrest
8 (R) Dan Dunn	Norman Marsh
12 (R) Little Orphan Annie	Harold Gray
16 (R) Freckles and his Friends	Merrill Blosser
20 (R) Dick Tracy	Chester Gould
24 (R) The Nebbs	Sol Hess, W.A. Carlson
28 (R) Terry and the Pirates	Milton Caniff
32 (R) Apple Mary and Dennis	Martha Orr
36 (R) Alley Oop	V.T. Hamlin
40 (R) Smitty	Walter Berndt
44 (R) Moon Mullins	Frank Willard
48 (R) Gasoline Alley	Frank King
52 (R) The Gumps	Gus Edson
56 (R) Don Winslow	Frank Martinek, Leon Beroth
60 (R) Boots and her Buddies	Edgar Martin
64 (R) Wash Tubbs	Roy Crane
67 (R) Winnie Winkle	Martin Branner
71 (R) Smilin' Jack	Zack Mosley
75 (R) Myra North, Special Nurse	Ray Thompson, Charles Coll
79 (R) Smokey Stover	Bill Holman

Advertisements
Super Comics; Big Little Books.

Compilation one-shot of newspaper strips syndicated by NEA Service, Chicago Tribune–New York News Syndicate, Publishers Syndicate, and Bell Syndicate. All strips are dailies, and the entire book is printed in black-and-white, except for the full-colour cover, which is repeated on the back page.

398 100 Pages of Comics

No. 1 (No. 101): 1937 (undated), 10¢, 100 pp. Publisher: Dell Publishing Co. Inc. (G.T. Delacorte Jr.), 149 Madison Avenue, New York.

Contents of No. 1

1 Cover	
2 (R) The Nut Bros: Our Boarding House	Bill Freyse (BW)
3 Tom Mix	
7 Og, Son of Fire	
11 (R) Apple Mary	Martha Orr
15 (R) Tailspin Tommy	Hal Forrest
19 Arizona Kid	
23 (R) Myra North, Special Nurse	Ray Thompson, Charles Coll
27 (R) Alley Oop	V.T. Hamlin
31 (R) Captain Easy	Roy Crane

35 Buffalo Bill
39 Flying the Sky Clipper
43 International Spy Featuring Doctor Doom
47 (R) The Nut Bros: Our Boarding House   Bill Freyse
51 (R) Freckles and His Friends   Merrill Blosser
55 Tom Beatty, Ace of the Service
59 Coast Guard
62 The Texas Ranger
66 (R) Herky   Clyde Lewis
68 (R) Wash Tubbs   Roy Crane
72 (R) Otto Honk   Bill Zaboly
72 (R) Out Our Way   J.R. Williams
74 G-Man and the Red X
78 Mac of the Marines
82 Lone Marshall and the Lost River
86 (R) Boots   Edgar Martin
90 Two Gun Montana
94 (R) School Days Out Our Way   J.R. Williams
96 (R) Dan Dunn, Secret Operative 48   Norman Marsh
99 Magic Tricks (BW)
100 (R) Dan Dunn   Norman Marsh

Although numbered on the back page as No. 101, this is a one-shot publication, compiled from strips previously published in Dell's *The Comics*. All syndicated strips come from the NEA Service Inc., and are dated 1935 and 1936. All original material stems from characters featured in *Big Little Books*, and the reader is exhorted to 'Read about' each character 'in the *Big Little Books*'.

399 The Second Strange As It Seems Scrapbook (formerly The John Hix Scrapbook)

No. 2: 1937 (undated). 10¢. 68 pp. 7½×10¼. Publisher: Eastern Color Printing Co., 61 Leavenworth Street, Waterbury, Connecticut. Artist: John Hix. Syndicate: McNaught.

Contents of No. 2 (first issue this title)
 1 Cover
 2 Optical X-Ray (R)
 3 Editorial
 4 Famous Facts of Football (R)
 6 Calendar Curiosities (R)
 8 What's in a Name (R)
10 Odd Appetites (R)
12 Famous Falls (R)
14 Unusual You (R)
16 Famous Felines (R)
18 Strange Bridges (R)
20 Odd Illumination (R)
22 Be It Ever So Humble (R)

24 Muscular Marvel (R)
26 Strange Sheep (R)
28 China (R)
30 The Birth of a Nation (R)
32 Strange Springs (R)
34 Strange As It Seems (R)
36 Foot Notes (R)
38 Old Time Champions (R)
40 Snail Tales (R)
42 Mental Marvels (R)
44 Midgets of Flight (R)
46 Beards and Mustaches (R)
48 Remarkable Rivers (R)
50 Funny Feminine Fashions (R)
52 Pig Tales (R)
54 Hole in Wonders (R)
56 Literature in Miniature (R)
58 Carnivorous Plants (R)
60 Coffee Curiosities (R)
62 Bird Dwellings (R)
64 Odd Optics (R)
66 Answers to Puzzles
68 Cover

Advertisements
Johnson Smith

First editorial
'"There is nothing so powerful as truth — and often nothing so strange . . ." Perhaps you will agree with Daniel Webster's statement after reading this book in which is presented some of the most amazing of the thousands of strange facts that have been unearthed during years of gathering material for the Strange As It Seems cartoons. I sincerely hope this and forthcoming issues of the *Scrap Book* meet with the same favor as did book number one . . . John Hix.'

Compilation reprinting the Sunday newspaper feature 'Strange As It Seems', syndicated by McNaught Syndicate Inc.

400 New Adventure Comics (formerly New Comics)

'The International Picture Story Magazine'
No. 12: January 1937–No. 31: October 1938. 10¢. 68 pp. 7¹/₄ × 10¹/₄. Publisher: Nicholson Publishing Co. Inc. (Malcolm Wheeler-Nicholson), 420 De Soto Avenue, St. Louis, Missouri. Editorial: 373 Fourth Avenue, New York; Malcolm Wheeler-Nicholson (editor); Vincent Sullivan (associate editor); Whitney Ellsworth (associate editor).

Title changed to *Adventure Comics* from No. 32.

Contents of No. 12 (first issue)

1 Cover	Whitney Ellsworth
3 Captain Jim of the Texas Rangers	Homer Fleming
6 Do You Know	
7 Janey	
8 Goofo the Great	Alger
10 The Vikings	Anthony
12 Don Coyote	Bill Patrick, Ed Beckwith
14 Captain Quick	Sven Elven
16 The Blood Pearls	Munson Paddock
20 Worth-while Pictures to Watch For (feature)	I.W Magovern (BW)
22 Rattlesnake Pete	Boody Rogers
24 17–20 on the Black	Tom Cooper (BW)
26 Andy Handy	Leo E. O'Mealia
28 Ebony	Bill Patrick (BW)
29 Straight from Hollywood	Laidlaw (BW)
30 Ol' Oz Bopp	Alger
32 The Charge of the Light Brigade	Henry Kiefer (BW)
34 Laughing at Life	Vincent Sullivan
36 She by H. Rider Haggard	Sven Elven (BW)
38 Loopy	Leroy Smith
40 Castaway Island	Tom Cooper (BW)
42 The Golden Dragon	Tom Hickey
44 Maginnis of the Mounties	Babe Mather (BW)
46 Rock-Age Roy	Boody Rogers
48 Jungle Town	Dick Ryan (BW)
49 The International Good Neighbor Club (feature) (BW)	
50 Steve Conrad	Creig Flessel
52 Cal 'n' Alice	Bill Patrick, Ed Beckwith
54 Sandor and the Lost Civilization	Homer Fleming
56 A Tale of Two Cities	Merna Gamble
58 Chikko Chakko	Ellis Edwards
60 Sam the Porter	Alger
61 Hardluck Harry	Bill Carney
62 Federal Men	Jerome Siegel, Joe Shuster
66 It's a Dern Lie	Bill Patrick

Advertisements

Johnson Smith; Hohner Harmonicas; Remington Noiseless Portable Typewriter; More Fun.

First editorial

'ANNOUNCING THE INTERNATIONAL GOOD NEIGHBOR CLUB

The formation of the International Good Neighbor Club is not merely a piece of editorial fol-de-rol; it is the outcome of a definite series of suggestions from you, the readers of *New Adventure Comics*. This publication, you may or may not realize, gets around to the far corners of the earth. It is read in Australia and New Zealand, England and South Africa, India and the Malay States, in fact everywhere that the English language is spoken. Too, most of the features are translated into Spanish and published in Mexico, Havana and all the South American countries. We get letters from all the far-flung places; not letters simply telling us that *New Adventure Comics* is liked wherever it is read, but letters showing that young folk all over this old globe of ours are interested in what their brothers and sisters in other countries are doing. A girl in Cape Town may be curious as to just how the day of a girl in, say, Wichita, Kansas, is spent; a boy in Sydney wants to know why American boys prefer baseball to cricket, and just how the games differ. Mostly they say they'd like to have a 'pen-pal' with whom they might correspond. Even non-English speaking countries yield lots of youngsters — and oldsters, too, for that matter — who'd like to have somebody to practise their English on in letters. It strikes us that the growing enthusiasm for the 'pen-pal' idea is an extremely healthy international feeling. If individual people all over the world are interested in other individuals of differing nationalities, if they feel a real kinship, if they have common interests, the result cannot help but be one of better, more peaceful relations between nations. Nations are composed of individuals, after all, and if those individuals like the individuals of other nations, there is no reason why they should take arms against one another. President Roosevelt realizes the value of friendly relations among nations, and he expends a great deal of energy toward the cementing of those friendships between the United States and other countries. The very least we, as citizens, can do is to cooperate with our chief executive in such a worthy endeavor. Let's make the International Good Neighbor Club a great success . . .'

Formerly *New Comics*, the change of title emphasizes the editorial switch away from humour to adventure strips. The word 'Adventure' was lettered quite small in the first issue (No. 12), but became dominant with No. 15, the word 'New' being reduced to a small diagonal band across the top left-hand corner of the cover. It disappeared entirely from No. 32, when the comic book was officially retitled *Adventure Comics*. New regular characters introduced during the run included: Nadir, Master of Magic by Will Ely (No. 17); Dale Daring by Will Ely; The Monastery of the Blue God by Malcolm Wheeler-Nicholson and Munson Paddock; Detective Sergeant Carey of the Chinatown Squad by Joe Donohoe; Barry O'Neill by Leo O'Mealia; Tom Brent by Jim Chambers; Captain Desmo by Win; Tod Hunter Jungle Master by Jim Chambers; Rusty and His Pals by Bob Kane; and Anchors Aweigh by Fred Guardineer. By the last issue (No. 31), Malcolm Wheeler-Nicholson was no longer editor-publisher. The comic had been taken over by Detective Comics Inc., and Vincent A. Sullivan was promoted to editor.

401 New Book of Comics

No. 1: January 1937–No. 2 Spring 1938. 10¢. 100 pp. 7¼×10. Publisher: Nicholson Publishing Co. Inc. (Malcolm Wheeler-Nicholson), 420 De Soto Avenue, St. Louis, Missouri.

Compilation of strips reprinted from *New Comics* Nos. 1–4 and *More Fun* No. 9, including Federal Men, Dr. Occult and Henri Duval by Jerome Siegel and Joe Shuster. This book was sold only through the stores of the F.W. Woolworth Company. The second edition was a compilation of strips reprinted from *More Fun Comics* Nos. 15 and 16, including Federal Men and Dr. Occult.

402 Wags

'Pages for All Ages'

No. 1: 1 January 1937–No. 88: 4 November 1938. 2*d*. (two pence). 32 pp. (1–16); 24 pp. (17–88). 10½ × 14¾. Publisher: Joshua B. Powers Inc., 220 East 42nd Street, New York. Distributor: T. V. Boardman/Joshua B. Powers Ltd. 14 Cockspur Street, London WC2.

Contents of No. 1

1 (R) Smitty	Walter Berndt
2 (R) Out Our Way: The Willets	J.R. Williams
(R) The Comic Zoo	George Scarbo
3 (R) Tarzan by Edgar Rice Burroughs	Hal Foster
4 (R) Smokey Stover; Spooky	Bill Holman
5 (R) Little Joe	Ed Leffingwell
(R) Smilin Jack	Zack Mosley
6 (R) Little Mary Mixup	Robert Brinkerhoff
7 (R) Little Orphan Annie; Maw Green	Harold Gray
8 (R) This Curious World	William Ferguson
(R) Freckles and His Friends	Merrill Blosser
9 (R) Myra North, Special Nurse	Ray Thompson, Charles Coll
10 (R) Broncho Bill; Bumps	Harry O'Neill
11 (R) Harold Teen	Carl Ed
12 (R) Annibelle	Virginia Krausmann
(R) Herky	Clyde Lewis
13 (R) Terry and the Pirates	Milton Caniff
14 (R) Moon Mullins; Kitty Higgins	Frank Willard
15 (R) Mutt and Jeff; Cicero's Cat	Bud Fisher
16 (R) The Enchanted Stone of Time	Adolphe Barreaux
17 (R) Boots: Bootkins	Edgar Martin
18 (R) Ted Strong	Al Carreno
19 (R) Dixie Dugan; Good Deed Dotty	J.P. McEvoy, J.H. Striebel
20 (R) Four Aces; Tailspin Tommy	Hal Forrest
21 (R) Alley Oop; Dinny's Family Album	V.T. Hamlin
22 (R) Tiny Tim; Dill and Daffy	Stanley Link
23 (R) Alice in Wonderland; Knurl the Gnome	Olive Scott, Ed Keukes
24 (R) The Gumps	Gus Edson
25 (R) Captain Easy	Roy Crane
26 (R) Joe Palooka; Fisher's History of Boxing	Ham Fisher
27 (R) Winnie Winkle; Looie	Martin Branner
28 (R) Mickey Finn; Nippie	Lank Leonard
29 (R) Highlights of History; Would You Believe It	J. Carroll Mansfield
30 (R) Rod Rian of the Sky Police	Paul Jepson
31 (R) The Nut Bros; Our Boarding House	Bill Freyse
32 (R) Dick Tracy	Chester Gould

Wags was an 'export only' comic book in tabloid format compiled from Sunday supplement comic pages copyrighted by the Chicago Tribune–New York News Syndicate, NEA Service, United Features Syndicate, George Matthew Adams, McNaught Syndicate, Bell Syndicate, H.C. Fisher, and J. Carroll Mansfield. It was printed in full colour throughout by the Greater Buffalo Press of Buffalo, New York, and shipped to the British Empire (Great Britain and Australia/New Zealand), where local agents distributed it every week. Original single-picture covers were introduced from No. 18 (30 April 1937) with Terry and the Pirates, and continued to No. 33 (13 August 1937) with Smitty. The weekly 32 pages were reduced to 24 pages from No. 17 (23 April 1937) and full-colour pages were reduced to 16 at the same time, the remainder being printed black-and-white. These pages contained new, original material supplied by the Universal Phoenix Feature Syndicate, an art and editorial agency founded by Samuel M. Iger, which from May 1938 became the Editors Press Service Inc. These new strips were unseen in the U.S.A. until they were reprinted in *Jumbo Comics* (No. 1: September 1938). Chronological listing of the new strips:

No. 16: 16 April 1937
Modern Planes and Model Building	Les Marshall (BW)
Puzzle Phun	Don De Conn (BW)
Peter Pupp and Sniffy	Bob Kane (BW)
Hawks of the Seas	Will Eisner (BW)
Adventures of Tom Sherrill	Don De Conn (BW)

No. 17: 23 April 1937
The Hunchback of Notre Dame	Dick Briefer (BW)

No. 24: 11 June 1937
Spencer Steel	Dennis Colebrook (BW)

No. 38: 19 Nov 1937
The Clock Strikes	George Brenner (BW)

No. 39: 26 Nov 1937
Scrappy by Charles Mintz	Will Eisner (BW)

No. 46: 14 Jan 1938
Sheena, Queen of the Jungle	Mort Meskin (BW)

No. 64: 20 May 1938
The Count of Monte Cristo	Jack Kirby (BW)
Gallant Knight	Vernon Henkel (BW)

There are a number of bibliographic confusions about the run of *Wags*. The new strips that made their first appearance in No. 16 started with their second episodes. This was corrected when their first episodes appeared in No. 17. Their second episodes were reprinted in No. 18. There seems to have been a gap in distribution between No. 33 (13 August 1937) and No. 34 (22 October 1937), between which at least one 'special edition' (unnumbered) was published. This 32-page *Wags* contained a number of textual feature pages from American Sunday newspaper magazine supplements, which replaced several of the comic strip pages. From No. 28 (9 July 1937) the U.K. distributor was listed as T.V. Boardman & Co. Ltd., of the same address as the previous publisher, Joshua B. Powers Ltd. The last issue of *Wags* known to have been distributed in Great Britain was No. 88 (4 November 1938), although publication continued for distribution in Australia and New Zealand.

403 Star Comics

'A Rapid View of Fun That's New'
No. 1: February 1937–Vol. 2, No. 7: August 1939. 10¢. 68 pp. (1–12); 52 pp. (13–23). 8×11¼ (1–6); 7×10. Publisher: Chesler Publications Inc. (Harry A. Chesler), 420 De Soto Avenue, St. Louis, Missouri. Editorial: 276 Fifth Avenue, New York; Harry A. Chesler (editor), George Nagle (associate editor).

Contents of No. 2

(*Note:* No. 1 unavailable for indexing)

Advertisements
Baby Ruth; Butterfinger; Star Ranger.

Handsome, oversize (for the first six issues) comic book, with full colour throughout. Companion to *Star Ranger*. Characters introduced in later issues include:

No. 3 Impy	Winsor McCay Jr.
No. 3 Third Class Male	Fred Schwab
No. 3 Bib and Tucker	Jack Romer
No. 3 Goobyland	Charles Biro
No. 5 Little Nemo in Slumberland	Winsor McCay Jr.
No. 5 Foxy Grandpa	Charles Biro
No. 5 Jungle-Town Show Boat	Dick Ryan
No. 5 Bows an' Arrows	Dick Ryan
No. 7 Trail of the Mammoth	Frank Frollo
No. 9 Colt Canyon	Frank Gruber, Fred Guardineer
No. 10 King's Revenge	Kenneth Ernst
No. 11 Rubber Plantation	Kenneth Ernst
No. 11 Don Marlow	Fred Guardineer
No. 11 Gertie the Cashier	Jack Cole
No. 12 Riders of the Golden West	Maurice Kashuba
No. 13 Surprise for Moe	Paul Gustavson
No. 14 Station Agent: Speed Silvers	Paul Gustavson
No. 15 Lucky Doyle, Master Detective	Maurice Gutwirth
No. 15 Speed Barton, Ace Reporter	Kenby
No. 15 Diana Deane in Hollywood	Tarpe Mills
No. 15 The Last Pirate	Carl Burgos
No. 16 The Phantom Rider	Al Petersen
No. 16 Davy Jones	Fred Schwab
No. 16 Brad Donovan at Rocky Hill	Amby
No. 16 Did You Ever	Gill Fox
V. 2 No. 1 Detective O'Leary	Paul Gustavson
V. 2 No. 1 Dash of the 100th Century	Fred Schwab
V. 2 No. 2 Windy	Martin Filchock
V. 2 No. 3 Homer Butts	Paul Gustavson
V. 2 No. 4 It's Really a Fact	Bob Wood
V. 2 No. 7 Jungle Queen	Claire S. Moe

The publisher changed from Chesler Publications to Ultem Publications (I.W. Ulman, Frank Z. Temerson) from No. 7 (November 1937), but the editorship remained with Harry A. Chesler and George Nagle. Ultem brought the format into line with regular comic books, but sold out to Centaur Publications (Joseph J. Hardie) with effect from No. 10 (March 1938). New Editor Lloyd Jacquet introduced a partial reprint programme, and the page count was reduced from 68 to 52 from No. 13 (July 1938). It is interesting that under Chesler two long-defunct comic strips were revived, Little Nemo (now by Winsor McCay's son Robert) and Foxy Grandpa (now by Charles Biro).

404 Star Ranger

'Pictorial Stories of the Golden West'
No. 1: February 1937–No. 12: May 1938. 10¢. 68 pp. 8×11¼ (1–6; 7×10 (7–12). Publisher: Chesler Publications Inc. (Harry A. Chesler), 420 De Soto Avenue, St. Louis, Missouri. Editorial: 276 Fifth Avenue, New York, Harry A. Chesler (editor), Kenneth Fitch (managing editor).

Title changed to *Cowboy Comics* from No. 13 (July 1938).

Contents of No. 1

1 Cover	W.M. Allison
3 Editorial: The Roundup	Ken Fitch
5 Jess Phoolin	Fred Schwab
6 Trailer Triggers	Rafael Astarita
8 Death's Head Range	Irving Frisch
10 Tenderfoot Joe	Fred Schwab
12 The Ghost Riders	Norman Daniels, W.M. Allison
15 Jesse James	
16 Trouble Hunters	Creig Flessel
18 Western Facts	W.M. Allison
19 The Winnah	Fred Schwab
20 Lobo	Fred Guardineer
22 Ace & Deuce, Saddle Pards	W.M. Allison
24 Copperhead Canyon	Fred Guardineer
26 Sitting Bull	
27 Waiting for a Sucker; Home on the Range	LaRue Edwards
28 Valley of Living Death	Creig Flessel
31 Horace Greeley	
32 Empty Six-Guns	Fred Guardineer
34 Fangs of Fate (story)	Omar Gwinn
38 Daffy Dills	Dick Ryan
39 Wrong Again	LaRue Edwards
40 Wanted Men	Creig Flessel
43 Dude McStude	Fred Schwab
44 Silver Saddle	Frank Gruber, Creig Flessel
46 Slim Pickens	C. Brigham
47 Out Where the West Begins	Fred Schwab
48 Air Patrol	Valens Moreno
51 The West That Was	W.M. Allison
52 The Joker	Tom Curry, Fred Guardineer
54 Stolen Gold	Fred Guardineer
57 Homeless Oscar	C. Brigham
58 Lariat Law	W.C. Miller, Creig Flessel
60 The Return of Tarzan	Dick Ryan
61 Watch Out	Fred Schwab
62 The Valley of Fear	Rafael Astarita
64 Buffalo Bill	
65 Hard Times	Fred Schwab

66 Lonesome Luke   Fred Schwab

Advertisements
Baby Ruth Curtiss Candy Co.; Mead Cycle Co.; Butterfinger; Bell Movie Camera; Star Comics.

First Editorial
'THE ROUNDUP: WE'RE A-CALLIN' YUH
Hi, Rangers! Jest tie yore broncs to th' hitchin' posts out thar an' push yore Stetsons back off yore foreheads! Thar ain't no sun a-gleamin' in yore eyes, an' the dust of th' prairies has plumb settled down, with nary a wind t' disturb it! Take yore six-guns out o' yore holsters an' hold 'em level, 'cause yore gonna do a bit o' action afore we're done with yuh. Thar! That's it, Rangers! Stand thar, jest so! We're a-goin' t' take yore pitchers an' put 'em in a book an' tell th' folks what yuh been doin' fer nigh on to a hundred y'ars! What's that, Cap'n? Yuh bet! A book like yuh ain't never seen afore! It's called Star Ranger an' it tells about yuh mostly in pitchers what artists draw an' color, an' we're a-calc'latin' it's a-goin' t' tell about yuh better'n anything ever done up t' now! Yore a-goin' t' ride them plains an' see them sunsets all over ag'in. The dust is a-goin' t' fly an' bullets is a-goin' t' zing through th' air while yo're pertectin' th' settlers ag'in th' Arapaho, th' Cheyenne, th' Kiowa an' th' Comanche Injuns. Them was hard ridin' days an' thar's a heap t' be told about yuh, Rangers . . . So thar yuh are, Rangers. Jest look over this here copy o' *Star Ranger*! Yore pitcher's in it. An' we hope you'll like what we're a-tellin' th' folks about yuh. 'Ken' Fitch.'

Handsome, oversize (for the first six issues) comic book, with full colour throughout. Companion book to *Star Comics*, but unlike that comic, *Star Ranger* concentrates on a single theme. Curiously, the first issue was published the same month as another comic book devoted to the west, *Western Picture Stories*. Strips and series in later issues include:

No. 2 The Ghosts of Ghost Town	Rafael Astarita
No. 2 Gun Boss	Creig Flessel
No. 2 Wanted for Murder	Fred Guardineer
No. 3 Wild West Junior	Charles Biro
No. 3 Six Shooter Justice	Jim Chambers
No. 4 Null and Void	Jack Romer
No. 5 Death Rides the Air Patrol	Rafael Astarita
No. 6 Baldy	Fred Guardineer
No. 7 Dynamite Trail	W.M. Allison
No. 8 Blood on the Rio Grande	Paul Gustavson
No. 9 Lee Trent	Frank Frollo
No. 10 Down the Trail	Jack Cole
No. 11 Two Gun Egbert	R.A. Burley
No. 12 Monarch of the Glen	Fred Guardineer

The publisher changed from Chesler Publications to Ultem Publications (I.W. Ulman, Frank Z. Temerson) from No. 7 (November 1937), but the editorship remained with Harry A. Chesler and Kenneth Fitch. Ultem brought the format into line with regular comic books, but sold out to Centaur Publications (Joseph J. Hardie) with effect from No. 10 (March 1938). Centaur tied the comic in with the Boy Rangers of America, enabling their front covers to be emblazoned with the official badge and the legend: 'Boy Rangers of America Official Magazine'. But after three issues, this tie-in was cancelled and the title of the comic book was changed to *Cowboy Comics*.

405 Western Picture Stories

No. 1: February 1937–No. 4: June 1937. 10¢. 68 pp. 7¼×10¼. Publisher: Comics Magazine Co. Inc., 1213 West 3rd Street, Cleveland, Ohio. Editorial: 11 West 42nd Street, New York.

Contents of No. 1

1 Cover	W.M. Allison
4 Treachery on the Trail	H. Muheim
11 Windy Parks' Kettle of Gold	Victor Dowling (BW)
18 Weapons of the West (feature)	W.M. Allison
20 Guns of Revenge	Arthur Pinajian (BW)
27 Blood and Iron	W.M. Allison, H. David
34 A Tense Moment	Rodney Thomson
36 Top Hand: A Wild Tex Martin Story	Will Eisner
43 A Killer's Conscience	G.G. Lewis, Tom McNamara (BW)
50 Famous Frontiersmen	R.A. Burley (BW)
52 The Lucifer Trail	Milton Wilcox (BW)
59 Tracks in the Snow	H.L. Hastings
66 Punchers	W.M. Allison

Advertisements

Johnson Smith; Crowell Publishing Co.; Remington Noiseless Portable Typewriter.

The first comic book on the single theme of the West. Apart from Will Eisner's 'Wild Tex Martin' and Victor Dowling's 'Windy Parks', the strips were mainly complete stories. These included 'Red Dolan Goes West' by Joseph Campbell (No. 2), 'The Innocent Horse Thief' by Tom McNamara (No. 3), and 'The Caveman Cowboy' by Joseph Buresch (No. 4). Many of the strips were later reprinted in Centaur's *Star Ranger Funnies* and *Cowboy Comics*.

406 The Comics

No. 1: March 1937–No. 11: January 1938. 10¢. 68 pp. 7¼×10¼. Publisher: Dell Publishing Co. Inc. (G.T. Delacorte Jr.), 149 Madison Avenue, New York. Editorial: Arthur Lawson (editor).

Contents of No. 1

1 Cover	
2 (R) You Wouldn't Believe It	John Hix (BW)
3 (R) Wash Tubbs	Roy Crane
7 In the Name of the Law	
11 (R) Cowboy Comics: Out Our Way	J.R. Williams
12 Sombrero Pete	
15 Tom Mix in Gunfighter's Range	
19 (R) Magic	Sandini
20 (R) Adventure Stamps	I.S. Klein
21 Erik Noble and the Forty-Niners	
25 Lone Marshal and the Border Rustlers	

29 Tom Beatty
33 Prairie Bill
36 Model Plane (feature)
39 G-Man Jim
43 (R) Cowboy Comics: Out Our Way · · · · · · · · · · · · · · · · J.R. Williams
44 Arizona Kid
47 (R) Myra North Special Nurse · · · · · · · · · · · · · · · · Ray Thompson, Charles Coll
51 (R) Cowboy Comics: Out Our Way · · · · · · · · · · · · · · · · J.R. Williams
52 Ford of the Foreign Legion (story)
54 Flying the Sky Clipper
57 The Shooting Sheriff
61 International Spy featuring Doctor Doom
64 Coast Guard and the Rajah's Ransom

Advertisements
Hecker Products Corp.; Crowell Publishing Co.; Little Giant Radio; Tinytone Radio; Claxo Trick Co.; Marvel Manufacturing Co.; Mead Cycle Co.; Johnson Smith; Ever Ready Batteries.

Although the covers emphasized familiar comic strip characters, this monthly comic book actually contained more original artwork than reprints. The new material was copyrighted by Stephen Slessinger Inc. and was uniformly poor. Further original strips included In the Name Of The Law, State Trooper (No. 4), Decks Awash by Augustus Robinson, Bill and Davey by James McCague, Man Hunt (No. 7), and several strip adaptations of movies including Tex Ritter in 'The Mystery of the Hooded Horsemen' by Norman Fallon (No. 7), 'Frontier Town' (No. 9) and 'Riders of the Rockies' (No. 10). Syndicated strip reprints included Alley Oop by V.T. Hamlin (No. 4), and from the George Matthew Adams Service Inc.: Ted Strong by Al Carreno, Rod Rian of the Sky Police by Paul Jepson, Gordon Fife by Bob Moore and Carl Pfeufer, Cap'n Cloud by Robert Weinstein, The Enchanted Stone of Time by Adolph Barreaux, and Pecos Bill by Jack A. Warren (No. 5). Several strips were reprinted from the early Dell comic *The Funnies*: Deadwood Gulch by Boody Rogers (No. 5), My Big Brudder by Tack Knight, Jimmy Jams by Victoria Pazmino, and Clancy the Cop by Pazmino (No. 7).

407 Detective Comics

No. 1: March 1937–. 10¢. 68 pp. 7¼×10¼. Publisher: Detective Comics Inc. (Malcolm Wheeler-Nicholson), 432 Fourth Avenue, New York. Editorial: 480 Lexington Avenue, New York; Malcolm Wheeler-Nicholson (editor); Vincent Sullivan, Whitney Ellsworth (associate editors).

Contents of No. 1
1 Cover · · · · · · · · · · · · · · · · Vincent Sullivan
Speed Saunders · · · · · · · · · · · · · · · · Creig Flessel
Cosmo the Phantom of Disguise · · · · · · · · · · · · · · · · Sven Elven
Buck Marshall, Range Detective · · · · · · · · · · · · · · · · Homer Fleming
Claws of the Red Dragon
Bruce Nelson · · · · · · · · · · · · · · · · Tom Hickey
Spy · · · · · · · · · · · · · · · · Jerome Siegel, Joe Shuster
Mr. Chang · · · · · · · · · · · · · · · · Ed Winiarski

Slam Bradley   Jerome Siegel, Joe Shuster
Flatfoot Flannigan   Paul Gustavson

Advertisements
Johnson Smith

Had *Detective Comics* been able to keep to its original publication schedule, it would have been the first American comic book to concentrate on one single theme, a claim often made for it by its publishers. But, although the first issue was advertised in the December 1936 issue of *More Fun Comics*, it was not until three months later that it finally appeared on America's newsstands — with the date on its front cover altered from December 1936 to March 1937. The first advertisement read:

> *You asked for it . . . and here it is! The most thrilling narrative-cartoon magazine in the comic field . . . Bang-up adventure yarns in thrilling pictures by your favorite artists . . . Novelettes! Short stories! Short shorts! Serials! — and only a dime at all newsstands!*

Series characters introduced in later issues include:

No. 5 Larry Steele, Private Detective   Will Ely
No. 15 Bring 'Em In Brannigan   Alger
No. 17 Doctor Fu Manchu   Leo O'Mealia
No. 20 The Crimson Avenger   Jim Chambers
No. 27 The Batman   Bob Kane
No. 34 Steve Malone, D.A.   Don Lynch
No. 37 Cliff Crosby
No. 60 Air Wave   George Roussos
No. 64 Boy Commandos   Joe Simon, Jack Kirby
No. 138 Robotman   Jimmy Thompson
No. 151 Pow Wow Smith
No. 225 Martian Manhunter
No. 293 Aquaman
No. 327 Elongated Man   Carmine Infantino
No. 437 New Manhunter   Walt Simonson
No. 443 The Creeper
No. 490 Black Lighting

The second most important comic book character after Superman, Bob Kane's Batman (later with Robin the Boy Wonder) made his debut in *Detective Comics* No. 27 (May 1939) and has appeared in every issue since. There have been several format changes: issues No. 438–445 contained 100 pages; from No. 481 the title was amalgamated with *Batman Family* and the price raised to $1.00. Two special editions, No. 500 and No. 526 (Batman's 500th appearance), cost $1.50 and contained 68 pages. Some issues were entitled *Batman's Detective Comics*. A facsimile edition of No. 27, but in tabloid size, was published in 1974 as *Famous First Edition* No. C28. A mint copy of No. 1 is valued at $10,000 and a mint copy of No. 27 is valued at $25,000 in the 1989 edition of Overstreet's *Comic Book Price Guide*.

408 Ace Comics

No. 1: April 1937–No. 151: October 1959. 10¢. 68 pp. 7½×10¼. Publisher: David McKay Co., 604 South Washington Square, Philadelphia. Editor: Ruth Plumly Thompson.

Contents of No. 1

1 Cover	Joe Musial
2 Editorial	Ace-Hi
3 (R) Tex Thorne by Zane Grey	Allen Dean
(R) Believe It or Not	Robert L. Ripley
(R) Jungle Jim	Alex Raymond
(R) Seein' Stars	Feg Murray
(R) Pete the Tramp	C.D. Russell
(R) The Katzenjammer Kids	H.H. Knerr
(R) The Pussycat Princess	Ed Anthony, Ruth Carroll
(R) Elmer	Doc Winner
(R) Sports in Pictures	Sords
(R) Tillie the Toiler	Russ Westover
(R) Nicodemus O'Malley; Just Kids	Ad Carter
(R) Tim Tyler's Luck	Lyman Young
(R) Col. Potterby; Blondie	Chic Young
Timberline Tales (story)	Rutherford Montgomery
The Stamp Spotlight (feature)	Jack King
(R) Curley Harper at Lakespur	Lyman Young
Teddy and Sitting Bull	Joe Musial
(R) Bunky; Barney Google	Billy De Beck
(R) Etta Kett	Paul Robinson
(R) Krazy Kat	George Herriman
(R) Room and Board	Gene Ahern

Contents This Issue

Advertisements
Johnson Smith.

The David McKay Company's second monthly comic book. Like its predecessor, *King Comics*, it reprinted Sunday supplement strips copyrighted by King Features Syndicate. Regular characters introduced later in the run include The Phantom by Lee Falk and Ray Moore (No. 11), Prince Valiant by Hal Foster (No. 26), Brick Bradford by William Ritt and Clarence Gray (No. 128), and The Lone Ranger by Fran Striker and Charles Flanders (No. 135). Original covers featuring the regular characters were drawn by Joe Musial, who also contributed the only original strip, Teddy and Sitting Bull. As with *King Comics*, the reduced Sunday pages were relettered for clarity, a practice which did great harm to such strips as George Herriman's Krazy Kat.

409 Western Action Thrillers

No. 1: April 1937. 10¢. 100 pp. Publisher: Dell Publishing Co. Inc. (G.T. Delacorte), 149 Madison Avenue, New York.

Contents
Compilation of strips on a western theme, including Buffalo Bill and the Texas Kid.

410 Feature Books

No. 1: May 1937–No. 57: 1948. 10¢. 52 pp. (1, 2); 100 pp. (3, 4); 76 pp. (5–25); 68 pp. (26–57). 8½×11½. Publisher: David McKay Co., 604 Washington Square, Philadelphia.

No. 1 May 1937 (R) *Zane Grey's King of the Royal Mounted*	Allen Dean
No. 2 Jun 1937 (R) *Popeye*	E.C. Segar
No. 3 Jul 1937 (R) *Popeye and the Jeep*	E.C. Segar
No. 4 Aug 1937 (R) *Dick Tracy the Detective*	Chester Gould
No. 5 Sep 1937 (R) *Popeye and His Poppa*	E.C. Segar
No. 6 Oct 1937 (R) *Dick Tracy the Detective*	Chester Gould
No. 7 Nov 1937 (R) *Little Orphan Annie*	Harold Gray
No. 8 Dec 1937 (R) *Secret Agent X-9*	Charles Flanders
No. 9 Jan 1938 (R) *Dick Tracy and the Famon Boys*	Chester Gould
No. 10 Feb 1938 (R) *Popeye and Susan*	E.C. Segar
No. 11 Mar 1938 (R) *Little Annie Rooney*	Brandon Walsh
No. 12 Apr 1938 (R) *Blondie*	Chic Young
No. 13 May 1938 (R) *Inspector Wade*	Lyman Anderson
No. 14 Jun 1938 (R) *Popeye*	E.C. Segar
No. 15 Jul 1938 (R) *Barney Baxter*	Frank Miller
No. 16 Aug 1938 (R) *Red Eagle*	Jimmy Thompson
No. 17 Sep 1938 (R) *Gangbusters*	
No. 18 Oct 1938 (R) *Mandrake the Magician*	Lee Falk, Phil Davis
No. 19 Nov 1938 (R) *Mandrake the Magician*	Lee Falk, Phil Davis
No. 20 Dec 1938 (R) *The Phantom*	Lee Falk, Ray Moore
No. 21 Jan 1939 (R) *The Lone Ranger*	Fran Striker, Charles Flanders
No. 22 1939 (R) *The Phantom under the Sea*	Lee Falk, Ray Moore
No. 23 1939 (R) *Mandrake the Magician in Teiba Castle*	Lee Falk, Phil Davis
No. 24 1939 (R) *The Lone Ranger*	Fran Striker, Charles Flanders
No. 25 1939 (R) *Flash Gordon*	Alex Raymond

Each *Feature Book* is a compilation of daily newspaper strips, printed in black-and-white and arranged at one and a half strips to the page. Strips are copyrighted to the King Features Syndicate and the Chicago Tribune–New York News Syndicate. The covers are in four colours and specially drawn, but not by the original artists. Covers are reprinted on the backs to No. 10, after which they are replaced by advertisements for the Johnson Smith Company. The two 100-page issues, Nos. 3 and 4, are reprints of earlier one-shot comic books, but with new covers and new numbering. The titles listed above are the issues falling in our given era, after which the *Feature Book* series changed format to regular comic book size and four-colour printing throughout.

411 Picture Crimes

No. 1: June 1937–. 10¢. 68 pp. 7¼×10¼. Publisher: David McKay Co., 604 South Washington Square, Philadelphia.

Contents of No. 1

1 Cover	Edgar Franklin
5 The Darkroom Murder	
11 A Champ Passes	
17 Death of a Gold Digger	
23 Marked for Murder	
30 Death at a Wooden Wedding	
36 The Green Jinx Strikes	
42 All Cops Are Dumb	
48 Revel of a Raffles	
55 Solutions	

Advertisements
Big Little Books; *King Comics*; *Ace Comics*.

Told entirely in specially posed photographs, this book can be considered the father of the modern 'fumetti' or photo-strip comics. Printed throughout in black-and-white, except for the full-colour cover, the only drawn picture in the book.

412 Gags

'The New Book of Jokes and Cartoons'
No. 1: July 1937–No. 10: October 1944. 10¢; 15¢ (9, 10). 52 pp.; 36 pp. (9, 10). $6^3/_4 \times 9^3/_4$; $10^3/_4 \times 13^3/_4$ (9, 10). Publisher: United Features Syndicate Inc., 220 East 42nd Street, New York. Editorial: 220 East 42nd Street, New York.

Contents of No. 1

1 Cover	George Lichty
3 (R) Grin and Bear It	George Lichty
5 Laugh This Off (jokes)	
6 (R) Grin and Bear It	George Lichty
8 Jokes (BW)	
14 (R) Grin and Bear It	George Lichty
15 (R) Fellow Citizens	Rossman
16 Jokes (BW)	
20 (R) Cartoons	John Pierotti (BW)
22 (R) Grin and Bear It	George Lichty
32 Joke's (BW)	
38 (R) Grin and Bear It	George Lichty
40 Jokes (BW)	
46 (R) Grin and Bear It	George Lichty
50 Jokes	

Advertisements
Pictorial Ring Co.; Transpix Picture Outfit; Economy Supply Co.; Johnson Smith; Tip Top Comics.

The first 'joke-book' to be published in comic book format. Mainly reprints of George Lichty's popular Sunday page of six individual cartoons, plus some daily panel cartoons from Rossman's 'Fellow Citizens' series, all syndicated by United Features. After No. 8 the publication was taken over by Triangle Publishing.

413 Feature Funnies

No. 1: October 1937–No. 20: May 1939. 10¢. 68 pp. 7½×10¼. Publisher: Comic Favorites Inc. (Everett Arnold, Frank Markey), 1213 West Third Street, Cleveland, Ohio. Editorial: 369 Lexington Avenue, New York; Edward Cronin (editor).

Title changed to *Feature Comics* from No. 21.

Contents of No. 1

1 Cover	
3 (R) Joe Palooka; Fisher's History of Boxing	Ham Fisher
(R) They're Still Talking	
(R) Jane Arden	Monte Barrett, Russell Ross
(R) Strange As It Seems	John Hix
(R) Off the Record	Ed Reed
(R) Lala Palooza	Rube Goldberg
(R) Modern Planes	Les Marshall
(R) Star Snapshots	Bernard Baily
(R) Good Deed Dotty; Dixie Dugan	J.P. McEvoy, J.H. Striebel
(R) Flossie	Zere
(R) Slim and Tubby	John Welch, J.W. McGuire
(R) Offside	Joe Metzer
(R) Ned Brant	Bob Zuppke, B.W. Depew
(R) Puzzle Phun	Don De Conn
(R) Little Brother; The Bungle Family	H.J. Tuthill
(R) Big Top	Ed Wheelan
(R) Toddy	George Marcoux
(R) Lena Pry	Russell Ross
Jim Swift	Ed Cronin
(R) Nippie; Mickey Finn	Lank Leonard

Advertisements
Johnson Smith; Remington Noiseless Portable Typewriter.

Compilation of newspaper strips reprinted from Sunday supplements and copyrighted by the McNaught Syndicate, Register and Tribune Syndicate, Frank Jay Markey Syndicate. The one original strip, Jim Swift and His Adventures, was drawn by the editor, Ed Cronin. No. 2 added The Hawk by George E. Brenner, who contributed a new adventure of his earlier character, The Clock Strikes, to No. 3. Will Eisner's strip, Hawks of the Seas, which had first appeared in *Wags*, the 'export only' comic, began in No. 3. Eisner used the pen-name 'Willis B. Rensie'. Gallant Knight by Vernon Henkel and Clip Chance at Cliffside by Scott Sheridan started in No. 7; Archie O'Toole by Bud

Thomas (another Eisner alias) began in No. 11, and Espionage Starring Black X by Erwin (yet another Eisner alias) started in No. 13. Reynolds of the Mounted by Arthur Pinajian was the last new strip to be added prior to the comic's change of title to *Feature Comics* (June 1939). The success of this comic book led to the foundation of Everett Arnold's Quality Comics Group.

414 Buddy Books

1938. Free (promotional). 126 pp. 3½×3½. Publisher: Whitman Publishing Co., Racine, Wisconsin.

No. 1 *Smokey Stover*	Bill Holman
No. 2 *Smilin' Jack and His Stratosphere Plane*	Zack Mosley
No. 3 *Tailspin Tommy on the Mountain of Human Sacrifice*	Hal Forrest
No. 4 *Terry and the Pirates Ashore in Singapore*	Milton Caniff
No. 5 *King of the Royal Mounted in the Far North*	Zane Grey
No. 6 *Dan Dunn, Secret Operative 48, and the Counterfeit Ring*	Norman Marsh
No. 7 *Kayo and Moon Mullins Down South*	Frank Willard
No. 11 *Dick Tracy Smashing the Famon Racket*	Chester Gould

Series of twelve small comic books reprinting pictures from daily newspaper strips. Soft covers in full colour, interior pages in black-and-white. The stories are told in text on the left-hand pages in the style of *Big Little Books*. Produced by Whitman as premiums given in return for twelve Buddy Book Tokens given away with ice-cream cones. *Note:* only those *Buddy Books* adapted from comics are included in the above list.

415 Charlie McCarthy in Comics. Full title: Edgar Bergen Presents Charlie McCarthy in Comics

No. 1 (764): 1938. 10¢. 36 pp. 10¼×15. Publisher: Whitman Publishing Co., Racine, Wisconsin.

Contents of No. 1
 1 Cover
 3 Charlie McCarthy
 9 The Private Life of Charlie McCarthy
29 Charlie McCarthy
36 Cover

Tabloid comic book containing single-page strips featuring ventriloquist Edgar Bergen and his dummy, Charlie McCarthy. Strips are copyrighted 1938 Charlie McCarthy Inc.

416 Cocomalt Big Book of Comics

1938. Free (promotional). 52 pp. 7¼×10

Contents
Original comic book created by the Harry A. Chesler studio as a premium for Cocomalt. Printed in four colours throughout, with cover drawn by Charles Biro. Characters include several regulars from earlier Chesler comic books (*Star Comics*, etc.): Dan Hastings by Fred Guardineer, Little Nemo by Winsor McCay Jr., etc., and the Broadway comedian, Joe Penner.

417 Famous Comic Strip Books

1938 (No. 1100A). 1¢. 36 pp. 2½×3½. Publisher: Whitman Publishing Co., Racine, Wisconsin.

1 *Dick Tracy Gets His Man*	Chester Gould
2 *Dick Tracy the Detective*	Chester Gould
3 *Adventures of Terry and the Pirates*	Milton Caniff
4 *Terry and the Prirates on Their Travels*	Milton Caniff
5 *Little Orphan Annie Gets into Trouble*	Harold Gray
6 *Little Orphan Annie Saves Sandy*	Harold Gray
7 *Don Winslow of the U.S. Navy and the Missing Admiral*	Leon Beroth
8 *Freckles and His Friends Stage a Play*	Merrill Blosser
9 *Alley Oop and the Missing King of Moo*	V.T. Hamlin
10 *Smokey Stover and the Fire Chief of Moo*	Bill Holman
12 *Dan Dunn, Secret Operative 48, and the Bank Hold-Up*	Norman Marsh
13 *Dan Dunn, Secret Operative 48, Plays a Lone Hand*	Norman Marsh
18 *Smilin' Jack Grounded on a Tropical Shore*	Zack Mosley

Series of 18 small comic booklets, all numbered 1100A, and sold at 1¢ each, or used as promotional giveaways with advertising overprinted on the back covers. Titles not listed above were original and not adapted from newspaper strips. Modelled on the same publisher's *Big Little Book* series, with one picture to each right-hand page, and narrative text on the left. Printed black-and-white with three-colour covers.

418 Famous Feature Stories

1938 (No. 1). 10¢. 68 pp. 7½×11. Publisher: Dell Publishing Co. (George T. Delacorte Jr.), 149 Madison Avenue, New York.

Contents

1 Cover	
3 Title Page	
4 Dick Tracy Shoots It Out	Chester Gould
10 Terry and the Pirates and the Chinese Bells	Milton Caniff
15 Little Orphan Annie and Her Apple Business	Harold Gray
21 Don Winslow of the Navy and the Invincible Disaster	Frank Martinek
26 Dan Dunn and the Hotel Washington Murder	Norman Marsh
31 King of the Royal Mounted and the Harper Gang	Zane Grey
37 Smilin' Jack and the Strato-Plane	Zack Mosley
42 Buck Jones and the Platteville Bank Robbery	Buck Wilson
48 G-Man and the Kidnap Ring	Milt Youngren
54 Tarzan of the Apes and the Hidden Treasure	Edgar Rice Burroughs
60 Tailspin Tommy and the San Felipe Revolution	Hal Forrest

Advertisement
Johnson Smith Co.

Experimental combination of *Big Little Book* and comic book formats: strips adapted into text stories illustrated with panels from the strips from which the speech balloons have been removed. There are two panels per page. Printed with full-colour covers, 16 pages in two colours (black and orange), the remainder black-and-white. The experiment evidently failed, as only No. 1 was published.

419 Fast Action Books

1938–1943. 10¢. 196 pp. 4×5¹/₂. Publisher: Dell Publishing Co. (George T. Delacorte Jr.), 149 Madison Avenue, New York.

1938
(1) *Adventures of Charlie McCarthy and Edgar Bergen*
(2) *Dan Dunn, Secret Operative 48, and the Zeppelin of Doom*   Norman Marsh
(3) *Zane Grey's King of the Royal Mounted Policing the Frozen North*   Jim Gary
(4) *Mickey Mouse, the Sheriff of Nugget Gulch*   Walt Disney
(5) *Dick Tracy and the Chain of Evidence*   Chester Gould
(6) *Donald Duck and the Ducklings*   Walt Disney
(7) *Little Orphan Annie under the Big Top*   Harold Gray
(8) *Tailspin Tommy in Flying Aces*   Hal Forrest
(9) *Dick Tracy and the Maroon Mask Gang*   Chester Gould
(10) *The Lone Ranger and the Lost Valley*   Fran Striker
(12) *Terry and the Pirates and the Mystery Ship*   Milton Caniff
1939
(14) *Little Orphan Annie in Rags to Riches*   Harold Gray
(15) *Mickey Mouse with Goofy and Mickey's Nephews*   Walt Disney
(16) *Tailspin Tommy and the Airliner Mystery*   Hal Forrest
(17) *Dick Tracy and the Blackmailers*   Chester Gould
(18) *Red Ryder Brings Law to Devil's Hole*   Fred Harman

Series of small comic books modelled on the *Big Little Book* series, reprinting daily newspaper strips with one picture to each right-hand page, the story being told in text on the left-hand page. Only those *Fast Action Books* featuring comic strips have been listed, the remainder being original illustrated stories, mainly westerns and Tarzan stories. None of the above series was numbered, the titles being released in monthly batches of four. Printed black-and-white with full-colour covers. *Note:* further titles were published between 1940 and 1943, but these have not been listed, as falling outside our period.

420 Jumbo Books

1938–1940. 10¢. 400 pp. 3¹/₂×4¹/₂. Publisher: Saalfield Publishing Co., Akron, Ohio.

No. 1150 *Napoleon and Uncle Elby*   Clifford McBride
No. 1166 *Napoleon, Uncle Elby and Little Mary*   Clifford McBride
No. 1167 *Dixie Dugan among the Cowboys*   J.H. Streibel

No. 1168 *Joe Palooka's Great Adventure*   Ham Fisher
No. 1169 *Bullet Benton*   J.W. McGuire
No. 1170 *Mickey Finn*   Lank Leonard
No. 1175 *Abbie an' Slats*   Raeburn Van Buren
No. 1176 *Gentleman Joe Palooka*   Ham Fisher
No. 1179 *Ned Brant Adventure Bound*   Bob Zuppke
No. 1180 *Jim Hardy Ace Reporter*   Dick Moores
No. 1181 *Broncho Bill*   Harry O'Neill
No. 1182 *Abbie an' Slats and Becky*   Raeburn Van Buren
No. 1183 *Tailspin Tommy Air Racer*   Hal Forrest
No. 1184 *Just Kids and Deep Sea Dan*   Ad Carter
No. 1186 *Inspector Wade of Scotland Yard*   Lyman Anderson
No. 1187 *Li'l Abner and the Ratfields*   Al Capp
No. 1188 *Dixie Dugan and Cuddles*   J.H. Streibel
No. 1190 *Major Hoople and His Horse*   Bill Freyse
No. 1192 *Little Mary Mixup and the Grocery Robberies*   R.M. Brinkerhoff
No. 1193 *Li'l Abner and Sadie Hawkins Day*   Al Capp
No. 1194 *Inspector Wade and the Feathered Serpent*   Lyman Anderson

Series of small comic books modelled on the *Big Little Book* series, reprinting daily newspaper strips with one picture on each right-hand page, and the story told in text on the left-hand page. Only those *Jumbo Books* featuring comic strips have been listed, the remainder being original illustrated stories, mostly westerns. *Jumbo Books* were a continuation of the same publisher's *Little Big Books*.

421 Nickel Comics

No. 1: 1938. 5¢. 68 pp. 7½×5½. Publisher: Dell Publishing Co., 149 Madison Avenue, New York. Editorial: Western Printing and Litho Co.

Contents of No. 1
1 (R) Cover (Wyoming Willy)   Harry Parlett
3 The Lie Detector
9 (R) Wyoming Willy   Harry Parlett
15 (R) Bob the Bugler   Reg Carter
17 (R) At the Mercy of the Sea
18 (R) Percy Go Bang   Harry Parlett
22 (R) The Secret of Pine Tree Point   John Woods
24 (R) Circus Capers   Reg Carter
25 (R) Bobby and Chip (Bobby Dazzler)   Otto Messmer
28 (R) Miss Adventure   Harry Parlett
32 A Picture Story of the United States
36 (R) Skit, Skat and the Captain   Basil Reynolds
42 Jack Stanton, Ace Detective
46 (R) Sir Endor the Knutty Knight
50 Pirate Gold (Treasure Island)
54 (R) Find the Spare Parts (puzzle)

55 (R) A Feathered Funster   Ern Shaw
56 (R) Riddle-Me-Ree
57 (R) Comical Carts   Ern Shaw
58 (R) This Is Going to Hurt   Leslie Marchant
59 (R) Chinamen (puzzle)
60 (R) Who Will Help Cinderella (puzzle)
61 (R) Wrong Again   Frank Lazenby
62 Tim McCoy: The Sign of the Tomahawk (story)
68 (R) Cover (Wyoming Willy)   Harry Parlett

Small comic book in oblong format, entirely black-and-white except for four-colour cover. A complete curiosity, it is almost entirely compiled from British comic strips originally published in *Mickey Mouse Weekly*. Even the American strip by Otto Messmer, 'Bobby Dazzler', appears here under its British title of 'Bobby and Chip'. Numbered 1, this is the only issue published. Evidently the half regular price was insufficient attraction to an audience with a taste for full-colour funnies.

422 Pan-Am Premium Comicbooks

1938. Free (promotional). 64 pp. $3^1/_2 \times 3^1/_4$. Publisher: Whitman Publishing Co., Racine, Wisconsin.

No. 1 *The Captain and the Kids: Boys Vill Be Boys*   Rudolph Dirks
No. 2 *Dan Dunn Meets Chang Loo*   Norman Marsh
No. 3 *G-Men and Kidnapped Justice*
No. 4 *Little Orphan Annie in Hollywood*   Harold Gray
No. 5 *Tarzan and the Daring Rescue*   Edgar Rice Burroughs
No. 6 *Tarzan and the Golden City*   Edgar Rice Burroughs

Series of six small books reprinting pictures from daily newspaper strips with additional text on the left-hand pages. Printed black-and-white with soft covers in full colour. Produced for Pan-Am Gasoline Co. as a promotional giveaway for children.

423 Tarzan Ice Cream Premium Comicbooks (Series Two)

1938. Free (promotional). 144 pp. $3^3/_4 \times 4$. Publisher: Whitman Publishing Co., Racine, Wisconsin.

No. 1 *Tailspin Tommy*   Hal Forrest
No. 2 *Broncho Bill*   Harry O'Neill
No. 3 *Zane Grey's Cowboys of the West*
No. 4 *Tarzan*   Edgar Rice Burroughs
No. 5 *Buck Rogers*   Dick Calkins
No. 6 *Ella Cinders*   Charlie Plumb

Series of six small comic books reprinting pictures from daily newspaper strips. Soft covers in full colour, inside pages in black-and-white. The stories are told in text on the left-hand pages in the style of *Big Little Books*. Produced by Whitman for the Lily-Tulip Corporation, who gave them away in return for twelve cup lids from their Tarzan ice-cream.

424 Up-To-Date Comics

1938. 10¢. 36 pp. 7¹/₂×10¹/₄. Syndicate: King Features.

Contents
Reprint (or recovering) of strips originally published in *King Comics*, including 'The Phantom' by Lee Falk and Ray Moore, 'Jungle Jim' and 'Flash Gordon' by Alex Raymond, 'The Katzenjammer Kids' by Harold Knerr, 'Curley Harper' and 'Tim Tyler's Luck' by Lyman Young, and others. Probably published as an advertising premium despite its cover price of 10¢. The cover is a one-colour redrawing of Popeye and Henry.

425 Comics on Parade

No. 1: April 1938–No. 104: February 1955. 10¢. 68 pp. 7¹/₂×10¹/₄. Publisher: United Features Syndicate Inc., 220 East 42nd Street, New York. Editorial: William Laas (editor); Harold Corbin (managing editor).

Contents of No. 1

1 Cover	Mo Leff
2 (R) Danny Dingle	Bernard Dibble
3 (R) Abbie an' Slats	Raeburn Van Buren
8 (R) The Captain and the Kids	Rudolph Dirks
12 (R) Tarzan of the Apes	Harold Foster
17 Wayne Webster of Waverly Prep (story)	Frank Methot
20 (R) Roads of Romance: James Cagney	Lee and Meggs
23 Jest di-Jest (jokes)	
24 (R) Cynical Susie	Becky Sharp, LaVerne Harding
26 (R) Broncho Bill	Harry O'Neill
30 (R) Looy Dot Dope; Colonel Wowser	John Devlin
34 (R) How To Make It	Harry Homan
35 (R) For Junior Readers	Dudley T. Fisher Jr.
36 (R) Joe Jinks Featuring Dynamite Dunn	Vic Forsythe
39 (R) Fritzi Ritz	Ernie Bushmiller
41 (R) Billy Make Believe	Harry Homan
45 Stamping Around in Malta (feature)	
46 (R) Bucky and His Pals; Mr. & Mrs. Beans	Robert L. Dickey
49 (R) Little Mary Mixup	Robert Brinkerhoff
52 (R) Benny; Opportunity Knox	J. Carver Pusey
55 (R) How It Began; If You Want to Know	Paul Berdanier
57 (R) Ella Cinders	Bill Conselman, Charlie Plumb
60 (R) Danny Dingle; Dub Dabs	Bernard Dibble

| 62 (R) Li'l Abner | Al Capp |
| 67 (R) Jasper | Frank Owen |

Advertisements
Lancaster County Seed Co.; Johnson Smith.

United Features Syndicate's second regular comic book (if we exclude the cartoon book, *Gags*), launched exactly two years after their first and very successful *Tip Top Comics*. As their original comic book contained the cream of their Sunday strip reprints, *Comics on Parade* had to be content with the daily strip versions of Broncho Bill, Joe Jinks, Fritzi Ritz, Little Mary Mixup, Ella Cinders, Li'l Abner, and Tarzan of the Apes. For this reprint United went back to their first ever newspaper strip, which began publication on 7 January 1929. Although United updated the copyright to 1938, they retained the original production credit: 'Produced by Famous Books and Plays, Distributed by United Feature Syndicate'. This was the first publication of the daily strip in full colour. It was followed by The Return of Tarzan, The Beasts of Tarzan, and The Son of Tarzan. Although this title ran 104 issues, from No. 30 (September 1940), it was combined with Single Series and concentrated on the adventures of one comic strip character each issue. Unsold issues of the first volume, Nos. 1–12, were bound in special pictorial boards and sold at Macy's Toyland in Children's World at the New York World's Fair from July 1939.

426 Super Comics

No. 1: May 1938–No. 121: February 1949. 10¢. 68 pp. 7½ × 10¼. Publisher: K.K. Publications Inc., Poughkeepsie, New York. Editor: Oskar Lebeck.

Contents of No. 1

1 Cover	
3 (R) Dick Tracy	Chester Gould
8 (R) Smokey Stover	Bill Holman
11 (R) Little Orphan Annie	Harold Gray
16 (R) Smitty	Walter Berndt
18 (R) Tiny Tim	Stanley Link
20 (R) Terry and the Pirates	Milton Caniff
25 (R) The Gumps	Gus Edson
29 (R) Spooky	Bill Holman
30 Crime a Hundred Years from Now	George Merkle
34 (R) Sweeney and Son	Al Posen
35 (R) Gasoline Alley	Frank King
39 (R) Small Stuff	Gus Jud
41 (R) Little Joe	Ed Leffingwell
44 Punchie	George Merkle
45 (R) Moon Mullins	Frank Willard
49 (R) Harold Teen	Carl Ed
52 Tyrone Ford, Air Adventurer	Dan Mer (George Merkle?)
56 (R) Winnie Winkle	Martin Branner
60 (R) Streaky	Loy Byrnes

62 Tootsie the Telephone Girl
63 (R) Smilin' Jack   Zack Mosley

Advertisements
Big Little Books; *Mickey Mouse Magazine*; Johnson Smith.

Although the indicia bears the line 'Entire contents copyright 1936, 1937, 1938 by Chicago Tribune–New York News Syndicate Inc.', this comic book reprint of Sunday pages does, in fact, contain a scattering of original material. Most, if not all, is drawn by George Merkle. This was the first U.S. comic book to reprint strips from British comics. In No. 2 appeared 'The Lost Colony of Atlantis' by William Ward, and 'Skit and Skat' by Basil Reynolds, and in No. 3, 'Wings of Fortune' by Reg Perrott and 'City of Jewels' by Jock McCail. 'The Phantom City' and 'Flashing Through', both by Stanley White, started in No. 6. All came from the British *Mickey Mouse Weekly*. Among other original strips introduced were 'Manuk the Arctic Crusoe', and 'Tim Todd the Boy Detective' (No. 9), and in the superhero era, 'Magic Morro' by Ken Ernst (No. 21). These strips were copyrighted to R.S. Callender, as were 'Jack Wander' by Ed Moore, and 'Jim Ellis' by R. Fletcher. 'Clyde Beatty, the Big Game Hunter', starred in a strip in later issues, copyright Famous Artists Syndicate. *Note:* from No. 2 the publisher became Whitman Publishing Co. at the same address. From the mid-1940s *Super Comics* was taken over by Dell Publishing Co.

427 Action Comics

No. 1: June 1938–. 10¢ (1–282); 12¢. 68 pp. $7^1/_2 \times 10^1/_2$. Publisher: Detective Comics Inc. (Harry Donenfield), 480 Lexington Avenue, New York. Editor: Vincent Sullivan.

Contents of No. 1

1 Cover	Joe Shuster
2 Color Page Contest (BW)	
3 Superman	Jerome Siegel, Joe Shuster
16 Chuck Dawson	Homer Fleming (BW)
22 Zatara, Master Magician	Fred Guardineer
34 South Sea Strategy (story)	Capt. Frank Thomas
36 Sticky-Mitt Stimson	Alger
40 The Adventures of Marco Polo	Sven Elven
44 Pep Morgan	Fred Guardineer
48 Scoop Scanlon, Five Star Reporter	Will Ely (BW)
54 Tex Thomson	Bernard Baily
66 Stardust	Star-gazer
67 Odds and Ends	Sheldon Moldoff (BW)

Advertisements
Johnson Smith.

This comic book has become the most important in the history of the genre. It introduced the original superhero, Superman, a type of character that changed the face of the American comic book, influencing virtually every successful title to come. Originally designed as a daily newspaper strip, author Siegel and artist Shuster failed to interest syndicates and eventually submitted it to Vincent Sullivan when informed he was putting together a new comic book on the lines of the already successful *Detective Comics*. The first 13-page, 98-panel episode was principally a paste-up of the daily strips. *Action Comics* No. 1 was reprinted in an enlarged (10×13¾) facsimile format as *Famous First Edition* (Limited Collectors' Golden Mint Series) No. C-26, copyright 1974 by National Periodical Publications Inc., price $1.00. A mint copy of the original No. 1 is valued in the 1989 edition of *The Comic Book Price Guide* by Robert M. Overstreet at $30,000. Regular characters introduced in later issues include:

No. 14 Clip Carson   Bob Kane
No. 18 Three Aces
No. 23 The Black Pirate   Sheldon Moldoff
No. 33 Mr. America   Bernard Baily
No. 37 Congo Bill
No. 40 The Star-Spangled Kid   Hal Sherman
No. 42 Vigilante   Mort Meskin
No. 127 Tommy Tomorrow
No. 242 Brainiac
No. 252 Supergirl

428 Circus

'The Comic Riot'
No. 1: June 1938–No. 3 August 1938. 10¢. 68 pp. 7¼×10¼. Publisher: Globe Syndicate Inc. (Monte Bourjaily), 16 East 48th Street, New York. Editor: Monte Bourjaily.

Contents of No. 1

1 Cover	Will Hammell
3 Peewee Throttle in Fuzzyland	Jack Cole
5 Dinty and Mope	James Pabian
6 Spacehawks	Basil Wolverton
8 Sea Imps	Henry Roesler
10 Disk-Eyes the Detective	Basil Wolverton
12 Leo the Great	Ralph Olian
14 Hal Hazard in the South Seas	Howard Norge
16 Honies	Henry Roesler
17 Natty Nats	Ed Nofziger (BW)
18 Circus Scramble	Will Hammell (BW)
20 Earn Money for Fun (quiz contest) (BW)	
21 Jiggers	Corinne Dillon
23 Flub Dub	Ed Nofziger
24 The Great Magoo	Terry Flagg
26 Sprinkle Puss	Dave Gerard
28 Ken Craig and the Lords of Crillon	Mort Cowen, Jay Jackson
32 Balmy Knight	Mark Ellison
34 Jack Hinton the Guardsman	Will Eisner

40 Beau Gus	Wesley Morse
42 Galahad Jones and His Lady	Eldon Frye
44 Van Bragger	Bob Kane
45 Donnie Stuart	Jean Hotchkiss
47 Sally MaGundy	V. Kirkpatrick
49 Picture Crossword Puzzle	Lee Paradiso (BW)
50 Circus Almanac for May (BW)	
51 The Hi-School Club (story) (BW)	
52 How Do You Rate (feature) (BW)	
53 Side Streets of New York	Bob Kane
54 The College Wrestler	Smada
56 Granpop's Workshop	Hal Wheatley
58 Spud Hilly	Chuck Dooling
62 It's Fun to Know	Horace Adams
64 Bob Venture	Herb Cornell

Advertisements
Johnson Smith; Crowell Publishing Co.

Although *Circus* contained some brilliant artwork and was full of bright ideas, it was spoiled by an editorial directive that decreed that each page should be laid out: 12 square panels of equal size, separated by a single black rule: no gutters. In addition, there were no drawn titles, all headings being typeset above the strips. A total of $201 was offered in a vast reader-participation contest for comic strips, cartoons, sketches, poems, limericks, short stories, letters, quizzes, Young Americana, etc., the winners to be published in a forthcoming 8-page section entitled 'Side Show'. Among the contributors to *Circus* will be noted such burgeoning comic book talent as Jack Cole, Basil Wolverton, Will Eisner, and Bob Kane.

429 Crackajack Funnies

No. 1: June 1938–No. 43: January 1942. 10¢. 68 pp. 7½×10¼. Publisher: Whitman Publishing Co. Inc., Poughkeepsie, New York. Editor: Oskar Lebeck.

Contents of No. 1

1 Cover	Oskar Lebeck
3 (R) Dan Dunn, Secret Operative 48	Norman Marsh
8 Capt. Frank Hawks, Air Ace	Al McWilliams
12 (R) Freckles and His Friends	Merrill Blosser
16 (R) Myra North, Special Nurse	Ray Thompson, Charles Coll
21 Columbus Goes West	Dan Balkin
24 (R) Wash Tubbs	Roy Crane
28 (R) Out Our Way	J.R. Williams
31 (R) Apple Mary and Dennie	Martha Orr
35 (R) The Nebbs	W.A. Carlson, Sol Hess
38 (R) Our Boarding House with Major Hoople	Bill Freyse
41 Clyde Beatty, Daredevil Lion Tamer	Al Lewin

44 (R) Don Winslow of the Navy	Frank Martinek, Leon Beroth
48 Tom Mix: Fence War in Painted Valley	Al Lewin
52 (R) Boots	L.B. Martin
56 Tom Traylor, G-Man X 32	
60 (R) Flapper Fanny	Sylvia
63 Buck Jones: Rock Creek Cattle War	Kenneth Ernst

Advertisements
Super Comics; *Mickey Mouse Magazine*; Johnson Smith.

First editorial (No. 7)
'Hello, Pals: First of all I want to thank those who have written to me in the past and tell them again how much their letters have meant to me and helped me to make the *Crackerjack Funnies* the fine magazine it is today. What do you say if we get together on this page once in a while and have a little Pow-Wow? You know this is your magazine and how else will I know what to do to make it better and give you the things you want unless we get together? So get your pens ready, your brain cells busy, and let's see what you have to suggest! Some letters I have received said — I think Dan Dunn is swell, let's have more pages of him! Why don't you have a Baseball page? and many many other suggestions. Well? What about it, Pals? Maybe your letter will win one of those Dollar Bills. Supposing you sit down and think for a second and then write down your idea of what we ought to have. You don't have to make it a long letter, just jot down your idea and put down your name, age and address and send it to me. Remember, Pals, this is your magazine! You are the ones who can make it a 100 per cent of what you want it to be. By the way, have you noticed that each and every page has a comic in full color? I knew that was one of the things you always wanted. Are we proud of it? You bet we are! Well, goodbye and let me hear from all of you real soon. Ed.'

Whitman's second comic book, a speedy follow-on to their *Super Comics*. It contained a selection of Sunday page reprints from Publishers Syndicate Inc., N.E.A. Service Inc. and Bell Syndicate Inc. The original material, which was mostly based on movie star personalities of the period, was supplied by Stephen Slesinger Inc. Fred Harman's 'Red Ryder' started in No. 9, as did original strips 'Speed Bolton Air Ace' by Al McWilliams, and 'Time Marches Back with Looney Luke' by Ole (Oskar Lebeck). 'Ed Tracer — G-Man X-32' by Will Ely (No. 11), 'Stratosphere Jim and His Flying Fortress' by Al McWilliams (No. 22), 'Ellery Queen' (No. 23) and 'The Owl' by Frank Thomas (No. 25) were also original series.

430 Cowboy Comics (formerly **Star Ranger**)
No. 13: July 1938–No. 14: August 1938. 10¢. 52 pp. 7×10. Publisher: Centaur Publications Inc. (Joseph J. Hardie), 420 De Soto Avenue, St Louis, Missouri. Editorial: Room 1821, 461 Eighth Avenue, New York. Lloyd Jacquet (editor); Raymond Kelly (business manager).

Contents of No. 13 (first issue)

1 Cover	A.P.
2 Editorial: Welcome Western Fans	
3 Slim Pickens	Jack Cole
4 (R) Chief Satanta	

5 (R) Ace and Deuce	W.M. Allison
10 (R) Little Maverick	Fred Guardineer
11 (R) Lyin' Lou	Fred Guardineer
13 (R) Air Patrol	Maurice Gutwirth
17 (R) Jess Phoolin'	Fred Schwab
18 (R) Wild West Junior	Charles Biro
20 (R) Aces High	Will Harr, Frank Frollo (BW)
25 (R) Medicine Man	Paul Gustavson
26 (R) A Close Call	Fred Guardineer
28 (R) Burros of the Hee-Haw Ranch (story)	Pat Allen (BW)
30 (R) Null and Void	Todmoro
32 (R) Cowboy Jake	Charles Biro
34 (R) Lonesome Luke	Fred Schwab
35 (R) Lee Trent	Frank Frollo
40 (R) Killer McGee	Fred Schwab
41 (R) Two Buckaroos	Will Harr, Paul Gustavson
46 (R) Daffy Dills	
47 (R) Trouble Hunters	Rafael Astarita

Advertisements
Ohio Novelty Co.; MMM Studios; Century Photo Service; Brazel Novelty Co.; Johnson Smith; Centaur Publications.

First editorial
'WELCOME WESTERN FANS!
Your Uncle Joe is certainly pleased to announce a big increase in our comic magazine family . . .'(identical editorial as for *Keen Detective Funnies*, below).

Cowboy Comics is basically a title change for *Star Ranger*, the Chesler publication which had been taken over by Centaur Publications from No. 10 (March 1938). Cover and title apart, the entire contents are reprints from earlier issues. The title ran only two issues before partial reversion to *Star Ranger Funnies*.

431 Keen Detective Funnies (formerly Detective Picture Stories)
No. 8: July 1938–No. 24 (September 1940). 10¢. 52 pp. 64 pp. (15–). 7×10. Publisher: Centaur Publications Inc. (Joseph J. Hardie), 420 De Soto Avenue, St. Louis, Missouri. Editorial: 461 Eighth Avenue, New York; Lloyd Jacquet (editor); Raymond Kelly (business manager).

Contents of No. 8 (first issue)

1 Cover	
2 Editorial: Welcome Keen Detectives	
3 (R) Alias the Clock	George Brenner
10 (R) Bayfront Cowboy	Ellis Edwards
17 (R) The Teen Age	Joe E. Buresch
18 (R) Terror of the Timber	Clyde Don

25 (R) Gag Way   Joe E. Buresch
26 (R) Weapons of the West (feature)   W.M. Allison
28 (R) Captain Jim and the Chinese Pirates   R.A. Burley
35 (R) Rocky Baird   Paul J. Lauretta
43 (R) The Spinner; The Case of the Broken Skull   Bert Christman

Advertisements
Ohio Novelty Co.; MMM Studios; Spencer Fireworks Co.; Century Photo Service; Brazel Novelty Co.; Johnson Smith; Centaur Publications.

First editorial
'WELCOME KEEN DETECTIVES!
Your Uncle Joe is certainly pleased to announce a big increase in our comic magazine family. In addition to *Funny Pages, Funny Picture Stories*, *Star Comics*, and *Star Ranger* with which you are all familiar, Uncle Joe now has enlarged the family to include three new magazines. These are as follows:
1: *Cowboy Comics* — which will bring you the cream of cowboy and western story funnies.
2: *Keen Detective Funnies* — chock full of hair-raising detective adventure comics to bring thrills galore.
3: *Little Giant Comics* — a new kind of comic magazine with 128 pages — twice as many comics — twice as thick — and twice as good and funny — in a new convenient pocket size!
I feel sure you will enjoy every one of our new comic magazines just as much as you have enjoyed our other publications. And, just wait until you see the many new features coming in future issues of *Keen Detective Funnies*!'

Despite the new title, new editor, and new publisher, regular readers of *Detective Picture Stories* must surely have found themselves in familiar territory: every one of the strips in the first issue of *Keen Detective Funnies* was a reprint from the earlier title. Gradually new material was added to the old, including:

No. 9 Doc Doyle, Scientific Detective   Maurice Gutwirth
No. 10 Dean Denton, Scientific Adventurer   Harry Francis Campbell
No. 10 Snoop and Stoop   Fred Schwab
V.2 No. 2 Little Dynamite   Jack Cole
V.2 No. 2 Stony Dawson   Carl Burgos
V.2 No. 3 Corporal Merrill of the Mounted   Terry Gilkison
V.2 No. 3 T.N.T. Todd, Ace G-Man   Victoria Pazmino
V.2 No. 3 Spy Hunters   Lachlan Field
V.2 No. 4 Gabby Flynn   Kenneth Ernst
V.2 No. 4 Crane of Scotland Yard   Paul Gustavson
V.2 No. 6 Dan Dennis F.B.I.   Sam Gilman
V.2 No. 6 Dan Dix, Ship's Detective   George Brousek
V.2 No. 6 Captain Steve Ransom   Arthur Hoffman
V.2 No. 7 The Masked Marvel, Super Sleuth   Ben Thompson
V.2 No. 10 Spark O'Leary, Radio Newshawk   Will Ely
V.2 No. 11 Dean Masters, D.A.   Claire S. Moe
V.2 No. 12 The Eye Sees   Frank Thomas

V.3 No. 1 Ed Colton	Max Neill
No. 18 Eyes of the Kumas; Dudley Dance	Jacqueline Martin
No. 19 Famous Spies	Malcolm Kildale
No. 23 Air Man	George Kapitan, Harry Sahle

432 Little Giant Comics

No. 1: July 1938–No. 4: February 1939. 10¢. 132 pp. (1–3); 68 pp. (4). 6¾×4¾ (1–3); 6½×9½ (4). Publisher: Centaur Publications Inc. (Joseph Hardie), 29 Worthington Street, Springfield, Massachusetts. Editorial: 461 Eighth Avenue, New York; Lloyd Jacquet (editor).

Contents of No. 1

1 Cover	Martin Filchock
2 Editorial: Cash in Ten Easy Prizes	
3 (R) Goofy Gags	Paul Gustafson
4 (R) Gil Galen, G-Man	Craig Fox
9 (R) Rough House Annie	Charles Biro
10 (R) Rustlers from the Sawtooth	Ross Martin, W.M. Allison
17 (R) Spider-Legs	Paul Gustafson
18 (R) Flood Valve 5	Frank Frollo
23 Can You Find 30 Mistakes	Martin Filchock
24 (R) Pot o' Gold	Rafael Astarita
27 (R) Phoney Crime	Bob Wood
32 (R) Cheerio Minstrels	Paul Gustafson
34 (R) Dormitory Daze	Bob Wood
35 (R) Ma and Pa	Paul Gustafson
36 (R) Cutter Carson	Creig Flessel
39 (R) Cop Killer	
41 (R) High Pressure Preston	Paul Gustafson
42 (R) Tin Mule	Rafael Astarita
46 15 Errors; 33 Dots	Martin Filchock
47 (R) Out on the Farm	Paul Gustafson
48 (R) Jack Strand	Frank Frollo
66 (R) Tim and Tom	
67 (R) Echo	
68 (R) Boomerang	Rafael Astarita
71 (R) Funny Fables	Dick Ryan
72 (R) The Little Black Bag	Bob Wood
77 (R) Bear Facts	Dick Ryan
78 (R) Top Guy (story)	Ken Fitch
90 (R) Fangs of the Cougar	Jim Chambers
93 (R) Tam O'Shanter	Jim Chambers
94 (R) Jig Saw Trail	Bob Wood
98 Riddle Rebus	Martin Filchock
99 (R) Ticklers	Fred Schwab
100 (R) Sonny Darling	Claire S. Moe
107 Magic Money	Martin Filchock

174

108 (R) Vacation Cowgirl	Bob Wood
113 Puzzles	Martin Filchock
114 (R) Sweet Revenge	Dick Ryan
119 (R) The Firehouse Gang	Paul Gustafson
120 (R) Lucky Coyne	Creig Flessel
123 Baseball Puzzle	Martin Filchock
124 (R) Bear Facts	Dick Ryan
125 (R) Arizona's Ace Trick	
130 Magic Money	Martin Filchock

Advertisements
Jo-Ra Products; Johnson Smith.

First editorial
'CASH IN — TEN EASY PRIZES!
Hello Boys and Girls!
You've been asking for something new and your Uncle Joe, who's been staying up nights thinking of ideas to amuse all his nieces and nephews, now hands you this *Little Giant Comics*, a brand new kind of magazine! *Little Giant Comics* is a whatchumcallit kind of magazine. It's a little book, yet it's a big magazine, all in one! It has giggles and gags, puzzles and tricks, funnies and stories, 128 pages of them . . . more than any other magazine. Your Uncle Joe has tried to give you the biggest buy — *Little Giant Comics* is it! Now, Uncle Joe is so proud of *Little Giant Comics*, he's been telling everybody that every one of you will read this big little magazine from cover to cover, and that you will write him a letter telling him to bring out a second *Little Giant Comics* right away. Would you like another issue of *Little Giant Comics* soon? Then, give Uncle Joe your reasons in a letter, and he will award the ten nieces and nephews who write him the best letters a brand new, crisp One Dollar Bill each. That's fun! All you have to do is read this *Little Giant Comics*, then decide why you want to see issue No. 2, and write the reasons! Do you like the new size? Is it easy to carry? Is it worth the dime? Do you like the comics, the puzzles, the tricks, or the stories — or all of them? Extra prize for promptness! First letter from anywhere gets a special souvenir surprise from Uncle Joe! Get going now!'

The first pocket-sized comic book, printed in oblong format and entirely black-and-white except for the three-colour cover. The contents were almost all reprints of strips that originally appeared in colour in earlier issues of comic books published by Centaur and its predecessors: Ultem, Chesler, and Comics Magazine Co. All the original strips were re-edited to fit the new oblong format. The fourth and final issue of this title reverted to regular format, but slightly smaller and still with the inside pages in black-and-white (uniform with *Uncle Joe's Funnies*).

433 Amazing Mystery Funnies

No. 1: August 1938–No. 24: September 1940. 10¢. 52 pp. 6³/₄× 10¹/₄. Publisher: Centaur Publications Inc. (Joseph Hardie), 420 De Soto Avenue, St. Louis, Missouri. Editorial: Room 1821, 461 Eighth Avenue, New York; Lloyd Jacquet (editor).

Contents of No. 1

1 Cover	Bill Everett

2 Editorial: Welcome Mystery Readers	Uncle Joe
3 (R) Tyrant's Gold	Arthur Pinajian
10 (R) The Master Mind	George Merkle
17 (R) Dragon Pass: Phantom o' the Hills	ArthurPinajian
24 (R) Tom Dawson Seascout	Steve Jussen
32 (R) Sapphire Seas (story)	C.W. Scott; W.M. Allison
34 (R) The Border War	Ed McD. Moore Jr.
42 (R) The Yellow Terror	Claire S. Moe

Advertisements
Columbian Music Publishers; Century Photo Service; MMM Studios; Johnson Smith; Centaur Publications.

First editorial
'WELCOME MYSTERY READERS!
It's always a pleasure for your Uncle Joe, editor of the Centaur Comics, to announce a new magazine — but it's really a treat to be able to welcome you as a reader to this, our latest magazine. Your Uncle Joe has felt, for a long time, that many, many boys and girls and grown ups too would welcome a comics magazine devoted to amazing and mystery stories. Therefore, after gathering together the bestest of the best material for this type of magazine, we present it herein for your approval. We hope you like *Amazing Mystery Funnies* and that you will tell all your friends and relatives about it.
Uncle Joe is also publishing another new magazine this month. It's called *Little Giant Movie Funnies* — and brings you something new in the way of magazines — a complete five-star movie program with swell comedies, great feature movies, a new style of newsreel, wild west features, adventure stories, mystery thrillers, and everything you've always liked to see in the movies — plus Giant-O Puzzles, Questions & Answers — a total of 128 pages of big, big features. There's also a big contest in this new magazine in which readers are asked to rate the movies according to five stars, four stars, etc. Make sure you see a copy and tell your friends about it! See you in our next issue!'

Despite the exciting editorial, the cover of No. 1 was the only new item in the entire issue. All the interior strips were reprints from *Funny Picture Stories*, and the other titles which Centaur Publications had taken over from Ultem Publications. However, the gradual introduction of science-fiction strips, and the reprinting of earlier science-fiction strips, warrant this title being dubbed the world's first science-fiction comic book. Characters introduced in subsequent issues include:

No. 2 Skyrocket Steele	Bill Everett
No. 2 2038 A.D.	A.S. Van Eerde
No. 3 Dirk the Demon, 24th Century Archaeologist	Bill Everett
No. 4 Jay Douglas in a Prehistoric World	Robert Golden
No. 7 Air-Sub D.X.	Carl Burgos
No. 8 Daredevil Barry Finn	Tarpe Mills
No. 11 The Fantom of the Fair	Paul Gustavson
No. 12 Speed Centaur	Malcolm Kildale
No. 12 Don Dixon and the Hidden Empire	Bob Moore, Carl Pfeufer
No. 14 Jon Linton, Flyer, Scientist, Adventurer	Harry Campbell
No. 16 Space Patrol	Basil Wolverton

434 Little Giant Movie Funnies

No. 1: August 1938–No. 2: October 1938. 10¢. 132 pp. 6³/₄×4¹/₂. Publisher: Centaur Publications Inc. (Joseph Hardie), 29 Worthington Street, Springfield, Massachusetts. Editorial: 461 Eighth Avenue, New York; Lloyd Jacquet (editor).

Contents of No. 1

1 Cover	Martin Filchock
3 (R) Minute Movies	Ed Wheelan
Puzzles	Martin Filchock

Advertisements
Johnson Smith.

Comment
Small oblong comic book reprinting the daily newspaper strip 'Minute Movies', by Ed Wheelan. Printed black-and-white with a three-colour cover. The second issue adds an animated cartoon 'Riffler' in the top right-hand corner. This is drawn by Martin Filchock and entitled 'The Amachoor'.

435 Jumbo Comics

'Bigger and Better Funnies'
No. 1: September 1938–No. 167: April 1953. 10¢. 68 pp. (1–3); 52 pp. (4–9); 68 pp. (10–). 10¹/₂×14¹/₂ (1–8); 8¹/₄×10¹/₄ (9); 7¹/₄×10¹/₄ (10–). Publisher: Real Adventures Publishing Co. Inc. (Thurman T. Scott), 461 8th Avenue, New York. Editorial: 805 East 42nd Street, New York; Malcolm Reiss (editor); William E. Eisner (art director); Samuel M. Iger (features editor).

Contents of No. 1

1 Cover	Will Eisner
2 Editorial: Hello Kids	Will Eisner
3 Peter Pupp	Bob Kane
7 Hawks of the Seas	Will Eisner
12 Bobby	Sam Iger
14 Puzzle Phun	Don De Conn
15 The Count of Monte Cristo	Jack Kirby
19 Spencer Steel	Dennis Colebrook
23 The Diary of Dr. Hayward	Jack Kirby
27 (R) Uncle Otto	Will Eisner
28 (R) Stars on Parade	Toni Rossett, Lora Lane
29 Jest Laffs	Bob Kane
30 (R) Pee Wee	Sam Iger
31 Sheena, Queen of the Jungle	Mort Meskin, W. Morgan Thomas
36 Modern Planes	Les Marshall
38 (R) Gilda Gay, the Modern Girl	
39 Puzzle Phun	Don De Conn
40 Lost in the Arctic (story)	Owen Finbar

42 The Hunchback of Notre Dame	Dick Briefer
47 The Adventures of Don Sherrill	Don De Conn
51 ZX5, Spies in Action	Will Eisner, W. Morgan Thomas
55 (R) Heroes of Sport	Will Eisner, Tom Swift
56 Island of Gold (story)	Dennis Drake
58 Jumbo Jim's Prize Party (feature)	Will Eisner
59 Inspector Dayton	Lou Fine, George Thatcher
63 Wilton of the West	Jack Kirby
67 Jest Laffs	Bob Kane
68 Cover	Will Eisner

First editorial
'HELLO KIDS! GREETINGS FROM JUMBO JIM
Grab your hats — hold on tight — here we go! You want comics with fun, adventure, thrills, laffs, puzzles, stories and prizes, and you can take your uncle Jumbo Jim's word for it, boys and girls, you'll find them in *Jumbo Comics*, a prize package if ever you've seen one. It has everything you want. Big pages, big clear pictures, big type, easy to read — a big magazine and a whale of a big dime's worth. And speaking of prizes, can you draw pictures or make up a joke? How would you like to see one of your cartoons or one of your funny gags printed in a future issue of *Jumbo Comics*? Well, boys and girls, just turn to page 56 and I'll tell you how you can do it and get paid for it too. Fair enough? Be seeing you, kids. I am sure you'll like *Jumbo Comics* and I hope you'll come and see me and my gang in the next issue. Watch for No. 2 on your newsstand. So-long and good fun! Jumbo Jim.'

Jumbo Comics, an aptly named outsize monthly, was designed to utilize the tabloid strips which had been originally published in *Wags*, the overseas export weekly and had not yet been seen in the U.S.A. As all the strips were designed in black-and-white, and it was considered too expensive to add four colours, the comic was printed on orange and green paper, only the cover and back page being printed in four colours. Some reprints of daily strips were included, dated from September to December 1937, copyrighted to Universal Phoenix Features Syndicate, founded by Samuel M. Iger, who was billed as features editor of *Jumbo Comics*. Few of the strips began from their first episodes, Peter Pupp commencing at episode 7, Hawks of the Seas at 41, Spencer Steel at 30, Sheena at 11, Inspector Dayton at 47, and Wilton of the West at 45. Eight issues were published in tabloid format; No. 9 was the first four-colour edition but at an odd size, regular comic-book-sized issues with full colour beginning with No. 10 (October 1939). A mint copy of No. 1 is valued at $2,600 in Overstreet's *Comic Book Price Guide* for 1989.

436 Uncle Joe's Funnies

'Magic Tricks — Games — Puzzles'
No. 1: September 1938. 10¢. 68 pp. 6³/₄×9¹/₂. Publisher: Centaur Publications Inc., 461 Eighth Avenue, New York. Editorial: 461 Eighth Avenue, New York, Joseph Hardie (editor).

Contents of No. 1

1 Cover	Bill Everett
3 Editorial: Uncle Joe's Funnies	Bill Everett, Joseph Hardie
4 Puzzle Detectives	Terry Gilkison

5 Easy Tricks up Our Sleeves	Fred Schwab
6 Puzzlettes	Terry Gilkison
7 Magicomics	Terry Gilkison
8 How to make a Zipper	Fred Schwab
9 Magic Made Easy	Fred Schwab
10 Try Your Hand as a Sky Writer	Terry Gilkison
11 Puzzle Pix	Terry Gilkison
12 Keeno the Great Magician	Fred Schwab
15 Kut-M-Up	Fred Schwab
16 Pix Pastime	Terry Gilkison
17 The Fun Spot	
18 (R) Here's Magic Tricks You Can Do	
23 Goofy Geography	
24 Draw Your Own	Terry Gilkison
25 Fun for All	
26 What Do You Remember	
27 Do You Mean It	
28 Enlarge an Elephant	
29 How to Make a Wooden Gun That Works	Fred Schwab
30 Game of Cuts	
31 Craft Corner	
32 Draw a Little	
33 Make Your Own	
34 Sandy MacMagic	Terry Gilkison
36 Stepping Stone Maze	
37 Craft Corner	
38 Roy the Rhymster	
39 Puzzle Patter	Terry Gilkison
40 Idle Hours	
41 Pix Your Pleasure	
42 Find Six Escaped Animals	
43 Brain Teasers	Terry Gilkison
44 Triangle Puzzle	Fred Schwab
45 Pastime Puzzles	Terry Gilkison
46 Cut Outs	Fred Schwab
47 Scrambled Sketches	Terry Gilkison
48 Finger Crafts	
49 Puzzletters	Terry Gilkison
50 Dots and Dashes	Terry Gilkison
51 Bill's Brain Teaser	Fred Schwab
52 Magic Cards	
53 How to Make a Racing Coaster	Fred Schwab
54 How Many Errors	
55 Pix Your Puzzles	Terry Gilkison
56 Play Ball	Fred Schwab
57 Magic Puzzles	Fred Schwab
59 Make an Enlargement of Rover	

60 Learn to Be a Sky Writer   Terry Gilkison
61 Uncle Ezra's Rebuses   Jingo
62 Enlarge Dolly Dove
63 Puzzle Sleuths   Terry Gilkison
64 Make a Big Rat
65 How Many Objects Start with the Letter B

Advertisements
Centaur Publications; Johnson Smith; Little Giant Comics

First editorial
'So many of Uncle Joe's nieces and nephews who have written to him have asked him to get out a
magic — puzzles — games — tricks and play magazine that — here it is!!! Uncle Joe's busy office has
been working for months gathering the pages that you will read in this issue. I hope the whole family
will enjoy puzzling over *Uncle Joe's Funnies* No. 1'

The first 'activity book' to be published in comic book format must be reckoned as a brave failure:
only No. One was published. Perhaps the fact that the entire book, save for the coloured cover, was
printed in black-and-white on cheap, thick newsprint paper contributed to its unpopularity.

437 **Little Giant Detective Funnies**

No. 1: October 1938–No. 4: February 1939. 10¢. 132 pp. (1–3); 36 pp. (4). $6^3/_4 \times 4^1/_2$ (1–3); $6^1/_2 \times 9^1/_2$ (4).
Publisher: Centaur Publications Inc. (Joseph Hardie), 29 Worthington Street, Springfield, Mas-
sachusetts. Editorial: 461 Eighth Avenue, New York; Lloyd Jacquet (editor).

Advertisements
Johnson Smith.

Small oblong comic book reprinting strips from earlier Centaur comic books: *Keen Detective
Funnies*, *Detective Picture Stories*, etc. Printed black-and-white with a three-colour cover. The final
issue is of regular comic book format, slightly undersize, but still printed black-and-white.

438 **Star Ranger Funnies** (formerly **Cowboy Comics**)
No. 15: October 1938–No. 20: October 1939. 10¢. 68 pp. 7×10. Publisher: Centaur Publications (Joseph
J. Hardie), 420 De Soto Avenue, St. Louis, Missouri. Editorial: 220 Fifth Avenue, New York: Lloyd
Jacquet (editor), Raymond Kelly (business manager).

Contents of No. 15 (first issue)
1 Cover   Terry Gilkison
2 Editorial: Eight Comic Magazines to Keep You
   Happy
3 Daffy Dills
4 True Westernotes   Terry Gilkison

5 Home in the Ozarks	Jack Cole
10 (R) Lyin Lou	Fred Guardineer
12 Tenderfoot Mary	Fred Schwab
13 The Ermine	Martin Filchock
17 Rangeography	Terry Gkilkison
18 (R) Wild West Junior	Charles Biro
20 (R) The Law of Caribou Country	Will Eisner (BW)
26 (R) Cowboy Jake	Charles Biro
28 (R) The Plugged Dummy	Arnold Hicks (BW)
33 The Riddle Roundup	
34 (R) Sunset	Fred Guardineer
36 The Rodeo Rope Rescue (story)	Pat Allen (BW)
39 How to Draw Comic Cowboys	Martin Filchock (BW)
40 (R) Jess Phoolin	Fred Schwab (BW)
42 One Buck and Two Bits	Martin Filchock
44 Famous Frontiersmen (BW)	
46 (R) Daffy Dills	Charles Biro
47 (R) Crime Doesn't Pay	
48 (R) Tenderfoot Mary	Fred Schwab (BW)
49 (R) Spurs	Paul Gustavson
50 (R) Red Coat	Maurice Kashuba
55 (R) Slim Pickens	Jack Cole
56 (R) Two Buckaroos	Will Harr, Paul Gustavson
61 (R) Jess Phoolin	Fred Schwab
62 (R) Trouble Hunters	Maurice Gutwirth
66 (R) Medicine Man	Paul Gustavson

Advertisements
Crowell Publishing Co.; Centaur Publications; Johnson Smith.

First editorial
'EIGHT COMIC MAGAZINES TO KEEP YOU HAPPY
Because so many boys and girls like funny pictures and comics, Uncle Joe now issues eight different comic magazines. Each magazine is issued once every two months so you can buy a different one at your newsstand every week. Just to make sure you know the names of all of Uncle Joe's Centaur Comic Magazines, here is the list:
Amazing Mystery Funnies — Thrilling stories of the future.
Funny Pages — Every page crammed with humorous pictures.
Funny Picture Stories — The magazine that keeps you smiling.
Keen Detective Funnies — Hair-raising, blood-curdling mysteries.
Little Giant Comics — 128 pages of comics, puzzles and magic.
Little Giant Movie Comics — A complete movie show — with comedies, newsreels, dramas, western pictures, etc. Also, a new feature — you turn the pages and see the Jitterbug dance. No fooling, it really does move!
Star Comics — All-star humor, laughs galore, and lots of fun!
Star Ranger Funnies — Exciting western features you'll enjoy.

There's the list — and I know you will like every one of my seven other magazines just as much as you like this one. They only cost you 10¢ — and your newsdealer will be glad to show them to you. Uncle Joe, Editor.'

After two editions as *Cowboy Comics*, this reverted in part to its original title (the title it had when Centaur Publications took it over from Chesler Publications), *Star Ranger*, adding the word *Funnies*. This title remained until the final issue, numbered Vol. 2, No. 5, actually the twentieth. The majority of the contents continued to be reprints from earlier issues of *Star Ranger*, but there were new episodes of Jack Cole's brilliantly eccentric 'Home in the Ozarks', plus occasional new characters of quality: 'Bill Hardin' by Al Mack (April 1939), Fred Schwab's 'Krazy Koot the Cowhand' (June 1939), and Art Pinajian's 'Red Man of the Rockies' (October 1939).

439 Adventure Comics (formerly New Adventure Comics)

No. 32: November 1938–No. 503: September 1983. 10¢. 68 pp. 7¼×10. Publisher: Detective Comics Inc. (Harry Donenfield), 420 De Soto Avenue, St. Louis, Missouri. Editorial: 480 Lexington Avenue, New York; Vincent Sullivan (editor).

Contents of No. 32 (first issue)

1 Cover	
Barry O'Neill	Leo O'Mealia
Tom Brent	Jim Chambers
Federal Men	Jerome Siegel, Joe Shuster
Junior Federal Men Club (feature)	
Captain Desmo	Ed Winiarski
Dale Daring	Will Ely
Cal 'n' Alec	Fred Schwab
Don Coyote	Fred Schwab
Tod Hunter, Jungle Master	Jim Chambers
The Golden Dragon	Tom Hickey
Rusty and His Pals	Bob Kane
Anchors Aweigh	Fred Guardineer

Advertisements
Johnson Smith.

Continuation of New Adventure Comics: the word 'New' is now dropped permanently from the title. Continuing characters introduced in later issues include:

No. 40 The Sandman	Bert Christman
No. 40 Socko Strong	
No. 47 Steve Conrad, Adventurer	Jack Lehti
No. 48 The Hourman	Bernard Baily
No. 58 Paul Kirk, Manhunter	Ed Moore
No. 61 Starman	Jack Burnley
No. 66 Shining Knight	Creig Flessel

No. 73 Manhunter	Joe Simon, Jack Kirby
No. 77 Genius Jones	Stan Kaye
No. 103 Aquaman	Paul Norris
No. 103 Green Arrow	George Papp
No. 103 Superboy	
No. 103 Johnny Quick	Mort Meskin
No. 247 Legion of Superheroes	
No. 381 Supergirl	
No. 425 Captain Fear	
No. 428 Black Orchid	
No. 431 The Spectre	
No. 449 Marine Marauder	
No. 459 The Flash	
No. 459 Deadman	
No. 459 Wonder Woman	
No. 459 Green Lantern	
No. 459 The New Gods	
No. 467 Plastic Man	
No. 479 Dial H for Hero	
No. 493 Challengers of the Unknown	George Tuska

There were several changes of format during this comic book's long run: 52 pages (409–420); 68 pages (459–162); 100-page 'digest' size (491–503), with one 148-page edition (500).

440 Single Series

No. 1: December 1938–No. 28: December 1940. 10¢. 68 pp. $7^1/_2 \times 10^1/_4$. Publisher: United Features Syndicate Inc., 220 East 42nd Street, New York.

No. 1 (R) *The Captain and the Kids*	Rudolph Dirks
No. 2 (R) *Broncho Bill*	Harry O'Neill
No. 3 (R) *Ella Cinders*	William Conselman, Charlie Plumb
No. 4 (R) *Li'l Abner*	Al Capp
No. 5 (R) *Fritzi Ritz*	Ernie Bushmiller
No. 6 (R) *Jim Hardy*	Dick Moores
No. 7 (R) *Frankie Doodle*	Ben Batsford
No. 8 (R) *Peter Pat*	Mo Leff
No. 9 (R) *Strange As It Seems*	John Hix
No. 10 (R) *Little Mary Mixup*	Robert Brinkerhoff
No. 11 (R) *Mr. and Mrs. Bumps*	Robert L. Dickey
No. 12 (R) *Joe Jinks*	Vic Forsythe
No. 13 (R) *Looy Dot Dope*	Johnny Devlin
No. 14 (R) *Billy Make Believe*	H.E. Homan
No. 15 (R) *How It Began*	Paul Berdanier
No. 16 (R) *Illustrated Gags*	
No. 17 (R) *Danny Dingle*	Bernard Dibble

No. 18 (R) *Li'l Abner*	Al Capp
No. 19 (R) *Broncho Bill* No. 2	Harry O'Neill
No. 20 (R) *Tarzan*	Hal Foster
No. 21 (R) *Ella Cinders* No. 2	William Conselman, Charlie Plumb
No. 22 (R) *Iron Vic*	Bernard Dibble
No. 23 (R) *Tailspin Tommy*	Hal Forrest
No. 24 (R) *Alice in Wonderland*	Olive Scott, Ed Keukes
No. 25 (R) *Abbie and Slats*	Raeburn Van Beuren
No. 26 (R) *Little Mary Mixup*	Robert Brinkerhoff
No. 27 (R) *Jim Hardy*	Dick Moores
No. 28 (R) *Ella Cinders/Abbie and Slats*	Plumb/Van Beuren

Contents
Each comic book in this series is a compilation of Sunday newspaper strips copyrighted by United Features Syndicate and previously published in that company's regular comic books, *Tip Top Comics* and *Comics On Parade*. Printed in full colour throughout, with specially drawn covers, often by the original artists. All issues undated.

441 Better Little Books

No. 1400: 1939–No. 1499: 1941. 10¢. 432 pp.; 300 pp. 3½×4½. Publisher: Whitman Publishing Co., Racine, Wisconsin.

No. 1400 *Red Ryder and the Little Beaver on Hoofs of Thunder*	Fred Harman
No. 1401 *Li'l Abner among the Millionaires*	Al Capp
No. 1402 *John Carter of Mars*	John C. Burroughs
No. 1403 *Apple Mary and Dennie's Lucky Apples*	Martha Orr
No. 1404 *Such a Life Says Donald Duck*	Walt Disney
No. 1407 *The Lone Ranger and Dead Men's Mine*	Fran Striker
No. 1409 *Buck Rogers and the Fiend of Space*	Dick Calkins
No. 1413 *Tailspin Tommy and the Lost Transport*	Hal Forrest
No. 1414 *Little Orphan Annie and the Ancient Treasure of Am*	Harold Gray
No. 1415 *Kayo and Moon Mullins and the One Man Gang*	Frank Willard
No. 1416 *Smilin' Jack in Wings Over the Pacific*	Zack Mosley
No. 1417 *Mickey Mouse on Sky Island*	Walt Disney
No. 1418 *Harold Teen Swinging at the Sugar Bowl*	Carl Ed
No. 1419 *Don Winslow of the Navy and the Scorpion Gang*	Leon Beroth
No. 1420 *Tom Beatty, Ace of the Service and the Big Brain Gang*	William Young
No. 1423 *Flash Gordon and the Perils of Mongo*	Alex Raymond
No. 1426 *Red Barry, Undercover Man*	Will Gould
No. 1428 *Mickey Mouse in the Foreign Legion*	Walt Disney
No. 1429 *Blondie and Baby Dumpling and Daisy*	Chic Young
No. 1431 *Mandrake the Magician and the Midnight Monster*	Phil Davis
No. 1434 *Donald Forgets to Duck*	Walt Disney
No. 1435 *Pinocchio and Jiminy Cricket*	Walt Disney
No. 1437 *Buck Rogers in the War with the Planet Venus*	Dick Calkins

No. 1439 *Skyroads with Clipper Williams of the Flying Legion*   Russell Keaton
No. 1440 *Red Ryder the Fighting Westerner*   Fred Harman
No. 1443 *Big Chief Wahoo*   Elmer Woggon
No. 1446 *Terry and the Pirates and the Giant's Vengeance*   Milton Caniff
No. 1450 *The Lone Ranger and the Black Shirt Highwayman*   Fran Striker
No. 1454 *Dick Tracy on the High Seas*   Chester Gould
No. 1460 *Foreign Spies: Doctor Doom and the Ghost Submarine*   Al McWilliams
No. 1463 *Mickey Mouse and the Pirate Submarine*   Walt Disney
No. 1470 *Junior Nebb Joins the Circus*   Sol Hess
No. 1472 *Secret Agent X9 and the Mad Assassin*
No. 1474 *The Phantom and the Sign of the Skull*   Ray Moore
No. 1476 *Mickey Mouse in a Race for Riches*   Walt Disney
No. 1478 *Inspector Charlie Chan of the Honolulu Police*   Alfred Andriola
No. 1479 *Tim Tyler's Luck and the Plot of the Exiled King*   Lyman Young
No. 1481 *Dan Dunn, Secret Operative 48, and the Border Smugglers*   Norman Marsh
No. 1486 *King of the Royal Mounted and the Great Jewel Mystery*   Jim Gary
No. 1487 *Perry Winkle and the Rinkeydinks Get a Horse*   Martin Branner
No. 1488 *Dick Tracy the Super Detective*   Chester Gould
No. 1489 *The Lone Ranger and the Red Renegades*   Fran Striker
No. 1492 *Flash Gordon and the Forest Kingdom*   Alex Raymond
No. 1493 *G-Man Breaking the Gambling Ring*   Jim Gary
No. 1496 *Radio Patrol Outwitting the Gang Chief*   Charlie Schmidt
No. 1497 *Myra North, Special Nurse, and Foreign Spies*   Charles Coll
No. 1498 *Jane Arden and the Vanished Princess*   Russell Ross
No. 1499 *Popeye and the Deep Sea Mystery*   E.C. Segar

Series of small-sized comic books following on from the same publisher's *Big Little Book* series. Of similar layout and design: one picture on the right-hand page, the story told in text on the left-hand page. Reprints from daily newspaper strips, printed black-and-white with specially drawn covers in full colour. *Note:* only those *Better Little Books* featuring comic strips have been included in this listing, the remainder being film and radio adaptations, western novels, etc. Nor does the above listing include those titles published after December 1939, as these fall outside our period.

442 Black and White Series

No. 1: 1939–No. 24: 1941. 10¢. 76 pp. (1–6); 52 pp. (7); 76 pp. (8, 9); 52 pp. (10–24). 8½×11¼. Publisher: Dell Publishing Co. (George T. Delacorte Jr.), 149 Madison Avenue, New York.

Title changed to *Large Feature Comic* from No. 25.

No. 1 (R) *Dick Tracy Meets the Blank*   Chester Gould
No. 2 (R) *Terry and the Pirates*   Milton Caniff
No. 3 (R) *Heigh-Yo Silver! The Lone Ranger*   Fran Striker
No. 4 (R) *Dick Tracy Gets His Man*   Chester Gould
No. 5 (R) *Tarzan by Edgar Rice Burroughs*   Hal Foster
No. 6 (R) *Terry and the Pirates and the Dragon Lady*   Milton Caniff

No. 7 (R) *Hi Yo Silver! The Lone Ranger to the Rescue*	Fran Striker
No. 8 (R) *Dick Tracy Racket Buster*	Chester Gould
No. 9 (R) *King of the Royal Mounted*	Allen Dean
No. 10 (R) *Gang Busters*	
No. 11 (R) *Dick Tracy Foils the Mad Doc Hump*	Chester Gould
No. 12 (R) *Smilin' Jack*	Zack Mosley
No. 13 (R) *Dick Tracy and Scotty of Scotland Yard*	Chester Gould
No. 14 (R) *Smilin' Jack*	Zack Mosley
No. 15 (R) *Dick Tracy and the Kidnapped Princess*	Chester Gould
No. 16 (R) *Donald Duck*	Walt Disney
No. 17 (R) *Gang Busters*	
No. 18 (R) *Phantasmo*	
No. 19 (R) *Dumbo Comic Paint Book*	Walt Disney
No. 20 (R) *Donald Duck Comic Paint Book*	Walt Disney
No. 21 (R) *Private Buck*	Clyde Lewis
No. 22 (R) *Nuts and Jolts*	Bill Holman
No. 23 (R) *The Nebbs*	Sol Hess, W.A. Carlson
No. 24 (R) *Thimble Theatre: Popeye*	E.C. Segar

Each comic book in the Dell Black and White Series is a compilation of daily newspaper strips arranged two to the page and printed throughout in black-and-white. Strips are copyright Chicago Tribune–New York News Syndicate and King Features Syndicate. The covers are in four colours and specially drawn, but not by the original artists. Slick paper covers replaced the thick paper covers from No. 10. All issues undated. Advertisements were for the Johnson Smith Company, and other Dell comic publications including *The Funnies*, *Popular Comics*, and *Fast Action Books*. Issues Nos. 1, 2, 4, 8, 9, 11, 13, 15 were published in 1982–1983 as facsimile editions by Tony Raiola of Long Beach, California.

443 Captain Easy

1939. 10¢. 68 pp. $7^1/_2 \times 10^1/_4$. Publisher: Hawley Publications. Artist: Roy Crane. Syndicate: N.E.A. Service.

Contents
Compilation of newspaper strips reprinted from Sunday supplements, and previously published in Dell Publishing's *The Funnies*.

444 Crackajack Funnies

1939. Free (promotional). 32 pp. $7^1/_2 \times 10^1/_4$. Publisher: Whitman Publishing Co. Inc., Poughkeepsie, New York.

Contents
(R) Dan Dunn   Norman Marsh

(R) Freckles and His Friends   Merrill Blosser
(R) Speed Bolton, Air Ace   Al McWilliams
(R) Buck Jones   Kenneth Ernst
(R) Clyde Beatty   Al Lewin
(R) The Nebbs   W.A. Carlson, Sol Hess
(R) Our Boarding House   Bill Freyse
(R) Wash Tubbs   Roy Crane

Reprint of half a regular issue of *Crackajack Funnies*, given away as a promotion for Malto-Meal.

445 Four Color Comics (Series One)

No. 1: 1939–No. 25: 1941. 10¢. 68 pp. $7^{1}/_{4} \times 10^{1}/_{4}$. Publisher: Dell Publishing Co. (George T. Delacorte Jr.), 149 Madison Avenue, New York.

Title changed to Four Color Comics (Series Two).

No. 1 (R) *Dick Tracy*   Chester Gould
No. 2 (R) *Don Winslow of the Navy*   Frank Martinek, Leon Beroth
No. 3 (R) *Myra North, Special Nurse*   Ray Thompson, Charles Coll
No. 4 (R) *Donald Duck*   Walt Disney
No. 5 (R) *Smilin' Jack*   Zack Mosley
No. 6 (R) *Dick Tracy*   Chester Gould
No. 7 (R) *Gang Busters*   Jim Gary
No. 8 (R) *Dick Tracy*   Chester Gould
No. 9 (R) *Terry and the Pirates*   Milton Caniff
No. 10 (R) *Smilin' Jack*   Zack Mosley
No. 11 (R) *Smitty*   Walter Berndt
No. 12 (R) *Little Orphan Annie*   Harold Gray
No. 13 (R) *The Reluctant Dragon*   Walt Disney; Al Taliaferro
No. 14 (R) *Moon Mullins*   Frank Willard
No. 15 (R) *Tillie the Toiler*   Russ Westover
No. 16 (R) *Mickey Mouse*   Walt Disney; Floyd Gottfredson
No. 17 (R) *Dumbo the Flying Elephant*   Walt Disney
No. 18 (R) *Jiggs and Maggie*   George McManus
No. 19 (R) *Barney Google & Snuffy Smith*   Billy De Beck
No. 20 (R) *Tiny Tim*   Stanley Link
No. 21 (R) *Dick Tracy*   Chester Gould
No. 22 (R) *Don Winslow of the Navy*   Frank Martinek, Leon Beroth
No. 23 (R) *Gang Busters*   Jim Gary
No. 24 (R) *Captain Easy*   Roy Crane
No. 25 (R) *Popeye*   Bela Zaboly

Contents
Each edition of Dell's *Four Color Comics* is a compilation of Sunday newspaper strips reprinted from earlier issues of the same company's regular comic books, *Super Comics* and *Popular Comics*. Printed in full colour throughout, none of the issues is dated, and the first three issues are not

numbered. The title Four Color Comics does not appear until issue No. 19. Series Two, starting again from No. 1, ran from 1941 to 1962, ending with No. 1354.

446 The Lone Ranger Comics

No. 1: 1939. Free (promotional). 52 pp. 7½×10¼. Publisher: Lone Ranger Inc., P.O. Box 6308, Baltimore, Maryland.

Contents of No. 1
1 Cover
2 Editorial: Howdy Pals!
3 The Lone Ranger and the Bar Line Rustlers   Ed Kressy

Advertisements
Lone Ranger ice-cream cones.

First editorial
'HOWDY PALS!
First we want to tell you how downright proud we are that you're eating Lone Ranger cones and that you sent for this book. We look at every letter that comes in, and get a mighty warm feeling around our hearts when we see how many true-blue friends we've made. We've tried to make this one of the most exciting books you've ever read, and we'll feel happy if you enjoy it as much as you do the Lone Ranger radio programs, moving pictures, and the regular comics in the newspapers. Whenever we get out something special like this, we always say, "Come on, fellows — let's give all our pals a little something extra — something that will surpise and please them." That's why you'll find a swell surprise right in this book! Just look at the back cover and the two pages in the middle. There you'll see some swell gifts that we've picked out — gifts that you can get as easy as pie, simply by eating Lone Ranger ice cream cones and saving the valuable coupons that come with them . . . The Lone Ranger.'

Although the cover bears the copyright date of 1938, the interior strips are copyrighted 1939. This book contains one single story spread over 46 pages of full-colour pictures, and thus may be considered the first of its kind.

447 That's My Pop Goes Nuts for Fair

1939. 76 pp. Publisher: Bystander Press. Artist: Milt Gross.

Contents
Compilation of Sunday supplement strips entitled 'That's My Pop!', reprinted in black-and-white, with a cover specially drawn by the artist, Milt Gross.

448 All-American Comics

No. 1: April 1939–No. 102: October 1948. 10¢. 68 pp. 7¼×10¼. Publisher: All-American Comics Inc. (Max C. Gaines), 480 Lexington Avenue, New York. Editorial: Max C. Gaines (managing editor); Sheldon Mayer (assistant editor).

Title changed to *All-American Western* from No. 103.

Contents of No. 1
1 Cover
3 Red, White and Blue   Will Arthur
13 (R) Mutt and Jeff   Bud Fisher
17 (R) Tippie   Edwina Dumm
18 (R) Always Belittlin'; Skippy   Percy L. Crosby
20 (R) Nugent's Original Puzzles   A.W. Nugent
21 (R) Reg'lar Fellers   Gene Byrnes
25 All-American Stamp Club (feature)
26 Hop Harrigan   Jon Elby
30 Scribbly   Sheldon Mayer
34 The Mystery Men of Mars   Carl H. Claudy
40 (R) Ben Webster   Edwin Alger
44 Spot Savage   Harry Lampert
45 (R) Daisybelle   Gene Byrnes
47 (R) Cicero's Cat   Bud Fisher
49 (R) Real Magic   A.W. Nugent
50 (R) Always Belittlin'; Skippy   Percy L. Crosby
52 (R) Tippie   Edwina Dumm
53 All-American Champs   Walter Galli
54 (R) Toonerville Folks   Fontaine Fox
57 (R) Bobby Thatcher   George Storm
60 A Real American (story)   Loring Dowst
62 (R) Wiley of West Point   Richard Rick
66 Editorial   Sheldon Mayer

Advertisements
Johnson Smith; Movie Comics.

First editorial
'ALL-AMERICAN COMICS
Dear Kids: — We hope you've had as much fun reading this first issue of *All-American Comics* as we have had making it for you. We'd like you to write and tell us how you like us — what you like best — and even what you don't like! We want to make *All-American Comics* the outstanding and favorite comic magazine in America, and any suggestions you send in will help. Address your letter to the Editor, *All-American Comics*, 480 Lexington Ave., New York City. Very sincerely, the *All-American Comics* Gang. P.S. Our next issue will be on sale about April 1st, no fooling! Be sure to get your copy early!'

All-American Comics No. 1 was the first comic book actually to carry the name of Max C. Gaines, the founding father of the comic book with *Famous Funnies* and its one-shot predecessors. He was billed as managing editor of All-American Comics Inc., a company that worked under the umbrella of Detective Comics Inc. (D.C.). The contents were an approximate fifty-fifty division between popular reprinted Sunday supplement strips and original strips created for the comic book. The reprint material was copyrighted by H.C. Fisher, the George Matthew Adams Syndicate, King Features, Gene Byrnes, Jay Jerome Williams, Fontaine Fox and Richard Rick.

Among the regular characters introduced during the comic book's long run were:

No. 5 The American Way	Walter Galli
No. 5 Popsicle Pete	Sheldon Mayer
No. 8 Gary Concord the Ultra-Man	Don Shelby
No. 16 Green Lantern	Bill Finger, Martin Nodell
No. 19 The Atom	Ben Flinton, Bill O'Connor
No. 25 Dr. Midnite	Stan Asch
No. 26 Sargon the Sorcerer	John Wentworth, Howard Purcell
No. 72 The Black Pirate	Sheldon Moldoff
No. 89 Harlequin	
No. 100 Johnny Thunder	Alex Toth

By 1941 the publisher was changed to J.R. Publishing Co., 225 Lafayette Street, New York and the legend 'A Superman D.C. Publication' apeared in the title logo. A mint copy of No. 1 is valued at $1,100 in the 1989 *Comic Book Price Guide* by R.M. Overstreet.

449 Movie Comics

'A Full Movie Show for Ten Cents'
No. 1: April 1939–No. 6: September 1939. 10¢. 68 pp. $7^{1}/_{2} \times 10^{1}/_{4}$. Publisher: Picture Comics Inc. (Max C. Gaines), 480 Lexington Avenue, New York. Editorial: Max C. Gaines (managing editor); C. Elbert (editor); Sheldon Mayer (assistant editor).

Contents of No. 1

1 Cover: 'Gunga Din'	
3 Editorial: Movie Comics — Now Showing	C. Elbert
4 'Gunga Din'	photos (RKO Radio)
15 'Fisherman's Wharf'	photos (RKO Radio)
23 'Scouts to the Rescue'	photos (Universal)
29 Scouting Trail	Remy Harrison
30 Killer on Location (story)	Loring Dowst
32 Movie Makeup	Boris Karloff (Universal)
33 Screen Scoops	Walter Galli
36 'The Great Man Votes'	photos (RKO Radio)
45 The Adventures of Phoozy	photos
46 Action Camera	Smitty Smith
47 (R) Minute Movies	Ed Wheelan
55 Movietown	Harry Lampert
58 'Son of Frankenstein'	photos (Universal)
66 Coming Attractions	

Advertisements
Johnson Smith; Rosati Accordians; *All-American Comics*.

First editorial
'NOW SHOWING
Here it is, boys and girls, the newest idea in Comics and Movie Books — a combination of both, which we believe you will like very much. We hope that it will give you many, many hours of interesting fun and pleasant reading. *Movie Comics* will present each month an idea of the outstanding pictures to be shown in your neighborhood theater so that you will better enjoy them when you see them on the screen. It will also serve as a permanent record of the pictures you have enjoyed, which you can refer to again and again with pleasure and entertainment. C. Elbert, Editor.'

Unique comic book using still photographs from current films instead of drawings, overprinting in full colour tints, and with hand-lettered captions and speech balloons. *Movie Comics* was not popular, and was discontinued after the sixth issue. Many years later Italian publishers rediscovered the technique with great success.

450 Keen Komics

Vol. 2, No. 1: May 1939–Vol 2, No. 3: November 1939. 10¢. $7^{1}/_{2} \times 11$ (1); $7 \times 10^{1}/_{4}$ (2, 3). Publisher: Centaur Publications Inc. (Joseph Hardie), 420 De Soto Avenue, St. Louis, Missouri. Editorial: 220 Fifth Avenue, New York; Lloyd Jacquet (editor).

Contents of No. 2

1 Cover	Fred Schwab
2 Keen Komedians: Edgar Bergen	Uncle Joe
3 Forbidden Idol of Machu Picchu	Charles Pearson
9 (R) Jack Potts	Fred Schwab
10 (R) Circus Days	Claire S. Moe
15 (R) Li'l Arthur	Bob Wood
16 (R) The Great Boodini	Fred Schwab
18 Cut Carson, Newsreel Man	Carl Burgos
22 (R) Mollie	Craig Fox
23 (R) King Kole's Kourt	Fred Schwab
26 (R) Robert Fulton	De Kerosett
28 (R) Jest Jokes	Martin Filchock
30 (R) Sweet Revenge	Dick Ryan
35 (R) Police Call	Claire S. Moe
41 (R) Jud	Kermit Ray
43 (R) Cheerio Minstrels	Paul Gustavson
45 (R) Range Poison	Jack Binder, W.M. Allison
50 (R) In Case You Didn't Know	Bob Wood

Advertisements
Johnson Smith; Remington Portable Typewriter.

Short-lived comic book, the first issue only of which was published in a slightly oversize format. Most of the strips were reprints from this publisher's earlier issues of *Funny Picture Stories*, etc. *Note:* No. 1 issue not available for indexing.

451 Wonder Comics

No. 1: May 1939–No. 2: June 1939. 10¢. 68 pp. 7¼×10¼. Publisher: Bruns Publications Inc. (Victor Fox), 480 Lexington Avenue, New York. Editorial: Will Eisner, Sam Iger.

Title changed to *Wonderworld Comics* From July 1939.

Contents of No. 2

1 Cover	
2 Winged Wonders	Floyd Kelly
3 Yarko the Great	Will Eisner
12 Minnie th' Mermaid	Nelson
14 Don Quixote in New York	Will Eisner
16 Wonders in the News	
17 Shorty Shortcake (Scrappy)	Will Eisner
25 Wonders That Are True	
26 Patty O'Day	Barreaux
30 Men Who Made the West	
32 Dr. Fung, Master Sleuth	Arthur Dean
38 The Children's Crusade (story)	Will Eisner
40 Tex Maxon	Cecelia Munson
45 Sport Album	Chuck Wilson
46 Filmore Dudd	Sam Iger
47 Movie Memos	Glenda Carol
48 K-51	Will Eisner
53 Gang Buster Robinson	Harold Vance
57 Short Subjects	
58 Spark Stevens of the Navy	Bob Kane
65 Belly Busters	Sam Iger

Advertisement
Johnson Smith.

The first comic book from Victor Fox/Fox Features Syndicate, who would become a successful if second-rate comic book publisher during the 1940s. No. 1 (unavailable for indexing) featured a superhero, 'Wonder Man', created by Will Eisner, but D.C. Comics considered the character too close to their own Superman for comfort. Litigation was also threatened by Hugo Gernsback, publisher of the science-fiction pulp magazine, *Wonder Stories*, and so the title was changed with effect from No. 3. Editor Sam Iger hastily hand-lettered an 'Announcement: Boys and girls, because of the many new features in this exciting magazine, and to make our name more complete, we are changing our title, beginning with the next issue, to *Wonder World Comics*. Watch for it!'

452 Feature Comics (formerly Feature Funnies)

No. 21: June 1939–No. 144: May 1950. 10¢. 68 pp. 7½×10¼. Publisher: Comic Favorites Inc. (Everett Arnold, Frank Markey), 1213 West Third Street, Cleveland, Ohio. Editorial: 369 Lexington Avenue, New York; Edward Cronin (editor).

Contents of No. 21 (first issue)

1 Cover	Edward Cronin

Gallant Knight	Vernon Henkel
(R) Good Deed Dotty; Dixie Dugan	J.P. McEvoy, J.H. Striebel
(R) Toddy	George Marcoux
(R) Mortimer Mum	Sakren
(R) Ned Brant	Bob Zuppke, B.W. Depew
(R) Slim and Tubby	John J. Welch, J.W. McGuire
(R) Off the Record	Ed Reed
The Clock Strikes	George Brenner
(R) Side Show	Rube Goldberg
(R) Nippie; Mickey Finn	Lank Leonard
(R) They're Still Talking	
(R) Jan Arden; Lena Pry	Monte Barrett, Russell Ross
(R) Little Brother; The Bungle Family	H.J. Tuthill
Reynolds of the Mounted	Arthur Pinajian
(R) Big Top	Ed Wheelan
(R) Lala Palooza	Rube Goldberg
Rance Keane	Will Arthur
(R) Joe Palooka	Ham Fisher

Continuation of *Feature Funnies* under a new title reflecting the difference in the buying public's mind between the terms 'funnies' and 'comics'. The former, by this time, definitely referred to Sunday comic supplements in newspapers, while the latter had become identified with comic books. *Feature Funnies* had begun as primarily a compilation reprint magazine with one token original strip, Ed Cronin's 'Jim Swift'. The new title indicated an increase of original content, although the next major strip to be introduced was, in fact, a reprint of Alfred Andriola's newspaper strip, 'Charlie Chan' (No. 23). Gradually original strips took over the comic: Will Eisner's 'Doll Man' (No. 27), Paul Gustavson's 'Rusty Ryan of Boyville' (No. 32), 'Samar' by John Charles (No. 32), 'The Ace of Space' (No. 38), 'The Destroying Demon' (No. 39), 'U.S.A. the Spirit of Old Glory' (No. 42), 'Zero the Ghost Detective' by Noel Fowler, 'Spin Shaw of the Naval Air Corps' by Rex Smith, 'Captain Bruce Blackburn — Counterspy' by Harry Francis Campbell, 'The Voice', 'Dusty Dane', 'The Spider Widow' by Frank Borth (No. 57), and 'Stuntman Stetson' (No. 140). The only traces of the original reprint characters to remain were 'Lala Palooza' and 'Big Top', and both of these characters were now drawn in entirely original episodes especially for the comic book, by Johnny Devlin and Bernard Dibble.

453 Superman

'The Complete Story of the Daring Exploits of the One and Only Superman'
No. 1: Summer 1939–. 10¢. 68 pp. $7^1/_2 \times 10^1/_2$. Publisher: Detective Comics Inc., 480 Lexington Avenue, New York. Editor: Vincent Sullivan.

Contents of No. 1

1 Cover	Joe Shuster
3 (R) Superman	Jerry Siegel, Joe Shuster
21 (R) Superman	Jerry Siegel, Joe Shuster
34 Supermen of America (club)	
36 (R) Scientific Explanation of Superman's Amazing Strength	Joe Shuster
37 (R) Superman	Jerry Siegel, Joe Shuster

50 (R) Superman   Jerry Siegel, Joe Shuster
63 Boys and Girls, Meet the Creators of Superman
64 Superman (story)   Jerry Siegel, Joe Shuster
68 Back cover   Joe Shuster

Advertisements
Johnson Smith; *Action Comics*.

The first solo comic book devoted to a single comic book character, reprinting the first four adventures of Superman from Nos. 1 to 4 of *Action Comics*, with some additional material. *Superman* No. 1 was reprinted in an enlarged ($10 \times 13^3/_4$) facsimile format as *Famous First Edition* (Limited Collector's Golden Mint Series) No. C-61 Volume 8, copyright 1978 by D.C. Comics Inc., price $1.00. A mint copy of *Superman* No. 1 is valued at $24,000 by the Overstreet *Comic Book Price Guide* for 1989.

454 Comic Pages (formerly **Funny Picture Stories**)
Vol. 3, No. 4: July 1939–Vol. 3, No. 6: December 1939. 10¢. 52 pp. $7 \times 10^1/_4$. Publisher: Centaur Publications Inc. (Joseph Hardie), 420 De Soto Avenue, St. Louis, Missouri. Editorial: 220 Fifth Avenue, New York; Lloyd Jacquet (editor).

This continuation of the long-running title, *Funny Picture Stories*, under a more modern name, *Comic Pages*, failed after only three bi-monthly editions.

455 Wonderworld Comics (formerly **Wonder Comics**)
No. 3: July 1939–No. 33: January 1942. 10¢. 68 pp. $7^1/_4 \times 10^1/_4$. Publisher: Bruns Publications Inc. (Victor Fox), 480 Lexington Avenue, New York. Editorial: Will Eisner, Sam Iger.

Contents of No. 3 (first issue)
1 Cover
Yarko the Great   Will Eisner
The Flame   Lou Fine
Dr. Fung, Master Sleuth   Robert Powell
K-51   Will Eisner
Spark Stevens of the Navy   Bob Kane

Continuation of the ill-fated *Wonder Comics*. Additional characters included 'The Black Lion' (No. 21) and 'Lu-Nar the Moon Man' (No. 28).

456 Magic Comics

No. 1: August 1939–No. 123: November 1949. 10¢. 68 pp. $7^1/_2 \times 10^1/_4$. Publisher: David McKay Co., 604 South Washington Square, Philadelphia. Editor: Ruth Plumly Thompson.

Contents of No. 1
1 Cover   Joe Musial

2 Editorial: The Wizard's Tower	G. Whiz
3 (R) Mandrake the Magician	Lee Falk, Phil Davis
(R) News in Sports	McKay
Jan and Aloysius	Joe Musial
(R) The Romance of Flying	Clayton Knight
(R) Bunky	Billy De Beck
(R) Tippie and Cap Stubbs	Edwina Dumm
(R) Inspector Wade	Edgar Wallace
(R) Secret Agent X-9	Robert Storm
Little Nature Stories (text)	Thornton Burgess
(R) Seein' Stars	Feg Murray
(R) Henry	Carl Anderson
Little Acorns	Bob Dunn
(R) Thimble Theatre Starring Popeye	Doc Winner
(R) Barney Baxter in the Air	Frank Miller
Indian Lore	Jimmy Thompson
(R) Blondie	Chic Young
Roger	Bob Dunn
Stamp Corner (feature)	Eugene Pollock
(R) Little Miss Muffet	Fanny Y. Cory
(R) Dinglehoofer und His Dog	Harold Knerr

Advertisement
Johnson Smith.

The third monthly comic book published by the McKay Company was, like its companions, a compilation of newspaper strips reprinted via King Features Syndicate. With all the most popular strips already appearing in *King Comics* and *Ace Comics*, *Magic Comics* was confined to daily strips rather than Sunday pages, although some Sunday 'top-strips' were used. Later additions to the roster included 'The Lone Ranger' by Fran Striker and Charles Flanders (No. 17), and 'Aladdin Jr'. by William Meade Prince and Les Forgrave. Original material was confined to covers and 'Jan and Aloysius', both by Joe Musial, who later introduced the competitive cartoon page, 'Dollar-a-Dither'.

457 Mystery Men Comics

No. 1: August 1939–No. 31: February 1942. 10¢. 68 pp. 7¼×10¼. Publisher: Bruns Publications Inc. (Victor S. Fox), 29 Worthington Street, Springfield, Massachusetts. Editorial: 480 Lexington Avenue, New York (Will Eisner, Sam Iger).

Contents of No. 1

1 Cover	
2 Editorial: An Open Letter to You	Will Eisner
3 The Green Mask	Walter Frehm
12 Rex Dexter of Mars	Dick Briefer
18 Billy Bounce the Kid Detective	Norman Lee
20 Chen Chang, Master Mind	Cecelia Munson

26 Wing Turner, Air Detective	
29 Famous Detectives	Lee Harris
30 Zanzibar the Magician	George Tuska
34 Hemlock Shomes and Dr. Potsam	Fred Schwab
38 The Haunted House (story)	Will Eisner
40 The Waco Kid	Arthur Peddy
44 Inspector Bancroft of Scotland Yard	
48 The Blue Beatle	Charles Nicholas
52 D-13, Secret Agent	Robert Powell
58 Captain Denny Scott of the Bengal Lancers	
61 Lt. Drake of the Naval Intelligence	F. Klaus

Advertisements
Remington Portable Typewriter; *Wonderworld Comics*.

First editorial
'AN OPEN LETTER TO YOU
Howdy, Boys and Girls! After months of hard work we've put together the swellest comic magazine in the world! We've included everything you want — thrills, action, fun, and mystery — 64 pages of New, complete action-packed stories. We want this to be your comic magazine, so we're going to give away One Dollar Each for the best 10 letters telling us the features you like best and your reasons, as well as your suggestions for new ones that you'd like to see in *Mystery Men Comics*.

The most popular and longest-lasting hero to have originated in this comic book is the Blue Beetle, who appeared in his own title from winter 1939 to August 1950, and from a different publisher, Charlton Comics, in his own title from February to September 1955, and again from June 1964 to November 1968. Blue Beetle is also believed to be the first comic book character to be adapted for a radio series. The Green Mask also achieved his own title from Summer 1942 to October 1946, with one additional issue in 1955, and *Rex Dexter of Mars* was also reprinted as a single comic book dated fall 1940. Later characters appearing in *Mystery Men Comics* included: The Moth (No. 9); Domino (No. 11); Lynx (No. 13; Miss X (No. 19); The Wraith (No. 26).

458 New York World's Fair Comics

No. 1: August 1939–No. 2: 1940. 25¢ (1); 15¢ (2). 100 pp. 7$\frac{1}{2}$times10$\frac{1}{2}$. Publisher: Detective Comics Inc., 480 Lexington Avenue, New York. Editor: Vincent Sullivan.

Contents of No. 1

1 Cover	Vincent Sullivan
4 Superman at the World's Fair	Jerry Siegel, Joe Shuster
16 Fairs 1851–1939	Sheldon Moldoff
17 From the Fair Corners	Sheldon Moldoff
18 Chuck Warren	Tom Hickey
24 Hanko goes to the World's Fair	Creig Flessel
26 History of the World's Fair(feature)	
32 Would You Believe It	Sheldon Moldoff

34 Butch the Pup	Fred Schwab
38 Cuffnotes from the Fair	Sheldon Moldoff
40 Ginger Snap	Bob Kane
42 Scoop Scanlon, Five Star Reporter	Will Ely
48 Wonders at the Fair	Sheldon Moldoff
50 A Day at the World's Fair	Creig Flessel
58 Tidbits from the Fair	Sheldon Moldoff
60 Slam Bradley at the World's Fair	Jerry Siegel, Joe Shuster
72 Curiosities from the Fair	Sheldon Moldoff
74 The Sandman	Larry Dean
84 Wonders at the Fair	Sheldon Moldoff
86 Zatara the Master Magician	Fred Guardineer
98 Editorial	Creig Flessel

First editorial
'We trust this book will serve to remind you of the many pleasant and happy hours you enjoyed at the New York World's Fair. And we sincerely hope, too, that it will assist, perhaps in some small fashion, in strengthening and promoting Peace and Friendship among the Nations of the World.'

The first 100-page comic book to contain all original material, created as a souvenir for young visitors to the New York World's Fair. The introductory page contained the legend 'Officially Licensed', plus the notice 'Theme Buildings, murals and sculpture, copyright New York World's Fair 1939 Inc.'. No. 1 was considered overpriced at 25¢, and when it failed to sell in quantity it was repriced at 15¢, by means of a sticky label. No. 2 published the following year, was priced at 15¢, and contained World's Fair adventures of such other D.C. Comics heroes as Batman, Hourman, Sandman and Johnny Thunderbolt. In 1974 facsimile editions of No. 1 and No. 2, but with all interior pages printed in black-and-white, were published by Special Edition Reprints (Alan L. Light) of East Moline, Illinois, as No. 12 and No. 20 in their Flashback series, priced at $3.00 each.

459 Smash Comics

No. 1: August 1939–No. 85: October 1949. 10¢. 68 pp. $7\frac{1}{2} \times 10\frac{1}{4}$. Publisher: Everett M. Arnold, 1213 West Third Street, Cleveland, Ohio. Editorial: 369 Lexington Avenue, New York; Edward Cronin (editor). Title changed to *Lady Luck* from No. 86.

Contents of No. 1

1 Cover	Edward Cronin
3 Espionage (Black Ace)	Will Eisner
12 Philpot Veep, Master Detective	John Devlin
14 Exciting Adventures	Terry
15 Chic Carter, Ace Reporter	Vernon Henkel
22 Simple Simon	Edward Cronin
26 Screen Snapshots	Bernard Baily
27 Wings Wendell of the Military Intelligence	Vernon Henkel
34 Archie O'Toole	Will Eisner
36 Hooded Justice	Arthur Pinajian

40 Clip Chance at Cliffside	George Brenner
46 Captain Cook of Scotland Yard	Will Arthur
50 Mystery at Catalina (story)	Jeffrey Spain
52 Sportraits	Gill Fox
53 Abdul the Arab	Vernon Henkel
60 Hugh Hazzard and His Iron Man	George Brenner

Advertisements
Morrow Coaster Brakes; Grips Athletic Club; Daisy Air Rifles.

First all-original comic book by these publishers, who would become better known as the Quality Comic Group. Later characters to be introduced were: 'The Lone Star Rider' (No. 2); 'Magno and Davey' (No. 13); 'The Ray' by Lou Fine (No. 14); 'Midnight' by Jack Cole (No. 18); 'The Jester' (No. 22); 'Wildfire' (No. 25); 'The Marksman' (No. 33); 'The Yankee Eagle' (No. 38); and 'Lady Luck' by Klaus Nordling (No. 42). This latter character would eventually take over the title from No. 86 (December 1949).

460 Amazing-Man Comics

No. 5: September 1939–No. 27: February 1942. 10¢. 68 pp. 7¼ times 10¼. Publisher: Comic Corporation of America, 29 Worthington Street, Springfield, Massachusetts. Editorial: 220 Fifth Avenue, New York; Lloyd Jacquet (editor).

Contents of No. 5 (first issue)

1 Cover	Bill Everett
3 The Amazing-Man	Bill Everett
13 The Cat Man	Tarpe Mills
18 River Subs Featuring Jack Rhodes	Riley
21 The Iron Skull	Carl Burgos
28 (R) Stranger Than Fiction	Walter Galli
30 The Tragic Note (story)	Matty Point
32 The Congo War Drum	Paul Gustavson
38 Minimidget the Miniature Man	John Kolb
45 Chuck Hardy	Frank Thomas
52 Slim Bradley, Forest Ranger	Dick Hayes
60 Mighty Man	Martin Filchock

Advertisements
Johnson Smith; *Keen Detective Funnies, Amazing Mystery Funnies.*

The first issue of this comic book is numbered 5. It is the first superhero comic book to be named for its leading character, following the sales success of D.C.'s *Superman* comic book. Later characters included:

No. 6 The Shark	Lew Glanz
No. 7 The Magician from Mars	

No. 11 Zardi the Eternal Man
No. 14 Dr Hypno
No. 18 Reef Kincaid   Frank Thomas
No. 22 Dash Dartwell the Human Meteor   Bob Lubbers
No. 23 The Marksman
No. 24 King of Darkness
No. 25 Meteor Martin   Basil Wolverton
No. 26 The Electric Ray

461 Motion Picture Funnies Weekly

No. 1: September 1939. Free (promotional). 36 pp. $7^{1}/_{4} \times 10^{1}/_{4}$. Publisher: First Funnies Inc. (Lloyd Jacquet, John Mahon, James Fitzsimmons), 45 West 45th Street, New York. Editor: Lloyd Jacquet.

Contents of No. 1
1 Cover
Sub-Mariner   Fred Schwab
Spy Ring (BW)   Bill Everett (BW)
American Ace (BW)

Planned as a promotional giveaway comic book to encourage children to attend their local movie house every week, but the experiment proved too costly and was abandoned after the first issue. It had full-colour covers with black-and-white inside pages. Some of the strips were salvaged by reprinting them in other comic books: Sub-Mariner in *Marvel Comics* No. 1 (October 1939); American Ace in *Marvel Mystery* No. 3 (January 1940). The obscurity of this comic book has given it an unnnatural high value to collectors, the 1989 *Comic Book Price Guide* by R.M. Overstreet quoting a figure of $5,000 for a copy in fine condition.

462 Mutt and Jeff

No. 1: September 1939–No. 148: November 1965. 10¢. 68 pp. $7^{1}/_{2} \times 10^{3}/_{4}$. Publisher: All-American Comics Inc. (Max C. Gaines), 480 Lexington Avenue, New York. Editorial: Max C. Gaines (managing editor); Sheldon Mayer (assistant editor).

Contents of No. 1
1 Cover
3 (R) Mutt and Jeff; Cicero's Cat   Sheldon Mayer
                                              Bud Fisher

The first publication of Bud Fisher's long-running 'Mutt and Jeff' strip in regular comic book format. The first issue is undated and unnumbered, and contains reprints of the Sunday supplement pages copyrighted by H.C. Fisher and distributed by the Bell Syndicate Inc. Only the cover cartoon is original artwork, drawn by Sheldon Mayer, the assistant editor of the comic. Issue No. 3 (Summer 1941) includes a two-page biography of the artist, and a four-colour reprint of a strip drawn by Fisher during his training in the Army during World War One. The comic book was taken over by National

Periodicals (D.C. Comics) from 1942, by Dell Publications from 1958 (No. 104), and by Harvey Publications from 1960 (No. 116).

463 Marvel Comics

No. 1: October 1939. 10¢. 68 pp. 7×10¼. Publisher: Timely Publications Inc. (Martin Goodman, Abraham Goodman), 330 West 42nd Street, New York. Editorial: Funnies Inc. (Lloyd Jacquet, editor), 45 West 45th Street, New York.

Title changed to *Marvel Mystery Comics* from No. 2.

Contents of No. 1

1 Cover	Frank R. Paul
Sub-Mariner	Bill Everett
The Human Torch	Carl Burgos
Kazar the Great	Ben Thompson
The Angel	Paul Gustavson
The Masked Raider	Al Anders
Burning Rubber (story)	Ray Gill
Jungle Terror	Thom Dixon

An historic comic book, the first to be issued by the publishers who would become known throughout the world as Marvel Comics, the title chosen for Martin Goodman's first effort. Ironically it lasted only one issue before being changed to *Marvel Mystery Comics*. The lead feature, Sub-Mariner, was an extended reprint of the same strip that had appeared in the failed *Motion Picture Comics Weekly*. One character, Ka-Zar, a Tarzan lookalike, was brought over from Goodman's line of fiction pulp magazines, which were issued under the imprints of Western Fiction Publishing Co., Manvis Publications, and Red Circle. The value of a mint copy of this comic book is quoted in the 1989 edition of Robert M. Overstreet's *Comic Book Price Guide* as $27,000. *Note:* printing difficulties caused publication delay and on most issues the October dateline was overprinted 'November'.

464 Speed Comics

'All Color — All Action — All Thrill'
No. 1: October 1939–No. 44: January 1947. 10¢. 68 pp. 7½×10¼. Publisher: Brookwood Publishing Co. Inc., 381 Fourth Avenue, New York.

Contents of No. 1

1 Cover	Will Eisner
3 Adventures of Shock Gibson	Maurice Scott
29 Crash, Cork and The Baron	Fred North
35 World Speed Records	
36 An Adventure with a Man-eating Plant (story)	Edward Lambert
38 Ted Parrish, the Man of a Thousand Faces	Bob Powell

42 Spike Marlin   Carl Larson
46 Smoke Carter   Cecelia Munson
52 Landor, Maker of Monsters
56 Texas Tyler   Harry Walters
60 Air Speed   Ace Shaw
61 Biff Bannon of the U.S. Marines   Remington Brant

Advertisements
Home Recording Co.; Remington Portable Typewriter; Speed Comics.

This comic book notched up its longest run under the Harvey Publications banner, including three editions (Nos. 14–16) in an unusual pocket-sized format of 100 pages. Characters appearing later in the series included: Mars Marson (No. 7); The Wasp (No. 12); Captain Freedom and the Young Defenders (No. 13); Girl Commandos (No. 13); Pat Parker, War Nurse (No. 13); Black Cat (No. 17).

465 Best Comics

No. 1: November 1939–No. 4: 1940. 10¢. Publisher: Better Publications Inc. (N.L. Pines), 22 West 48th Street, New York.

The first comic book of many to be published by N.L. Pines of Better Publications, a house famous for its line of 'Thrilling' pulp magazines (*Thrilling Detective*, *Thrilling Love*, *Thrilling Wonder Stories*, etc.). This first effort sought to break the now regular comic book format by printing on slightly oversize paper and arranging the entire contents, including the cover, sideways so that it was necessary to turn the hinged spine to the top in order to read the book! The novelty failed, and after four issues the comic was discontinued in favour of new titles in standard format.

466 Blue Ribbon Comics

'Action — Mystery — Thrills'
No. 1: November 1939–No. 22: March 1942. 10¢. 68 pp. 7¹/₄×10¹/₄. Publisher: M.L.J. Magazines Inc. (Morris Coyne, Louis Silberkleit, John Goldwater), 420 De Soto Avenue, St. Louis, Missouri. Editorial: 160 West Broadway, New York; Harry A. Chesler (editor).

Contents of No. 1
1 Cover
2 Hold That Line   Jack Cole
3 Editorial: Just a Moment
4 Rang-A-Tang the Wonder Dog   Norman Danberg
10 Dan Hastings
20 (R) Buck Stacey   W.M. Allison (BW)
25 Brain Teasers
26 Foxy Grandpa   Jack Cole
28 Sugar, Honey and Huggin   Dick Ryan (BW)

30 Ima Slooth, Secret Agent B.O.	Jack Cole
33 (R) Laughs	Dick Ryan
34 (R) Boodini the Great	Fred Schwab
36 Burk of the Briny (BW)	
41 (R) Ages of Animals	
42 King Kole's Kourt	Jack Cole, George Nagle
44 Village of Missing Men	Cliff Thorndyke (BW)
50 Death around the Bend (story)	Pat Gleason
55 Little Nemo	Winsor McCay Jr.
59 It's Really a Fact	
60 Crime on the Run	Jack Cole

Advertisements
Johnson Smith; Home Recording Co.

First editorial
'JUST A MOMENT
"Hello" is the very best word we could think of in greeting you in this, our first issue of *Blue Ribbon Comics*. For we believe that "hello" is the finest word in the English language. It means that something new is beginning, be it a new greeting of old friends, or an entirely new set of circumstances crossing the horizon. We believe that *Blue Ribbon Comics* is going to bring you something in comic magazines that you have never quite seen before. It will, in the first place, thrill you in a way you never before have been thrilled. Because every picture story in the magazine is planned to make each page count the fullest in exciting drama. Every story in *Blue Ribbon Comics* is complete. You won't have any long, drawn-out plots to try to remember from one month to the next. When you have read the last page of this snappy magazine you will have seen all there is to see of that issue, and can look forward to the next with confidence that brand new excitement awaits you. Another thing. You'll never find in these pages any reprints. Every feature in this magazine is entirely original and has never before appeared in any other magazine. And you can rest assured, too, that when you have read *Blue Ribbon Comics* you will not find its stories cropping up in other books with different titles. Some people do that, you know, and at times you pay your money for a comic magazine and find that you have read a great many of its features in some other comic book. That will never happen to any *Blue Ribbon* feature! And then there are sixty-four full pages in this book. We suggest that you count them and see for yourself. Just because you do not see the pages numbered is no reason why you need fear that we will ever give you less for your money than you are entitled to. That has happened with other comic books, but *Blue Ribbon Comics* will be on the level with you first, last and all the time. So for the first time we present this streamlined, double-action, extra-special, up-to-the-minute, high-class issue of *Blue Ribbon Comics* by saying "Hello!" and we'll be seeing you every month.'

Packaged by the Harry A. Chesler 'shop' (studio) for a newcomer to comic book publishing, M.L.J. Magazines (who would eventually change their name to Archie Comics Publications). The contents of this comic book did not exactly match the 'honest' editorial. Many of the characters had previously seen action in earlier Chesler comic books such as *Star Comics*, and several of the strips and feature pages were reprints. Later characters to appear in this title included: Bob Phantom (No. 2); Silver Fox (No. 2); Doc Strong (No. 4); The Green Falcon (No. 4); Hercules (No. 4); Ty-Gor, Son of the Tiger (No. 4); Mr. Justice (No. 9); Inferno the Flame Breather (No. 13); and Captain Flag (No. 16). The title of *Blue*

Ribbon Comics was revived by St. John Publications (February–August 1949) and in 1983 by Archie Enterprises Inc.

467 Fantastic Comics

No. 1: December 1939–No. 23: November 1941. 10¢. 68 pp. $7^{1}/_{4} \times 10^{1}/_{4}$. Publisher: Fox Publications Inc. (Victor Fox), 29 Worthington Street, Springfield, Massachusetts. Editorial: Will Eisner, Sam Iger, 480 Lexington Avenue, New York.

Contents of No. 1
1 Cover
Samson
Stardust the Super Wizard
Space Smith
Sub Saunders
Captain Kidd
Yank Wilson, Super Spy

Lou Fine
Alex Blum
H. Fletcher

Third regular title from the burgeoning Fox Publications, which gave them the following publishing schedule: *Fantastic Comics* on the 10th of the month, *Mystery Men Comics* on the 15th of the month, *Wonderworld Comics* on the 28th of the month. This latter publication date would be shared by *Science Comics*, which although dated February 1940 actually went on sale on 28 December 1939. It is worth mentioning here that from the beginning (with *Famous Funnies* No. 1), publishing practice was to date comic books one month ahead of the month of sale. By the end of our period, the practice was beginning to slip towards two months. By the 1980s, a three-month gap between on-sale date and publication date had become not uncommon.

468 Marvel Mystery Comics (formerly Marvel Comics)

No. 2: December 1939–No. 92: June 1949. 10¢. 68 pp. $7 \times 10^{1}/_{4}$. Publisher: Timely Publications Inc. (Martin Goodman, Abraham Goodman), 8 Lord Street, Buffalo, New York. Editorial: Funnies Inc. (Lloyd Jacquet, editor), 330 West 42nd Street, New York.

Title changed to *Marvel Tales* from No. 93.

Contents of No. 2 (first issue)
1 Cover
3 The Human Torch
19 The Angel
27 Sub-Mariner
39 The Masked Raider
47 (R) American Ace
53 Death Head Squadron (story)
55 Ka-Zar the Great
67 All in Fun

Claire S. Moe
Carl Burgos
Paul Gustavson
Bill Everett
Al Anders
Paul Lauretta
David Cooke
Ben Thompson
Fred Schwab

68 Loony Laffs   Ben Thompson

Continuation of *Marvel Comics*, the first comic book in the long-running Marvel Comics publications. 'American Ace' was reprinted from the failed *Motion Picture Funnies Weekly*. Other regular characters introduced during this comic book's run include:

No. 4 Electro, Marvel of the Age   Steve Dahlman
No. 4 The Ferret, Mystery Detective   Stockbridge Winslow
No. 10 Terry Vance the Schoolboy Sleuth   Bob Oksner
No. 13 The Vision   Joe Simon, Jack Kirby
No. 21 The Patriot   Art Gates
No. 28 Jimmy Jupiter in the Land of Nowhere   Ed Robins
No. 49 Miss America
No. 75 The Young Allies
No. 80 Captain America   Sid Shores
No. 84 Blonde Phantom   Sid Shores

469 Merry Christmas From Mickey Mouse

December 1939. Free (promotional). 16 pp. 7½×10¼. Publisher: K.K. Publications Inc. (Kay Kamen), Poughkeepsie, New York.

Contents
Pictures and text stories of the Walt Disney characters (Mickey Mouse, Donald Duck, Pluto) in comic book format, printed part black-and-white, part full color. Produced as a seasonal giveaway for shoe stores.

470 Merry Christmas From Sears Toyland

December 1939. Free (promotional). 16 pp. 7½×10¼. Publisher: Sears Roebuck Co.

Contents
Comic book produced as a seasonal giveaway for the Sears Roebuck stores toy departments including Sunday strip reprints of 'Dick Tracy' by Chester Gould, 'Little Orphan Annie' by Harold Gray, 'The Gumps' by Gus Edson, and 'Terry and the Pirates' by Milton Caniff. Probably a reprint of *Super Comics*.

471 Top-Notch Comics

'Thrills — Action — Adventure'
No. 1: December 1939–No. 45: June 1944. 10¢. 68 pp. 7¼×10¼. Publisher: M.L.J. Magazines Inc. (Morris Coyne, Louis Silberkleit, John Goldwater), 420 De Soto Avenue, St. Louis, Missouri. Editorial: 160 West Broadway, New York; Harry A. Chesler (editor).

Title changed to *Laugh Comics* from No. 46.

Contents of No. 1

1	Cover	
3	The Wizard	Edd Ashe Jr.
14	Laughing At Life	Jack Cole
15	Scott Rand in the Worlds of Time	Eando Binder, Jack Binder
21	Sportopics	Irving Hasen
22	Swift of the Secret Service	Charles Biro
28	(R) Jungle Town Show Boat	Dick Ryan
30	Air Patrol: Wings Johnson	Ed Smalle
35	Murder Rap (story)	Ken Fitch
39	(R) It's Really a Fact	Bob Wood
40	Lucky Coyne, Undercover Man	
45	(R) Lonesome Luke	Fred Schwab
46	The Mystic	
51	Puzzlettes	
52	The West Pointer	
57	(R) Impy	Winsor McCay Jr.
58	(R) Speaking of Sports	Bob Wood
59	Manhunters	Jack Cole
65	(R) Pokey Forgets to Remember	Dick Ryan
66	Editorial: Yours Truly	

Advertisements
Johnson Smith; Home Recording Co.; Blue Ribbon Comics

First editorial
'YOURS TRULY: SPROUTING WINGS
This first great issue of *Top Notch Comics* reminds us of a bird that has sprouted wings. It feels proud of them until it tries to use them and then finds that there is much to learn about flying before Mr. Bird is ready to leave the ground. Not that we feel in any way unfit for flying the banner of *Top Notch Comics*! Here's what we do mean. Remember the old saying that you've got to learn to walk before you can fly? Well, that's the way we felt. So we went into session with ourselves and decided that before we should put *Top Notch Comics* on the market we should find out just what the best type of picture stories and fiction should be to entertain you. We feel that now we have the formula . . . but unlike the bird with the sprouting wings, we went into hiding until we had decided just what to do, so that before we came before you we'd know already how to fly. It took a lot of testing and investigating and planning to know what you like best. Of course, we are not perfect, but we feel that we have the kind of magazine now that you are going to read for a long time to come and enjoy it each time you read. There will be no dragging stories in *Top Notch Comics*, no stories that carry on without rhyme or reason, month after month. For in this magazine each issue will be complete in itself. It's going to run on and on, all right, but each new issue will have a completely new set of stories, and each story in each issue will be complete.
Again, there will be no reprints in *Top Notch Comics*. You have never seen the stories you read here in any other magazine or in any other newspaper! Besides that, the stories you read here will not crop up again in some other magazine. You'll see for yourself in this and each succeeding issue how really

superior *Top Notch Comics* is. Streamlined fiction, stepped up to meet today's fast pace of living. Exciting action, thrilling drama. Real life characters. All working together to give you the biggest value in comics that you have ever witnessed. So let's all whoop it up together for *Top Notch* — the World's Greatest Comic Book! We'll be seeing you!'

M.L.J. Magazines' speedy follow-up to No. 1 of *Blue Ribbon Comics*, once again packaged by the Harry A. Chesler 'shop'. And once again the contents did not match Chesler's editorial statements, for already established characters (such as Lucky Coyne) as well as previously published strips were included from earlier Chesler publications (*Star Comics*, etc.). Later characters introduced into this title included: Bob Phantom (No. 3); The Shield (No. 6); The Firefly and Roy the Super Boy (No. 8); The Black Hood (No. 9); and Suzie (No. 28). Suzie made her debut in the same issue that changed the title slightly to *Top-Notch Laugh Comics* (No. 28). Humour content was increased from this issue, and the title was changed completely from No. 46 to *Laugh Comics*

472 The Blue Beetle

No. 1: Winter 1939–No. 60: August 1950. 10¢. 68 pp. $7^1/_4 \times 10^1/_4$. Publisher: Fox Publications Inc. (Victor Fox), 29 Worthington Street, Springfield, Massachusetts. Editorial: Will Eisner, Sam Iger, 247 Park Avenue, New York.

Contents of No. 1

1 Cover	Will Eisner
3 (R) The Blue Beetle	Charles Nicholas
16 (R) The Blue Beetle	Charles Nicholas
20 (R) The Blue Beetle	Charles Nicholas
24 (R) The Blue Beetle	Charles Nicholas
28 (R) The Blue Beetle	Charles Nicholas
32 (R) The Blue Beetle	Charles Nicholas
36 Death Rides on Horseback (story)	
38 (R) Yarko the Great	Will Eisner
46 (R) Yarko the Great	Will Eisner
53 (R) Yarko the Great	Will Eisner
61 (R) Yarko the Great	Will Eisner

Advertisements
Daisy Air Rifles; Comic-Scope Projector.

Quarterly comic book reprinting earlier adventures of its title character from *Mystery Men Comics*, and 'Yarko the Great' from *Wonderworld Comics*. *Blue Beetle* had a long career: after Fox discontinued the title in 1950, Charlton Comics revived it in 1955 and again in 1964.

Title Index

Name Index